THE INVISIBLE FIELD

The Invisible Field
THE DEFINITIVE HYPER-LOCAL ECONOMIC CONCEPT.

THE INVISIBLE FIELD

HOW HIDDEN CONSTRAINTS SHAPE YOUR LIFE - AND WHAT TO DO ABOUT THEM

A. H. REYNOSO

The Invisible Field
How Hidden Constraints Shape Your Life - and What to Do About Them

Written by **A. H. Reynoso**

KDP Paperback ISBN: 979-8-90340-022-5

Library of Congress Control Number: 2026903119
Library of Congress Classification: BF637.S4 R49 2026

Dewey Decimal Classification: 158.1

First Edition, April 2026

Obvious Things Publishing
111 Town Square Pl Ste#1238 PMB 650110
Jersey City, New Jersey 07310, USA

www.obviousthingspublishing.com

Important: Field Safety & Professional Boundaries

This work is an educational framework, not a clinical intervention. The concepts presented here are designed to supplement, not replace, professional medical, psychological, legal, or financial guidance.

Immediate Risk: If you are currently in a high-risk environment or facing immediate danger, whether physical, emotional, or situational, please bypass this material and contact your local emergency services or a qualified crisis professional immediately.

Privacy & Mechanics: To protect the privacy of individuals while preserving the integrity of the behavioral mechanics, all case studies and examples in this book are composites. Names, identities, and specific timelines have been altered.

Inclusivity & Context: The Invisible Field applies to all human systems, regardless of background, identity, or location. However, its effectiveness depends on a foundation of safety. If your current Field is compromised by acute health, legal, or safety threats, prioritize specialized professional support to stabilize your environment before applying these strategies.

Use this book as a high-level strategic supplement to your existing support systems.

For Mom and Dad,
who absorbed the costs so I could negotiate the Field.

Contents

Introduction

YOU ARE NOT LAZY. YOU ARE PRICED.

Before you made a single real choice, terms were already in force. You arrived with a body, a name, a language, a family system, a place, and a nervous system already adapting to conditions you did not choose. You did not negotiate those terms. You still pay for them.

That is the first hidden clause of a human life: you do not begin on a blank page. You begin inside a contract you did not write.

Most people are handed a cleaner lie. If you are struggling, the lie says you must be flawed. If you are winning, it says you must be superior. It is a simple story, and it does profitable work. It flatters winners, humiliates strugglers, and keeps the mechanism invisible.

This is not a book of inspiration. It is not a book of excuses.

It is a book of leverage: a way to read recurring outcomes without confusing them for character, and a way to change the conditions that keep producing them.

Defaults are not mysteries. Most of them are invoices.

They are the moves your system learned to survive, belong, reduce danger, manage overload, preserve attachment, or simply get through the day under the terms it was given. They are not random. They are not moral verdicts. They are not proof of who you are. They are the bargains your system learned to trust.

This matters because most people try to change behavior by shaming it. They call themselves lazy, weak, avoidant, selfish, chaotic, needy, undisciplined. They attack the visible move and leave the hidden price list untouched. Then they wonder why the pattern returns.

But behavior follows cost.

Some actions cost money. Some cost time. Some cost energy. Some cost sleep. Some cost dignity. Some cost belonging. Some cost conflict. Some cost safety. Some cost reputation.

And when the real price of the better move is higher than your system can currently pay, you do not make the better move.

You make the move the system can afford.

That does not excuse harm. It explains recurrence. And explanation is what makes redesign possible.

I built this model by noticing the same hidden pricing logic in places people usually keep separate: family conflict, work schedules, unpaid bills, legal notices, panic spirals, and sexual choices made for relief instead of closeness.

Different rooms. Same arithmetic.

It is clearest where the same outcome keeps returning under pressure: the same fight, the same collapse, the same avoidance, the same invoice.

The formula is simple:

UNCHOSEN TERMS + REPEATED COSTS = THE LIFE YOU ARE LIVING

By the end of this book, you will be able to identify the Default your system keeps making cheap, see what it buys you, see what it costs you, and begin changing the Terms so the better move becomes easier to repeat.

Read this book slowly. Read it with a pen. Mark what applies. Ignore what does not. Do not read it like motivational content. Read it like a contract that finally matters.

The point is not to admire the model. The point is to catch the hidden clause before it catches you again.

THE PRICE OF CHOICE

Most people think their life is the record of what they chose. That story flatters willpower and hides structure.

People do make choices. But the live menu in any moment is shaped by pressure, capacity, cost, and consequence. Some moves are available. Some are technically available but too expensive to repeat. Some are visible only to people with more margin than you have. Some never appear at all.

Your life is not only a record of what you wanted. It is also a record of what your system could afford - in money, time, energy, attention, shame, risk, belonging, safety, and recovery.

I call that pricing environment the Field.

The Field is the network of Terms shaping your life at any given moment: family rules, money, work, law, culture, relationships, biology, and the current state of your body. Those Terms price behavior in multiple currencies - time, energy, risk, shame, belonging, and enforcement.

The move that repeatedly lowers immediate cost becomes the Default. Once that move brings enough relief, the nervous system starts trusting it.

Relief becomes reinforcement.

Reinforcement becomes recurrence.

That loop is simple. Its consequences are not.

This is why people feel stuck. The problem is often not a lack of values. The problem is that the Field keeps making the same move cheap.

At work, a deadline slips, the demand is framed like a favor, and the real cost of saying no sits in the room even if nobody says it aloud. You comply because the bill is obvious.

That same logic runs in families, in money, in law, and in private habits. The surface changes. The pricing logic repeats.

When people misread priced behavior, they call it laziness, weakness, or self-sabotage. That moral vocabulary hides structure.

Better questions are these:

What does this move buy immediately?

What does it protect you from immediately?

What invoice does it send later?

Once you can answer those questions, shame becomes less useful and responsibility becomes more precise. You stop arguing with yourself in the dark and start changing the conditions that make the harmful move cheap.

The method of this book is simple: identify the Default, price it honestly, find the Terms that keep it cheap, edit what you can, and run small experiments until the better move becomes the cheapest reliable option.

This book is not asking you to become a different species. It is asking you to read the price list accurately, then edit it where you are.

How to Read This Book

As you read, keep one recurring frustration in view: one work loop, one family conflict, one money habit, one relationship pattern, or one private behavior that keeps returning. Use the framework questions from the previous section as your lens.

What does this move buy me now?

What does it protect me from now?

What does it cost later?

What would have to change to make the better move cheaper?

A better move that only works on a good day is not designed yet. When it works on a bad day, the Field has started to change.

Three Lives in View

ELENA IS TWENTY-EIGHT, THE ELDEST DAUGHTER IN A FIRST-GENERATION FAMILY, FLUENT IN RESPONSIBILITY AND SHORT ON MARGIN. HER FIELD IS MONEY, MIGRATION, FAMILY LOYALTY, AND THE QUIET TAX OF BEING THE DEPENDABLE ONE.

Marcus is thirty-four, successful enough to be admired and tired enough to be vanishing inside his own schedule. His Field is status, work, attention, and the bargain that turns exhaustion into proof.

Rafi is thirty-one, bright, intermittently sober, and better at getting through nights than building a life he can stay inside. His Field is loneliness, desire, shame, and the search for relief that does not become another debt.

They are composites. Keep them in view. The point is not biography for its own sake. The point is to watch how the same logic behaves in different rooms.

What Pricing Looks Like in Real Time

If the phrase priced behavior still feels abstract, make it smaller. In any pressured moment, the system is running a fast comparison: Which move buys relief fastest? Which move avoids the largest immediate bill? Which move can this body, in this room, under these Terms, actually afford? The answer is often not the wisest move. It is the move with the lowest immediate price.

That price is never just money. A move can be cheap in cash and expensive in dignity. Cheap in status and expensive in sleep. Cheap in belonging and expensive in self-respect. Cheap in immediate relief and ruinous by morning. Behavior can be priced in money, time, energy, attention, shame, conflict, belonging, safety, reputation, and recovery. That is why the same act can look irrational from far away and perfectly coherent from inside the person living it.

Elena: Duty, Money, and Belonging

For Elena, the cheapest move is often compliance. When her manager asks for Saturday, yes buys cash, supervisor approval, proof that she is not difficult, and temporary relief from the fear of being the worker who can be replaced. No does not arrive as one clean word. No arrives priced as lost pay, possible retaliation, maternal disappointment, more household strain, and the shame of being the one who could have helped but did not. From outside, yes looks passive. Inside her Field, yes is a bundled purchase: rent protection, identity protection, and conflict delay.

Family rescue is priced the same way. If a cousin needs money, a sibling needs a ride, or a parent needs translation at an office, Elena's automatic move is not only generosity. It is cost management. Sending the money buys belonging now, relieves guilt now, protects her role as the dependable one now, and prevents the accusation - spoken or unspoken - that she has become selfish. Holding the boundary buys almost nothing in the first hour except anxiety. The later invoice reverses: the rescue creates overdraft, exhaustion, resentment, and a life built around other people's emergencies. But the nervous system discounts later pain when today's belonging feels unstable.

Even rest is priced for her. An evening off should be free. It is not. Rest costs Elena the sensation of usefulness. It costs her control over the next problem. It risks criticism from people who treat constant availability as love. So the cheap move becomes one more errand, one more text answered, one more problem absorbed. Then observers call her stressed or martyr-like, as if the pattern were vanity. Often it is simpler than that: in her Field, stillness is expensive because stillness leaves guilt unpaid.

Relationships inherit the same terms. A partner asking for more time, more honesty, or more softness can sound to Elena like one more demand on a system already at capacity. Saying, "I can't do that this week," may be emotionally healthier, but it feels expensive in the short term because it risks disappointing someone she loves. Over-functioning feels cheaper. She pays by managing, anticipating, smoothing, explaining, and rescuing until closeness itself starts feeling like another bill.

The redesign for Elena is not abstract self-worth. It is repricing. More cash buffer makes no cheaper. Shared responsibility at home makes rescue less mandatory. Prepared scripts make boundaries less improvisational. A second translator, a backup ride, a clearer work limit, a day protected before collapse - these are not small comforts. They lower the immediate price of the better move. Once the better move stops threatening rent, belonging, and identity at the same time, Elena can repeat it.

Marcus: Status, speed, and identity

For Marcus, the cheap move is performance. The late-night email buys certainty. The extra revision buys protection against judgment. The quick yes buys status, admiration, and the fantasy that he can stay ahead of replacement if he never stops moving. No single act looks catastrophic. That is why the loop hides. One more message, one more deck, one more dinner missed, one more Sunday half-lost to recovery. Each individual move is cheap in the moment because it avoids the acute pain of seeming slow, ordinary, or dispensable.

Overwork also buys identity. Marcus is not only paid by work. He is named by it. The body learns that exhaustion produces praise, and praise produces temporary calm. That means the job is doing two things at once: generating income and regulating self-doubt. Once work is regulating worth, stepping back feels much more expensive than the salary spreadsheet shows. It threatens the story that he is serious, wanted, and safe. People around him may even reward the pattern, which makes the short-term math look excellent right up until the body, marriage, or attention span sends the larger invoice.

Attention is priced the same way for him. The phone buys stimulation, urgency, and the feeling of relevance. Quiet buys almost nothing at first except the return of whatever he has been outrunning. So the cheap move becomes checking, scanning, refreshing, reading one more message, tracking one more signal. From outside it looks like ambition or habit. Inside the Field it is a regulation loop: certainty now, fragmentation later. The later invoice arrives as worse decisions, thinner patience, poorer intimacy, shallower thinking, and the eerie feeling of succeeding at a life he is barely inhabiting.

Closeness gets priced by the same prestige logic. Telling the truth - "I am tired, I do not want this, I am afraid I'm disappearing" - is emotionally expensive because it risks puncturing competence. Staying polished is cheaper. Staying useful is cheaper. Staying impressive is cheaper. Then the relationship starves while the image stays well fed. The outside world sees a high performer. The inner system is paying with honesty, tenderness, and recovery.

Marcus does not need more insight into burnout. He needs a different cost structure. Hard stops that are actually kept. Fewer false urgencies. Team norms that do not reward midnight proof. Protected sleep. A phone that sleeps in another room. Real friendships that are not organized around competition. Work that has scope instead of sprawl. The better move becomes repeatable when it stops looking like career suicide every time he chooses it.

Rafi: Relief, shame, and the night

For Rafi, the cheap move is not laziness. It is relief. On a lonely evening, texting the wrong person, opening the app, finding the substance, chasing the hookup, or disappearing into the screen buys immediate state change. That matters. The move lowers noise, creates sensation, interrupts shame, and gives the body something clear to do. The healthier move - calling a safe person, staying still, naming the craving, going to sleep sober - often feels unbearably expensive because it asks him to endure the very state the old move was built to erase.

Desire is priced inside that loop. When desire is fused with loneliness, boredom, self-hatred, or the need to feel chosen, the body stops reading it cleanly. The fast sexual or chemical move becomes a discount regulator. It buys proof of existence, proof of desirability, proof that the night can still be altered. The bill arrives later as shame, danger, depleted trust, money gone, sleep gone, or a fresh reason to hide. But by then the immediate relief has already taught the nervous system the lesson that matters most to it: this worked fast.

Secrecy makes the move cheaper in the moment and far more expensive afterward. Lying, ghosting, minimizing, or saying "I'm fine" buys temporary protection from being seen in a bad state. That is the short-term discount. The later invoice is brutal: less support, more isolation, fewer witnesses, more opportunity for the old loop to become automatic. This is how relief becomes debt. The person is not only paying for the original behavior. The person is paying for the collapse of the relationships and structures that might have helped interrupt it next time.

The night matters because timing matters. Rafi may believe one thing at 3 p.m. and another at 11:40 p.m. Hunger, fatigue, aloneness, shame, and boredom change the price list. Under those conditions the old move becomes artificially cheap. The future disappears. Morning becomes abstract. This is why promises made in daylight often fail by midnight. The problem is not insincerity. The problem is that the night is a different Field.

Rafi's redesign is therefore concrete. Less cash in the wrong window. More structure before nightfall. A call list already chosen. One person who gets the truth early. Routes not taken. Apps blocked. Food already in the apartment. A room arranged for sleep instead of drift. A form of intensity that does not destroy tomorrow. The better move does not win because it is morally superior. It wins when it becomes faster, closer, and more believable than the old relief.

That is how pricing works across all three lives. The Default is not the move the person loves most. It is the move that is cheapest right now in the currencies their Field makes urgent. Elena pays mostly in guilt, duty, and belonging. Marcus pays mostly in status, certainty, and identity. Rafi pays mostly in shame, loneliness, and immediate state change. Different rooms. Same arithmetic.

And that is how repricing is done. You do not argue with the system first. You change the immediate math. Lower the short-term cost of the better move. Raise the ease of the destructive one. Add buffer. Add structure. Add witnesses. Add replacement rewards. Remove the false urgency. Remove the secrecy. Give the body evidence that the wiser move is survivable. Once the wiser move is survivable often enough, it stops feeling noble and starts feeling normal.

Read for recognition. Read for leverage. Read to find the price list under the pattern. Because once the hidden Terms are visible, change stops being a pep talk and becomes a redesign. Keep one pattern in view. Let's begin.

The One Page Model

YOU ARE NOT LAZY.
YOU ARE PRICED.

Behavior = Adaptation Under Constraint

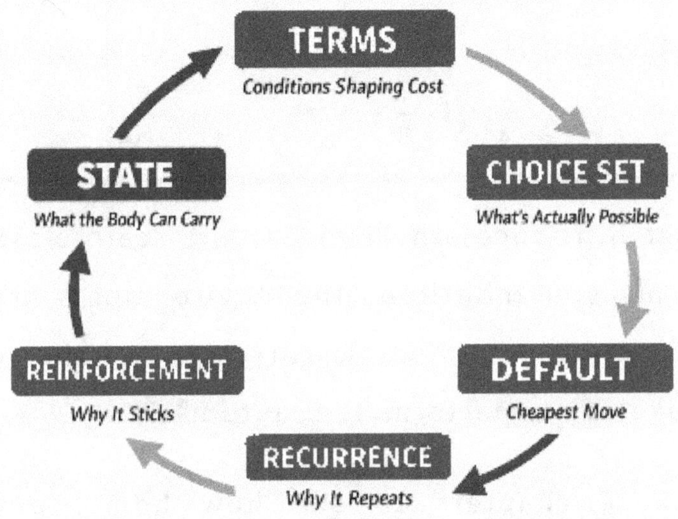

- **Capacity** = Resources – Load
- **Behavior** = Cost-Driven
- **Freedom** = Capacity, **Not** Permission
- **Recurrence** = *Cheap Relief Loop*

- Behavior Follows Cost
- **Relief** Beats Ideals
- **State** Limits Choice
- **Environment** Sets Price
- **What Repeats** Becomes *Identity*
- Replace Function or It Returns

IF YOU WANT A DIFFERENT LIFE → MAKE BETTER MOVES CHEAPER.

PART I - THE FIELD

This Part introduces the Field at the scale closest to life: the Terms you inherited, the environments training you now, the state your body is carrying, and the relief loops that make costly patterns feel automatic.

Read these chapters to see how home, environment, physiology, relief, and shame price what becomes possible before you ever call it choice.

1

The Terms You Never Chose

At 6:14 on a Thursday, Elena stands in the bathroom with the fan running so her younger brother will not hear the call.

Her manager wants Saturday. Her mother needs her at a housing office. Rent is due in four days. Saying yes will cost peace at home. Saying no will cost cash the household is already counting.

From the outside, the decision will look trivial. She says yes. A single word. Inside the Field, it is already crowded with money, obligation, time, and belonging.

That is where this book starts. Before Elena chooses, the Terms have already priced the move.

When Advice Refuses to Price the Move

People love advice that starts with just. Just leave. Just stop. Just forgive. The word *just* is a refusal to price the move.

Before you choose, the Terms set the price. Terms are the constraints, incentives, and enforcement conditions beneath the story: what feels possible, what feels dangerous, what feels worth it, and what will get punished.

The cost can be energy, threat, time, money, conflict, shame, or belonging. Under pressure, behavior follows cost more reliably than ideals. A Default is the move your system selects when it is trying to minimize expected cost under load. Once you see that, a lot of "mystery" behavior stops looking mysterious. Terms have layers. Start with physiology.

A skeptic might say this makes people sound predictable, as if incentives explain everything. They do not. People vary. Some choose against cost on principle. Some absorb pain for loyalty, love, faith, or pride. This book is not claiming that structure is destiny. It is claiming that structure is usually the heavier weight on the scale. When the same result keeps returning, pricing is the first place to look.

Start with the body. Some nervous systems spike fast and recover slow. Sleep debt, hunger, pain, caffeine, alcohol, noise, and conflict all change what you can carry without snapping.

Add training. What got you relief, praise, safety, or attention (and what got you punished) became your instruction manual. The nervous system learns through consequence, not through your values statement.

Add the room: crowding, privacy, commute, temperature, light, food, silence, and whether you have a third space that isn't work or home. A person living with crowding, poor privacy, and constant noise does not get the same decision menu as someone with a quiet door and some control over space.

Add the tribe. Belonging isn't a soft preference. It's a survival system. The nervous system can register social exclusion as threat because, historically, exclusion often endangered survival.

Status decides access: to safety, resources, opportunity, and dignity. The social layer prices what you're allowed to become without losing your people. And which emotions, questions, and boundaries are punished.

These layers compound. A reactive body in a chaotic room inside a high-shame culture runs a different life than a calmer body in a stable room inside a forgiving culture. Calling both "choices" and judging them equally is not ethics. It is mismeasurement. The Field is what you are inside when all of this is true at once.

It is also the reason simple advice fails. "Just leave." "Just forgive." "Just set boundaries." "Just stop caring." "Just quit." "Just be confident." "Just love yourself."

Those commands assume costless options. In real life, options have prices. In real life, leaving can mean homelessness, retaliation, custody battles, deportation risk, losing community, losing health insurance, losing identity. Forgiving can mean being unarmed. Setting boundaries can mean being alone. Quitting can mean losing food. Confidence can mean getting targeted. Loving yourself can mean betraying a family story that required self-erasure to survive.

Terms aren't personality. They're the constraints and incentives that shape who you become. They decide what feels natural, what feels risky, and what feels impossible. That's why two people can hear the same advice and walk away with different bodies. Modern self-help culture often worships intention. Intention is treated like a magic wand: if a person wants something badly enough, the person will do it. If a person fails, the failure must mean weakness, laziness, bad character, or a lack of love.

That story sells. It also breaks people. When stability is threatened, the system tightens. It reaches for whatever kept it alive before. This isn't a metaphor. It is a property of complex adaptive systems: under uncertainty, the cheapest reliable strategy becomes attractive.

Why Cheap Moves Repeat

Repeated behavior under repeated constraints forms a pull. When familiar Terms recur, the system reaches for the same Default. The world repeats, and the body repeats.

In human terms, a return clause can look like: The same kind of partner. The same kind of job conflict. The same kind of self-sabotage right before progress. The same kind of friend group. The same kind of binge after restraint. The same kind of disappearing when closeness arrives. The same kind of rage when respect feels threatened.

To change the basin, the landscape has to change: incentives, environment, relationships, timing, body state, and meaning. This is why changing a life often looks like changing what surrounds the Default, not only fighting the Default itself. It is not dramatic. It is structural.

This is also why many people feel cursed. When recurring patterns are not read structurally, they often feel like fate.

A teenager in the Bronx, a lawyer in Midtown, a janitor on a night shift, a new immigrant with a suitcase, a PhD student living on coffee, a person in recovery counting days. Different worlds, same mechanics. The surface differs. The Field logic repeats. Under threat, attention narrows. Under uncertainty, the system reaches backward. Under shame, the system hides. Under loneliness, the system bargains. Under overstimulation, the system numbs. When constraint and enforcement risk drop, underlying incentives and preferences become easier to observe.

Most people do not know why they do what they do. They know the story they tell about why they do what they do. Narratives are not useless; they keep the mind coherent. But the mind can tell a beautiful story while the body quietly runs the opposite program. A person says, "Love should be easy," then confuses intensity with intimacy and calls calm "boring."

Words are cheap. The body is expensive. This is why the most honest data in a life is not the self-description. The most honest data is the repeat. The Default shows itself in what happens when the same trigger arrives again. An email from the boss. A late text.

A door slamming. A compliment. A bill. A holiday. A silent room. A bed at night. A moment of success. A moment of rejection.

The trigger arrives, and the body makes a move. The move happens faster than ideology. That speed matters. Much of human behavior is not slow, deliberate reasoning. Much of it is rapid prediction and correction. The brain is a forecasting engine. It learned, through repetition, what tends to happen next in each situation. It anticipates. It prepares. It acts.

The system learns fast: what reduces pain, what buys belonging, what avoids threat. It repeats the move that worked, even when you hate the aftermath.

Relief Is Reinforcement

"Reward" is not always pleasure. Sometimes the reward is relief. Relief is the nervous system's favorite drug.

Relief is also why the wrong choices can feel right. If a person grew up being ignored until something dramatic happened, drama becomes a signal flare. The nervous system learns:

Intensity equals connection. Years later, calm will feel like neglect. The person will choose partners who recreate the old conditions, then call it chemistry. None of this requires pathology. This is normal adaptation. A human being is a learning system dropped into a world. The world teaches through consequence. The consequence does not have to be fair. It only has to be consistent enough to teach.

Intelligence increases the ability to justify. It builds elegant explanations for why a Default is unavoidable. Analysis can become a defense: a way to stay inside the same life while feeling as if progress is happening. One person disappears into substances. Another disappears into interpretation. Both may be avoiding the same state. Better branding does not make the Default different.

The Same Default Wears New Clothes

A human must be humble about this: the same Default can wear a thousand outfits. A single mother working two jobs is not choosing exhaustion as a personality. Exhaustion is the Field. A teenager in a violent neighborhood is not choosing hypervigilance as a vibe. Hypervigilance is the Field. A first-generation immigrant translating adult life at sixteen is not choosing maturity for fun. Premature responsibility is the Field. A physician in a broken system is not choosing numbness because of weak character.

Numbness is the Field. When constraints are hidden, observers often attribute outcomes to character and respond with blame instead of redesign.

This model makes the Field visible without removing responsibility. In practice, environment design often outperforms raw self-control. Self-control is state-dependent. It degrades under load and improves with sleep, safety, and slack. Change the environment so the better move costs less: reduce friction, remove triggers, build timing and structure, add accountability, and give the system a replacement reward. People tend to do what is easier, more immediate, and more socially reinforced.

Under stress, planning gets expensive and habit gets cheap. In groups, people copy what is rewarded and hide what is punished.

The question is not "why is there not more willpower?" The question is "why is the system living outside its window so often?" Sleep debt, chronic conflict, isolation, caffeine, alcohol, poor nutrition, constant digital stimulation, financial precarity, unsafe relationships, and unprocessed grief all narrow the window. Once the window narrows, minor triggers feel major. Life turns into a survival drill, and a survival drill cannot produce a free life.

VISIBLE CHOICE = OPTIONS PRICED BY HIDDEN TERMS

Preventative choice looks boring. That boredom is a sign of stability. Modern culture hates boring because boring does not sell. Boring is also where freedom lives. The Field is not a personality test. It is a lens: a way to see the invisible forces that shape a day so that the day stops shaping the person by default.

One modern force can intensify these loops: attention markets. Recommendation systems do not have ethics; they have objectives. Many platforms and media systems are optimized around engagement metrics because engagement monetizes. When ranking systems learn what keeps attention, they often privilege high-arousal content (outrage, fear, desire, comparison, and conflict) because those signals retain users. The nervous system then gets trained by repeated exposure to whatever reliably spikes arousal.

This is not a conspiracy. It is incentive. A person scrolls not only because the person is weak, but because the feed is engineered to monetize attention. Intermittent rewards keep a nervous system checking: maybe the next swipe pays out.

If a Field supplies constant micro-triggers, the nervous system stays activated. Activated systems choose short-term relief. Short-term relief reinforces loops. Loops become identity. Identity becomes defense. Defense becomes culture. That is how a personal Default becomes a social Default. The Field includes these systems because the modern self is not living in nature. The modern self is living inside engineered environments. Designed homes, designed cities, designed markets, designed media.

A theory that ignores engineered Fields is incomplete. The moment that matters is the moment a person stops treating engineered triggers like personal weakness and starts treating them like climate. Climate is managed through design: boundaries, schedule, environment curation, community selection, and conscious substitution.

A life is made in small intervals: the five seconds after a trigger, the ten minutes before sleep, the hour after rejection, the drift of attention when nobody is watching. The system runs those intervals. If survival has been expensive, the system keeps charging.

The work is not "be a better person." The work is "become a different system." Naming Terms does not eliminate dignity. It restores accurate responsibility.

If behavior is only "choice," then every struggling person becomes contemptible. If behavior is only "trauma," then every person becomes helpless. If behavior is Terms inside a Field, then struggle becomes understandable and change becomes designable. This is the middle path: accountability without cruelty. Cruelty confuses pain for pedagogy. Cruelty is lazy. It demands change without providing conditions. It tells a drowning person to swim better while holding the head under water. The Field refuses that logic.

It treats every human as a system doing its best with the costs it can perceive. Perception can be upgraded. Costs can be shifted. Environments can be redesigned. Groups can be changed. Meaning can be rebuilt. That is where freedom lives: not in denial of constraint, but in learning how constraint actually works.

Systems can change. That is the point. Naming the constraints, payoffs, and enforcement conditions makes Defaults legible and therefore adjustable. Invisibility is where Defaults hide.

A clause becomes visible when the same cost shows up in different rooms. Same fight, different partner. Same burnout, different job. Same panic, different deadline. That isn't fate. It's Terms.

Treat your life like a system you can finally see. The goal isn't to blame the past. The goal is to stop repeating the same clause in new ink. Start by noticing what repeats. That's the doorway.

2

Home Writes the First Terms

ELENA LEARNED EARLY THAT SILENCE IN A KITCHEN CAN BE A RULE BEFORE IT BECOMES A MEMORY.

Every human life begins mid-sentence. No one arrives as a blank page. A person arrives as a continuation.

Before the first memory, there is already calibration: caregiving patterns, stress exposure, and family survival strategies arriving before language. Some of that history is recorded. Most of it is not. The body carries it anyway. Through habits taught at the dinner table, through what gets praised or punished, through what counts as "normal," through what the nervous system expects when the world gets quiet.

This is not poetry. It is mechanics. A body is shaped by repeated exposure. Genes set ranges; early conditions help set baselines and stress thresholds. If food was scarce, the body learns to store. If danger was common, the body learns to scan. If love was conditional, the body learns to bargain, perform, or freeze. These are not moral choices. They are calibrations. Inheritance also arrives as rules that were never spoken.

The Rules You Inherited Before You Could Refuse Them

Families transmit how money is handled, how conflict is handled, how affection is earned, what gets punished, what gets ignored, and what counts as "normal." Not by lectures, but by repetition. A child watches what happens when someone asks a question, says no, cries, rests, fails, succeeds, tells the truth, tells a lie. The nervous system takes notes. By adulthood, those notes become priors: expectations about what the world will do next.

The person then chooses inside those priors, which is why different people can be handed the same opportunity and experience different costs. One person hears "risk" and feels possibility. Another hears "risk" and feels catastrophe. Inheritance is not only wealth or trauma. It is timing, tone, tolerance, and threat thresholds. It is what your body treats as safe, what your attention hunts for, and what your mind calls "me." You can change it.

But first you have to stop calling it destiny and start calling it training. Two siblings can grow up in the same home and inherit different priors because they were assigned different roles: the peacemaker, the achiever, the problem. Each role comes with its own payoff and its own threat. When the role becomes identity, the adult keeps paying for it long after the original home is gone.

This is one of the earliest truths of the Field: A person is not an isolated unit. A person is a node in a chain. Chains of the Field matter because chains enforce loyalty. A lineage is not only family. A lineage is also class. In one Field, a missed rent payment is a crisis that threatens housing. In another Field, a missed payment is an inconvenience.

In one Field, a broken arm threatens work and food. In another Field, a broken arm threatens only comfort. These differences shape psychology. They shape risk tolerance. They shape trust. They shape ambition. They shape the nervous system's Default state. Institutions extend lineage.

Schools, churches, policing, hospitals, immigration systems, workplaces, media ecosystems. These are not neutral backdrops. They reward certain behaviors and punish others. They shape what kinds of people "make sense" and what kinds of people are labeled problems. A child who grows up inside unstable institutions learns: authority is unreliable. A child who grows up inside protective institutions learns: authority can be trusted. A child who grows up inside corrupt institutions learns: rules are theater. A child who grows up inside consistent institutions learns: rules can be navigated.

Those lessons get carried into adulthood as priors. This is why it is possible for two adults to argue about "responsibility" while living in different realities. One adult means responsibility inside a Field where effort is rewarded. Another adult means responsibility inside a Field where effort is exploited. Both are describing lived data. Neither is describing the whole map.

The Field requires honesty about this: some people are born into a Field that makes change cheaper, and some are born into a Field that makes change expensive. Naming that is not defeat. It is accuracy. Accuracy is required for design. Loyalty is not only a virtue. Loyalty is also a constraint. A system will often prefer familiar suffering over unfamiliar freedom if freedom would mean separation from the group that provided identity and safety.

Not because success is bad. Because success can be lonely. In each case, the new behavior threatens belonging. The nervous system experiences that threat as real, even if the mind calls it irrational. That is lineage at work: a living system defending continuity.

Debt habits. Food habits. Conflict habits. Love habits. Work habits. Substance habits. Parenting habits. Gender habits. Shame habits. Money is one of the clearest inheritance channels because money reveals fear.

Money scripts are rarely taught directly. They are absorbed. A child watches whether bills create panic or routine. A child watches whether spending is celebrated, punished, or hidden. A child watches whether asking for help brings warmth or contempt. A child watches whether generosity is safe or exploited. Those observations become a financial nervous system. In behavioral economics, there is a concept called loss aversion: losses feel heavier than gains. In scarcity, loss aversion intensifies.

The system becomes more sensitive to potential loss than to potential growth. That produces conservative choices, or desperate choices, or both. That is why two people can receive the same paycheck and feel two different realities. One feels abundance and plans long-term. Another feels temporary safety and spends immediately, not out of immaturity, but out of training: resources disappear; take what can be taken now.

These Defaults are reinforced by experience. If a person grew up watching money vanish through job loss, illness, or rent hikes, then "save for later" feels naïve. The body says: later is not promised. History can be updated, but only through repeated evidence of stability, redundancy, support, and plans that work. These patterns repeat because they were learned as survival strategies, and in many environments they still are.

The nervous system does not choose partners only through conscious preference. It chooses through familiarity. Familiarity is not the same as health. Familiarity is simply recognizable. In psychology, the mere exposure effect describes how repeated exposure can increase preference. In attachment dynamics, repeated early relational Defaults can shape what feels like "chemistry." Chemistry is often the nervous system recognizing a template.

A person from a volatile home can feel a calm partner as "missing something" because the template expects intensity. A person from an emotionally cold home can feel an emotionally available partner as suspicious because the template expects distance. A person from a critical home can feel a supportive partner as unrealistic because the template expects correction.

People who genuinely want stability can still walk toward chaos. The walk is not a conscious plan. It is a prior pulling the system toward the known basin. This does not mean attraction is fake. It means attraction is trained. Training can be updated. But the update requires a willingness to tolerate unfamiliar safety long enough for it to stop feeling unfamiliar. That tolerance is not a slogan. It is a practice.

It is also a social decision: stable choices are easier when stable people surround you. That is one of the hidden reasons community matters. Community is not only emotional. Community is regulatory. The group sets the nervous system's baseline. A lineage built for village life can be dropped into a city. A lineage built for predictable seasons can be dropped into digital chaos. A lineage built for collective survival can be dropped into individualistic capitalism.

The old strategies still run, but the Field is different. The strategies begin to misfire because the body is still using old templates in new conditions.

Templates become unconscious instruction manuals. They dictate what "love" looks like, what "respect" looks like, what "safety" looks like, what "success" looks like, what "shame" looks like. Language is one of the most underrated inheritance mechanisms. Language does not only name objects. Language shapes what can be thought without strain. A person raised in a language that has a dozen words for family roles will notice relational nuance that another person might miss. A person raised in a language where respect is built into grammar will carry a different posture toward elders and authority.

Then adulthood arrives and exposes the cost. The Defaults are consistent. The labels change. This is where the phrase "just be yourself" becomes dangerous. Which self?

The goal is not to shame the inheritance. The goal is to see it accurately so it can be used intentionally.

Childhood is not only memory. It is calibration. The surface memory fades. The calibration stays.

Two adults can live in the same city, with the same access to information, and interpret the same interaction as either harmless or threatening. The interpretation is not a personality quirk. It is the nervous system running a model built in the first environment where survival mattered. That first environment is the house.

THE HOUSE BECOMES A LAB

The house is a laboratory. It trains the organism. The training happens through two learning systems at once. Classical conditioning links cues to body states. A slammed door becomes a cue. A certain tone becomes a cue. A parent's footsteps in the hallway become a cue. The cue arrives, and the body prepares before the mind knows why. Years later, a similar cue appears: a partner's sigh, a boss's pause, a friend going quiet - and the same preparation happens.

Those are not moral categories. Those are strategies. They become templates for later relationships because the nervous system prefers familiar rules, even when the rules hurt. The body learns through Default. It does not require a headline.

A house can provide food, education, and a safe neighborhood while still producing chronic dysregulation if emotional reality is denied. A child can grow up with material stability and still learn: feelings are unsafe, needs are shameful, conflict is catastrophic, love is conditional. The world then looks at the adult and says, "Nothing bad happened to you." The nervous system disagrees.

Traumatic stress can follow events that overwhelm coping capacity in the moment, and repeated adversity can accumulate over time.

DEFAULT =

$$(\text{IMPACT} \times \text{DURATION} \times \text{ISOLATION}) \div (\text{SUPPORT} \times \text{MEANING} \times \text{OPTIONS})$$

The developing nervous system is plastic. Plasticity is power. Plasticity is vulnerability. At a biological level, development includes processes like synaptic pruning, myelination, and the tuning of threat detection circuits. The details are not required to feel the truth: what repeats becomes wiring. Homes also assign roles: the responsible one, the funny one, the achiever, the invisible one, the caretaker, the rebel. Roles can look like personality because they are practiced for years. They are not personality. They are survival strategies that made the house more navigable. The point of naming them is not to collect labels. The point is to recognize Defaults so adulthood can choose something better.

Secure attachment is not a perfect childhood. It is a childhood with enough consistency that the child learns: needs can be expressed, repair happens after rupture, and closeness is not a trap. Disorganized attachment can emerge when the caregiver is both the source of comfort and the source of fear. The child's system cannot reconcile the contradiction. The result can be a push-pull Default: craving closeness and panicking when it arrives, wanting love and sabotaging it, seeking safety and choosing danger because danger is predictable.

The tragedy is that roles harden. The Default is stable because it solves a problem the nervous system still believes exists. That belief is often unconscious.

Conscious memory can be clean while the body is still running the old map. That is why "talking about childhood" is not always enough.

Fawning Buys Temporary Safety

Narrative memory can be updated while implicit memory remains unchanged. The body keeps its own ledger. There is also a survival strategy that rarely gets named because it looks like "being nice." Fawning is the Default of appeasing threat by becoming pleasing. It can look like agreement, charm, excessive empathy, sexual compliance, humor, caretaking, or constant apology. The goal is not true connection. The goal is de-escalation. The child learns: if the adult is pleased, the danger decreases. Fawning is not weakness.

It is a sophisticated survival strategy. It also becomes a trap in adult life because it attracts people who feel entitled to be served. The exit is not becoming cold. The exit is learning that safety does not require constant appeasement. The moment safety arrives, the system relaxes, and the stored material surfaces: panic, grief, rage, emptiness, exhaustion. The person says, "Why now?" The answer: the body waited until it could afford to feel. A child who had to keep going learned to postpone feeling.

That child can grow into an adult who stays outwardly functional while chronic stress keeps billing the body in the background.

Nervous system stability from adults. That process is called co-regulation. A calm adult in a child's storm teaches the child: feelings can be held without disaster. An overwhelmed adult teaches the opposite: feelings are emergencies.

When regulation is missing, the system looks for substitutes. These substitutes are not random. They are attempts to manage arousal and emotion with whatever tools were available. A person who cannot rest without guilt is not lazy. The nervous system is still negotiating with an old authority figure that lived in the house. That authority figure may be gone. The internalized voice remains. The Field treats that voice as data: it reveals what the house demanded.

A child learns whether signals are allowed. When signals are not allowed, the body finds alternative channels: headaches, gut issues, insomnia, chronic tension, skin problems, dissociation, compulsive behaviors. This is not "mind over matter." It is an organism trying to discharge load through any available pathway. The developing self also learns what love costs.

In some homes, the body is celebrated: food is pleasure, movement is normal, illness is treated with care, sexuality is discussed with honesty, and aging is not mocked. In other homes, the body is a problem: weight is criticized, hunger is shamed, sickness is ignored, sexuality is treated as dirty or dangerous, and appearance becomes a currency. Those lessons become adult body relationships. Again: not morality. Training.

The Field treats eating, sex, sleep, and movement as psychological topics. These are not side issues. These are the nervous system's main interfaces with regulation and reward. Love can cost obedience. Love can cost performance. Love can cost caretaking. Love can cost silence. Love can cost being easy. Love can cost shrinking.

Updating the House Model

Evidence takes time. That is why early change feels fake. The body has not collected enough proof yet. Updating the childhood model requires three kinds of new experience. First: new relationships. A stable relationship is not only comfort. It is corrective data.

It teaches the body that closeness can be safe, conflict can be repaired, and honesty can survive. Second: new environments. The nervous system is context-sensitive. A chaotic environment keeps the old program active. A calmer environment gives the body room to update. This is not "running away." This is changing the Field so the system can learn something new.

Third: new repetition. You behave differently in the same kind of situation until the nervous system changes its prediction. That is why gentle exposure works and flooding backfires. The goal is new evidence inside the window of tolerance. The mind can argue with alarms. The body does not listen to arguments. The body listens to outcomes. Build small moments where the reaction starts, then do something different: pause, breathe, ask, clarify, leave, hold a boundary, name the emotion, tolerate the discomfort. Repeat until the body learns the catastrophe is not guaranteed.

That is the practical meaning of healing: creating situations where the old prediction fails repeatedly, safely, until the nervous system revises its expectations.

Building a new lab does not require a perfect childhood rewrite. It requires deliberate inputs.

Boundaries that are enforced consistently, not boundaries declared once and abandoned. Different lives will design differently. A teenager living in a crowded home might need a library, a gym, a park bench, a mentor. Some third space where the nervous system can uncoil. A lawyer on call might need strict device boundaries and protected sleep, not more motivational quotes about discipline. A janitor working nights might need daylight exposure, routine meals, and community contact to prevent the body from drifting into chronic isolation.

A parent with limited money might need predictable rituals more than expensive interventions: dinner at the table, bedtime stories, honest apology after conflict. A person in recovery might need a new social Field entirely, because the old one is engineered around relapse.

The details vary. The principle does not: design the inputs until the outputs change. The Field does not ask for perfection. It asks for conditions. Change the conditions, and the Default changes. Refuse to change the conditions, and the Default will keep proving itself "true."

Childhood wrote the first draft. Adulthood decides whether the draft becomes a life sentence.

The point of reading childhood this way is not to live in it. The point is to stop living from it without knowing. A Default that remains unnamed keeps recruiting new evidence. The person enters adulthood and unconsciously chooses situations that prove the old model: unsafe partners, chaotic jobs, friendships built on rescue, lifestyles built on exhaustion, habits built on relief. Each repetition feels like fate. It is the nervous system seeking what it already knows how to survive. The exit begins when the model is named in plain language: the cue, the body response, the prediction, the survival move.

That language is power because it turns fog into a map. A map does not erase the past. It keeps the past from running the future by default. A person can carry history with respect and still refuse to repeat it.

3

Your Current Environment

MARCUS NOTICES THE ROOM BEFORE HE NOTICES HIS THOUGHTS: FLUORESCENT LIGHT, STALE AIR, AND CONSTANT NOISE.

Before you learn rules, your body learns the room. Air. Light. Noise. Sleep. Threat. The first environment is not an idea. It is the conditions your nervous system has to survive.

A human body arrives and immediately begins adapting to what it meets first. Not as philosophy. As chemistry, heat, pressure, pathogens, and the presence or absence of threat. That sampling is calibration. Calibration means the system sets its Defaults based on what it meets first. It decides what counts as "normal" load.

It decides how quickly to mobilize. It decides what level of noise is ignorable. It decides what level of light feels safe to rest under. It decides what kind of air makes breathing feel easy, and what kind makes breathing feel like work. Those are Terms before you have language for them. The story comes later.

The Room Sets the Baseline

No one chooses those settings. A nervous system does not get a vote. It adapts. Start with the simplest fact: the air you breathe is a physiological input.

The first breath is not symbolic. It is literal intake of the local world. The body learns the taste of the air where life begins. Ocean salt.

Dry dust. Diesel. Smoke. Mold. Pine. Bleach. Perfume. Industrial solvent.

Roasted food. Damp concrete. A hospital's antiseptic sting. A basement's wet rot. A city summer's trash heat. A winter's sharp cold. Those molecules do two things at once. They build the body, and they teach the body what kind of world this is. When impulse is cheap and regulation is expensive, a life can look like "bad choices" from the outside.

This is the first place the Field shows itself without metaphor. The Field is not only people. It is particulate matter. It is humidity.

It is allergens. It is the density of bodies in a room. It is whether windows open. It is whether streets are lined with trees or exhaust pipes.

It is whether a child sleeps with a fan to drown out sirens, or sleeps with the window cracked to hear crickets.

The body does not need the concept. It lives the constraint. Some lives begin inside an abundance of quiet and clean. Some begin inside an abundance of stress and noise. Those beginnings do not guarantee a destiny, but they do tilt the starting conditions. They set the starting interest rate on the nervous system's loans. Allostasis is the body's budgeting process: the way it stays stable by spending energy. When the environment is harsh, the body spends more to stay stable.

That spending accumulates. It becomes allostatic load, a ledger of adaptation. This is why two people can want the same change and pay different prices for it. One can stay stable on five hours of broken sleep. Another becomes unstable quickly, not because of weakness, but because the baseline costs are already high.

Light Sets the Clock

The Field is doing arithmetic. It is not judging. Light is another quiet architect. Before the brain learns concepts, it learns day and night. It learns brightness and shadow. It learns whether night means rest or vigilance. It learns whether light comes from the sun or from flickering fluorescents. It learns whether mornings arrive with ease or arrive after a night of noise, disruption, and emergency.

The circadian system is not a motivational quote. It is hardware. It is a timing mechanism that coordinates hormones, temperature, appetite, immune function, alertness, and mood.

The story is cheap. The mechanism is expensive. Modern life is a light experiment on a species built for sunrise and darkness. A person can be born under tropical sun and grow up inside neon. A person can be born under long winter nights and grow up in a city that never turns off. A person can spend adolescence staring into a rectangle at midnight, training the brain to treat night as daytime, and then wonder why mornings feel like punishment.

Light does not only shape sleep. It shapes dignity. Some people can control light. They can dim a room, close a laptop, and let night be night. Other people live inside schedules that treat darkness as irrelevant: hospitals, warehouses, security booths, restaurants, transit systems, the endless care work that keeps cities alive. For those lives, the night shift is not a personality. It is an imposed circadian tax.

A circadian tax is the hidden interest paid when a body is forced to run at the wrong hour. It shows up as hunger at odd times, a shorter fuse, a weaker immune response, a foggy mind, a need for stimulants, a need for sedatives, and a constant sense that effort yields less return than it should. Chronotype is not identity. It is distribution. Some bodies peak early. Some bodies peak late.

Modern life treats one of those distributions as moral and the other as defective. The result is predictable: a whole class of people blaming themselves for a mismatch between biology and schedule.

That mismatch has a name in the literature: social jet lag. The body is waking on one clock and living on another, the way it would after flying across time zones. Except there is no vacation at the destination. There is only another week of misalignment. Misalignment changes behavior. A tired brain is less flexible. A tired brain Defaults to the cheap option: sugar, scrolling, anger, avoidance, impulse spending, relapse. Then the person gets judged as undisciplined.

The same Field conditions can produce the behavior and then punish the person for it. Light is also a signal war. The retina does not care that a phone is not the sun. It responds to brightness and timing. Late-night light tells the brain that morning has arrived. Early-morning darkness tells the brain that night is still here. The organism follows the signals it receives, not the intentions it recites.

Many people cannot think clearly in the morning and cannot shut down at night. They are not broken. They are living inside an experiment. Industrial schedules, artificial light, and screens optimized to keep attention awake long after the body was built to power down. Children learn this first. A child who falls asleep to a television learns that sleep is something that happens inside stimulation. A child who grows up under constant streetlight learns that darkness is foreign.

Later, quiet and dark can feel unsafe, even when the adult insists they want peace. Calibration often wins the argument. Until repeated evidence, skills, and support shift what safety costs.

Temperature is another unglamorous architect. Heat can change sleep, appetite, and irritability; cold can do the same in a different direction. Tension, contraction, a constant fight for comfort. Effects vary by body, acclimation, clothing, and context, but baseline discomfort makes every other choice more expensive.

When a body is negotiating temperature all day, attention becomes expensive and patience becomes rare. This is why some people cannot "focus" in a room that never cools down. The nervous system is spending its budget on regulation. That spending is invisible to observers who have always had stable heat, stable cooling, stable comfort. They call it laziness. The body calls it load.

Crowding is the final quiet architect. Crowding is not only bodies in a room. It is the absence of recovery space. It is the inability to be alone without being monitored. It is having nowhere to drop the mask. When privacy is expensive, self-regulation becomes expensive. The system stays half-on because it never gets permission to fully downshift.

NOISE TRAINS VIGILANCE

Air, light, noise, temperature, and crowding are the Field in its purest form: inputs that train the body before the mind ever forms a philosophy. When those inputs are ignored, people build stories to explain outputs. When those inputs are changed, outputs change without speeches. None of this is moral. It is calibration. Noise is the third architect people ignore. A siren at 3 a.m. is noise. A parent's yelling is noise. A roommate slamming doors is noise.

An upstairs neighbor pacing is noise. A television that never turns off is noise. A group chat that never stops vibrating is noise. A constant low-grade threat that something will happen is noise. Noise trains the brain to scan. Scanning is costly.

It consumes attention. It consumes energy. It makes concentration feel like effort. It makes stillness feel unsafe. It makes silence feel loud. This is why some people cannot work in quiet.

Quiet leaves the body alone with itself. A body trained under noise often needs noise to feel normal. That is not preference. It is imprint. The brain's threat system does not need a dramatic trauma to become vigilant. Chronic interruption is enough. Chronic unpredictability is enough. Chronic overstimulation is enough. The nervous system learns: stay ready. Readiness becomes identity if it is never named. From the outside it can look like intensity.

From the inside it feels like never fully landing. A person can carry that readiness into a job and be praised for being "on it" and "fast" and "always available." The praise reinforces the Default. The Default becomes a career. Then the cost arrives: exhaustion, irritability, insomnia, hypertension, compulsions, numbness, a sudden collapse that looks random but was being billed for years. The Field is the name for that billing system. This is why the same advice lands differently across lives. "Just relax" is not advice. It is a confession that the speaker has never had to fight for baseline safety.

Relaxation is a skill, but it is also an environment. A regulated nervous system is not only a personal achievement. It is a product of conditions: stable housing, predictable schedules, enough food, enough sleep, low violence exposure, manageable noise, supportive relationships, and the simple experience of being able to make a mistake without catastrophe. Those conditions are not equally distributed. This is where the fantasy of equal choice does the most damage.

It tells people to blame themselves for the cost of their own environment. That does not produce change. It produces shame. Shame creates more noise in the system. More noise makes the Default tighter. Baseline is set by the body's environment early and often. Use timing as a variable, not a verdict.

Moving can be a psychological event even when nothing "bad" happens. The Field changes, which means the cost map changes. Mismatch is a cost.

People love to talk about resilience, but resilience is not pretending mismatch is fine. Resilience is building capacity to tolerate mismatch without losing coherence. Coherence is a system's ability to keep its signals aligned. When sleep, stress, appetite, mood, attention, and meaning move in different directions, coherence collapses. Collapse drives the system to reach for cheap stabilizers. Cheap stabilizers are Defaults. A person in a high-noise environment will often choose high-intensity stabilizers because subtle stabilizers cannot compete.

Slow breathing is real, but it is hard to access when the environment never stops signaling danger. Meditation works, but it is not designed to compete with a landlord threat, a violent block, a screaming household, or a schedule that breaks sleep for money. Air, light, and noise also shape meaning.

Meaning follows sensation. The stories a person tells later are often rationalizations of early calibration. This is why moral arguments rarely change people. Moral arguments speak to the story layer. Calibration lives beneath story.

The faster route is not preaching. It is changing input. One of the most reliable interventions in a human life is often boring: changing air, changing light, changing noise, changing sleep, changing the number of interruptions per day. Boring is exactly why it works. A system updates from outcomes. Outcomes change when conditions change.

ENVIRONMENTAL LOAD = NOISE + THREAT + FRICTION - RECOVERY

Some conditions are changeable. Some are not. That is reality, not pessimism. A person can add blackout curtains and stop waking up in a flood of streetlight. A person can buy earplugs and finally sleep through a neighbor's chaos. A person can set a screen boundary and let melatonin do its job. A person can spend more time outdoors and let the body remember that day is day. A person can clean mold and stop living in a low-grade inflammatory fog.

A person can also be trapped. Many are. A person can be born into a neighborhood where the air is toxic because the highway cuts through it. A person can be priced out of quiet. A person can live under a landlord who will not fix mold. A person can work nights because the bills do not accept philosophy. A person can raise children under constant noise because the building is old and the city is loud and the options are limited.

Environmental fine print is dosage. Air is not "just air." Noise is not "just noise." Light, temperature, crowding, and allergens are not background. They are inputs. Inputs become biology.

Two people can live in the same city, work the same hours, and still end up with different nervous systems because their rooms are different. One sleeps beside a highway, under a streetlamp, with a neighbor's bass coming through the wall. The other sleeps in relative dark and quiet. Give it three months. One person is more irritable, more impulsive, and more reactive, and then gets told it is "attitude." It is sleep debt plus stress exposure.

Treat your environment like a lab. Change one variable for one week and measure the result. Earplugs. A fan for white noise. Blackout curtains. A cheap hygrometer to see if the room is too dry or too damp. Open the window, or do not. Walk outside in the morning light, or do not. Track two things: how long it takes to fall asleep, and how you feel at 11 a.m. Defaults will show up fast.

Sometimes the experiment proves a hard truth: the room is making you sick. Mold, heat, pests, constant conflict, constant noise. If you cannot change the room, you have to change the arrangement: more time elsewhere, different hours, different housing, different neighborhood, different city. That is not drama. That is arithmetic.

As heat waves, smoke, flooding, and energy volatility increase in many regions, "environment" increasingly behaves like a monthly fee. People who can read the Field treat shelter, air, and quiet like baseline infrastructure, not luxury.

Some Terms cannot be solved by personal optimization. If a neighborhood is loud because of policy, or unsafe because of neglect, or unhealthy because of pollution, the "fix" is not meditation. The fix is collective: enforcement, investment, design, and accountability. Until then, a person's job is to stop confusing endurance with virtue. If the room is the problem, treat leaving as intelligence.

The clause is real whether you believe it or not. That is not a personal failure. That is the Field. The honest move is to name what can be changed, and what cannot, and to stop pretending both are the same. This is not a demand for purity. It is a demand for accuracy. If the goal is freedom, freedom begins with seeing the actual inputs shaping the system. Air, light, and noise are inputs. They are not background. They are not decor.

They are part of the Terms. Free will exists inside a body that is either taxed or supported by the environment. When the environment supports the body, the body has slack. Slack makes choices cheaper. Cheaper choices become more frequent. More frequent good choices become a life. When the environment taxes the body, the body runs hot. Running hot makes narrow choices. Narrow choices repeat. Repetition becomes identity.

Repeated Defaults, under stable Terms, start to look like identity and become predictive; they are environment-trained patterns, not fate. The exit is rarely heroic. The exit is usually environmental. The most underestimated question in a human life is not identity. It is: what is being breathed, what light is shaping sleep, and what kind of noise is training the nervous system every day? Those answers are not inspirational. They are decisive.

4

The Body's Ledger: State and Capacity

RAFI'S BODY REMEMBERS NIGHTS HIS MIND KEEPS TRYING TO RENAME.

The body does not forget because the body stores what it had to do to survive. A mind can rewrite a story. A nervous system cannot be argued out of a reflex. That is the first reason many people feel trapped inside "choices" that do not behave like choices. The moment the system detects a familiar threat Default, it moves first and explains later.

Under acute stress, slower planning and language functions narrow while faster survival responses dominate. The explanation feels like personality. The movement is physiology. This is what it means to say the body keeps a record. The record is not mystical. It is procedural. It is the accumulation of predictions that kept the organism alive.

A nervous system is a forecasting machine. It constantly asks: what is about to happen, and what should be done now to survive it? The brain does not wait for certainty because certainty often arrives too late.

Experience does not only mean what happened. It means what happened repeatedly. It means what happened when no help arrived. It means what happened when help arrived and made things worse. It means what happened in the body at the moment of threat: heart rate, breath, muscle tension, freezing, appeasing, running, fighting, collapsing. Those responses become templates.

When the Body Predicts Before the Mind Does

Templates are powerful because they bypass debate. Debate is slow. Templates are fast. There are different kinds of memory, and confusing them is how people end up arguing with their own bodies. Declarative memory is the story layer: names, dates, scenes, facts. It can be incomplete or even absent. A person can forget details and still be shaped by what happened.

That is not denial. That is how the brain protects function. Procedural memory is the body layer: the sequence, the reflex, the timing. It is the learned algorithm that runs without asking permission. The record described here is procedural. It is not a diary. It is a playbook.

A body can forget the day, the face, the room, and still flinch at a tone of voice that matches the old room. A body can insist it is fine and still tighten its jaw when the same kind of silence returns. The system does not need a narrative to run a program. This is why triggers look irrational from the outside. The trigger is not always the obvious event.

The trigger is the Default match: the smell, the lighting, the cadence of footsteps, the shape of a hallway, the kind of laughter that used to precede humiliation. Default matching is cheap. That is the point. If the system had to reason through every danger from scratch, it would die. It overgeneralizes. It treats similarity as signal. It fires early to avoid paying late. Interoception is the sense of the inside: hunger, thirst, breath, tension, heartbeat, heat, nausea, fatigue.

The brain is not only predicting the outside world. It is predicting the internal world and deciding what those signals mean. A person with a calm record can feel a fast heart and think: caffeine, excitement, stairs, a normal body doing normal things. A person with a threat-trained record can feel the same heart rate and think: danger, judgment, collapse, rejection. The same signal. A different model. A different life. This is how panic happens.

That is not a moral failure. It is an operating mode. The body record also explains why some people chase intensity. Intensity can be a self-made trigger. If the baseline state is under-stimulated numbness, intensity feels like life. If the baseline state is chronic vigilance, intensity feels like confirmation. Either way, the system is matching the internal state to a familiar Default so it can predict what comes next.

An adult can swear they want peace and still pick partners who feel like the old house. Not because peace is unwanted, but because peace is unfamiliar. Unfamiliar is expensive. Familiar is cheap. Cheap is chosen Under load. Once this is clear, the goal changes. The goal is not to become a different person through force. The goal is to give the nervous system new data (repeatedly) until the old playbook becomes more expensive than the new one.

New data is not only emotional. It is sensory. It is sleep that actually restores. It is meals that arrive regularly. It is a room that stays quiet. It is a relationship where repair happens after rupture. It is an environment where the body stops bracing for impact.

A person can be "successful" on paper and still feel unsafe in a quiet room. A person can be loved and still brace for abandonment. A person can be stable and still reach for chaos. A person can be praised and still hear accusation. Allostasis is how the body stays stable by changing. Heart rate rises to meet demand. Cortisol mobilizes energy. Attention narrows to track threat.

Digestion slows to prioritize survival. Sleep becomes shallow to stay ready. Pain sensitivity changes. Immune function shifts. These are not flaws. They are adaptations. An adaptation becomes a problem when it outlives its environment. A body trained under chronic threat can keep running threat protocols long after danger is gone. The protocol becomes the personality label: anxious, intense, guarded, avoidant, controlling, lazy, addicted.

The label is often wrong. The label describes the symptom of a prediction system that has never been given enough evidence to update. A nervous system updates when a familiar trigger occurs and the expected catastrophe does not. It updates when safety is not a concept but a lived sequence: the door closes, the body relaxes, nothing bad happens, the next day arrives, the world continues.

One calm day is not evidence. It is noise. A system needs repetition to revise its model. When safety is inconsistent, the nervous system predicts a bill: relational debt. The person withdraws or becomes performative, trying to pay the debt preemptively.

Then relationships feel exhausting, not because love is flawed, but because love is being processed through an old accounting system.

A person who learned that mistakes meant humiliation can feel panic in any evaluative situation: interviews, exams, feedback, even praise. Praise is not safe because praise raises expectations. Expectations raise the cost of failure. The body responds by sabotaging, avoiding, or attacking first. A person who lived through real violence can react to normal conflict as if it is lethal. Tone shifts, footsteps, a slammed cabinet, a hand movement. The body fires the same alarm. The mind arrives late and calls it overreaction. The body calls it survival.

None of those outcomes are guaranteed in any one person. The point is not certainty. The point is that the body and the story are not separate departments. A human life is one system. The Field is the name for the system-level view: how behavior, body, relationships, time, and environment form a single pressure landscape. The budget is shaped by the record. A person reaches for alcohol to turn down noise.

A person reaches for food to create comfort. A person reaches for work to avoid emptiness. A person reaches for sex to feel alive. A person reaches for scrolling to avoid thinking. A person reaches for rage to feel power. A person reaches for sleep to disappear. Relief becomes evidence. Evidence reinforces the record.

This is the most misunderstood loop in modern life. People treat compulsion as moral failure. Moralizing increases shame. Shame increases load. Load increases the need for relief. Relief reinforces compulsion.

The loop tightens. A person can become trapped in this loop while appearing functional. High-status addictions exist. Workaholism is an addiction. Achievement can be an addiction. Being needed can be an addiction.

The bill usually arrives eventually, even if it shows up late or gets externalized, because the body's record does not care about applause. The record is also social.

A body learns safety partly through other bodies. Attachment is physiology, not sentiment. When care is consistent, the nervous system learns co-regulation: the ability to return to baseline through connection. When care is inconsistent, manipulative, or absent, the nervous system learns that connection is not reliable. That becomes a baseline setting.

That is a high bar. It is also a practical one. That can happen through therapy. It can happen through a safe relationship. It can happen through changing environment. It can happen through learning skills that increase control.

It can happen through building financial stability. It can happen through sobriety. It can happen through leaving a violent place. It can happen through finally sleeping. It can happen through medication. It can happen through community.

Understanding is not forgiveness for harm. Harm still counts. Understanding is Leverage. It allows the system to be addressed at the level it lives: inputs, prediction, cost. A person who wants a new life has to stop negotiating only with the story. That is the quiet miracle beneath every "overnight" transformation. Nothing was overnight. Interoception is the nervous system's perception of internal state: heartbeat, breath, temperature, hunger, nausea, tension. A person lives inside these signals.

When the signals are chronically elevated, the world looks different. A crowded room looks hostile. A neutral face looks judgmental. A quiet pause looks like rejection. The body's signal becomes the lens. Panic is not an opinion.

It is a full-body state. In that state, the brain prioritizes survival. Attention narrows. Time feels distorted. The ability to think in long arcs collapses. The mind starts hunting for an explanation to match the intensity of the signal.

If it cannot find one, it invents one. Logic does not win against a state it cannot enter. A person can know, intellectually, that a flight is safe, and still shake. A person can know, intellectually, that a partner is not abandoning them, and still spiral. A person can know, intellectually, that a supervisor's email is neutral, and still feel attacked. The record is firing. The mind is trying to keep up.

This is also why some people cannot access their best selves on demand. The "best self" requires regulation: enough calm to think, enough safety to be honest, enough slack to choose the expensive option. When the record is loud, the nervous system chooses the cheap option. Cheap options are often social strategies. Fight, flight, freeze, fawn are not buzzwords. They are categories of cost management. Fighting can create control. Fleeing can reduce exposure. Freezing can avoid detection.

Appeasing can prevent escalation. A person learns which strategy worked in the early Field and repeats it later even when it no longer fits.

A brilliant adult can still appease a mediocre bully because the record learned appeasement was the cheapest path to safety. A competent leader can still freeze in conflict because the record learned that movement invited punishment. A kind person can still attack first because the record learned that being soft was expensive. The record does not care about self-image. It cares about outcomes.

There is a reason people often change fastest after a true break. A break is when the old strategy stops paying. The relationship ends. The job collapses. The body gets sick. The addiction stops delivering relief and starts delivering pain. The cost flips. The system finally has incentive to learn a new strategy because the old one is no longer cheap.

That is brutal. It is also mechanical. The earlier alternative is learning by choice: building a new record before the old one collapses. That requires patience, structure, and usually support, because the system is being asked to tolerate discomfort without the emergency forcing it. The ledger under the skin is why some compliments feel like threats. If praise used to precede demands, praise becomes expensive.

If calm used to precede an explosion, calm becomes expensive. If love used to be conditional, love becomes expensive. The body is not being dramatic. It is keeping an audit trail. An audit trail is not a grievance list. It is a risk model. It is the nervous system saying: this happened before, which means it might happen again.

The model can be wrong. The model can also be accurate. Either way, arguing with it without changing conditions is wasted breath.

The cleanest question is never "Why am I like this?" The cleanest question is "What did this protect, and what is it costing now?" Protection is the origin. Cost is the present. When protection is honored and cost is named, the system can consider a new strategy without feeling like it is betraying itself.

A receipt is proof of purchase. The body is proof of exposure. It records what you have been breathing, eating, swallowing emotionally, and carrying. It records it in muscle tone, inflammation, digestion, skin, sleep, and baseline mood. The body does not keep secrets politely.

This is where measurement becomes dignity. Track what you can: sleep hours, resting heart rate, steps, alcohol, caffeine, time in daylight, time in conflict, time alone. You are not trying to become a robot. You are trying to stop gaslighting yourself about inputs.

BODY LEDGER = REPEATED EXPOSURE - REPAIR

History shows this clearly. When food was seasonal, sleep was darker, and community was closer, baseline regulation was different. Modern life traded some dangers for new ones: artificial light, processed food, isolation, nonstop information. The receipt printer never stopped.

Another way to say it: your symptoms are not a personality review. They are telemetry. If you read telemetry early, you can adjust before the engine overheats. Most people wait until the breakdown forces a change. The Field is teaching earlier maintenance.

The work is not mystical. It is mechanical: build enough safety, over enough repetitions, that the nervous system stops treating the present like the past. That can involve therapy. It can involve medication. It can involve changing who is allowed near the body. It can involve sleep, movement, and the unglamorous rebuilding of daily rhythm. The method varies. The requirement does not: new evidence, repeated, under conditions the body can tolerate. That is what real maturity is: paying for learning before crisis collects the debt.

A person does not "intend" to overreact when a certain tone is used. Overreaction is an old prediction firing before the conscious mind arrives. The system does not ask what is true. It asks what is cheap. Cheap means: what reduces threat quickly, what restores predictability quickly, what restores belonging quickly, what restores control quickly, what restores sensation quickly.

Conservative means: less exploration, more repetition. Less flexibility, more reflex. Less long-term thinking, more short-term relief. In cognitive science, this shows up as narrowed attention. In stress physiology, it shows up as sympathetic activation. In daily life, it shows up as snapping, binging, withdrawing, spending, fighting, scrolling, drinking, disappearing, or working until the body shuts down. Most people mislabel these moves as personality. They are often state-dependent strategies.

Some people become numb when stressed. Numbness is cheaper than constant alarm. These are not random quirks. They are strategies. They are also visible in the body. A stressed system has a signature. It shows up in jaw tension, gut tightness, shallow breath, cold hands, hot face, insomnia, headaches, back pain, racing thoughts, irritability, shutdown, or a constant sense of urgency that does not match the actual day. Ignoring the dashboard is expensive.

This matters because perception is upstream of choice. People do not react to reality. People react to their nervous system's model of reality. Under load, the model becomes more pessimistic, more suspicious, more absolute.

A body in pain interprets the world as less safe because it is less capable. The mind then builds a story to justify the feeling. When state is skewed, accuracy is harder.

Capacity Has a Price

Marcus can think clearly on Sunday afternoon and lose access to that clarity by Tuesday night. A clean approach to human behavior starts with state literacy. It also means refusing to make permanent conclusions from temporary states.

Simplification reduces uncertainty. It also reduces possibility. State literacy cuts through that. It is also why the most practical interventions are often boring: sleep, food, hydration, movement, daylight, lowering noise, stabilizing routine, reducing conflict exposure, increasing social safety, designing rest.

A person can know exactly what to do and still not do it. The knowledge is not the constraint. The state is.

They pay for it in private: insomnia, irritability, digestive issues, cravings, collapse on weekends, or the inability to enjoy what they worked for. The state layer also explains why environments matter more than affirmations.

A person cannot out-mantra a night-shift schedule that destroys sleep. Biology is not cruel. Biology is honest. A person might be a teen in a crowded apartment, studying with headphones while adults argue through walls. A person might be a nurse finishing a double shift, walking into a home where someone still wants a fight.

A person might be an analyst staring at a screen all day, under fluorescent light, in a chair that locks the hips, while the body quietly accumulates exhaustion. A person might be a recent immigrant navigating bureaucracy in a second language, carrying fear in the jaw all day because one mistake feels catastrophic. Different lives. Same principle: state is shaped before "choice" arrives.

Elena knows this version too: a week of promising Saturday to work and Sunday to family, then wondering why every small task feels hostile by Tuesday. Her jaw tightens, patience shortens, and even the grocery line feels adversarial. Low capacity does not announce itself as a theory. It arrives as a life that suddenly feels impossible to hold.

This is also why the phrase "be your best self" is meaningless without specifying conditions.

Inside the window, the person can pause, reflect, and choose. The exact boundaries differ by person. The logic does not.

Under enough load, even high-functioning people lose access to the version of themselves they like.

Do Not Negotiate from a Flooded State

The important implication is this: change that depends on the best state only is fragile. Durable change is the behavior that survives the bad states. That requires designing around state, not pretending state does not exist. The first design move is timing. Most catastrophic decisions happen in predictable windows: late night, post-conflict, post-rejection, post-exhaustion, post-boredom, post-shame. Those windows are not moral tests. They are high-risk environments. A system can be built around that truth. Rules are not for the good days. Rules are for the days when state makes bad options cheap.

A practical rule: never renegotiate the relationship at midnight. Never send the message that will haunt you when sleep returns. Never spend money to regulate a state that could be regulated with food, water, movement, or sleep. Never decide the future from the moment the body is panicking. That is not avoidance. That is respect for signal quality.

Another design move is pre-commitment. A pre-commitment is a decision made in a good state that protects you in a bad state: automatic savings, blocked apps at night, a packed lunch, a workout scheduled with a friend, an appointment already on the calendar, a boundary already stated, a supportive person already told the plan.

Pre-commitment is intelligence applied to the nervous system. It assumes the future state will not cooperate. It designs anyway. The third move is friction. Friction makes destructive actions slightly harder to execute. It does not have to be dramatic. It can be removing saved payment methods, keeping substances out of the home, storing gambling apps behind passwords, putting devices outside the bedroom, building a routine that includes a buffer before stress peaks.

Power, in the Field, means usable options under pressure. That is why freedom is capacity. Capacity is the set of resources that makes a choice repeatable. Repeatable is the real test. Many people can do almost anything once. What matters is what becomes repeatable under real constraints.

What matters here is usable choice. A menu that exists only in theory is not freedom; it is decoration. Capacity is what turns options into something the body can actually repeat under load.

Resources Minus Load

Capacity can be described as a simple equation: capacity equals resources minus load. Resources can be external (money, time, safety, support) and internal (sleep, health, skills, regulation). Load can be external (work demands, violence, bureaucracy, caretaking) and internal (pain, anxiety, depression, craving, rumination).

When load outruns resources, the system contracts around survival. It reaches for immediate regulation before long-horizon values. That contraction is what people often mislabel as weak character.

A person can be allowed to rest, leave, study, or get sober and still be unable to execute because the underlying capacity is missing. This is why state belongs in any honest account of freedom.

Physiological capacity: sleep, nutrition, movement, nervous system regulation, health, absence of chronic depletion. Cognitive capacity: attention, working memory, ability to plan, ability to hold the future, clarity under stress. Emotional capacity: tolerance for discomfort, ability to repair, ability to stay present, ability to name internal states. Social capacity: safe relationships, support, community, belonging that does not require self-betrayal. Economic capacity: money, buffer, predictable income, access to resources. Environmental capacity: a safe place, quiet, stability, a calendar with rhythm. Institutional capacity: documentation, legal protection, access to healthcare, access to education, access to transportation.

Increase load only after you have already deposited capacity. Do not try to build the muscle in the same moment you add weight. If you need a bigger life, ramp it: deposit → test → deposit → expand.

Stable routines are not "boring lifestyle content." They are capacity production.

The practical question is not whether recurrence is shameful. It is which variable would make the safer move cheaper the next time pressure rises.

Once that is clear, the task stops being heroic self-denial and becomes condition-building: more sleep, more buffer, more structure, less exposure to what keeps the old move cheap.

Friction works because systems are lazy. If an option becomes more expensive, the system will try a cheaper one, especially if a cheaper one exists. That is the key: create alternatives. The fourth move is replacement.

The correct question is: what job is the behavior doing? Is it lowering anxiety? Is it creating sensation? Is it creating control?

Is it creating belonging? Is it creating silence? Is it creating identity? Is it creating protection from vulnerability? Once the job is named, replacement becomes possible. If the job is belonging, replace with people who do not require self-betrayal.

If the job is control, replace with structure. If the job is identity, replace with values-based action. State determines what replacements are available. This is why small changes are powerful. Small changes can widen the Choice Set by lowering baseline cost. This is also why the fastest growth sometimes looks like becoming basic.

Sleep. Eat. Walk. Drink water. Leave the room. Say no.

Turn off the phone. Take the nap. Stop arguing with the past. People underestimate how revolutionary this is because it is not poetic. It is mechanics. A final move is measurement. State lies to the memory.

A stressed body remembers the world as worse than it was. A euphoric body remembers the world as better than it was. A depressed body remembers the world as emptier than it was. Measurement is the antidote. Measurement does not need to be scientific. It can be a short daily log: sleep hours, hunger level, stress level, movement, social contact, and a one-line note about the day. Defaults appear quickly When data is honest. A person begins to see: every time sleep drops below six hours for three days, the relationship conflict spikes.

Every time money gets tight, avoidance increases. Every time there is no daylight, mood collapses. Every time there is a certain person, the chest tightens. That is not fate. That is state interacting with Field. Once seen, it becomes negotiable. The most aggressive form of self-respect is refusing to interpret taxed state as truth.

That does not mean ignoring reality. It means refusing to confuse temporary chemistry with permanent identity. Those versions are states. The work is to lower the frequency and intensity of the states that hijack the life, and to build strategies that function even when state is imperfect. That is how choice becomes real.

That is the point of the ledger. State sets the price. Learn the pricing, and the whole life becomes easier to steer. State also has timing. A body is not equally capable at every hour. Cortisol, temperature, alertness, and impulse control move in cycles. Late night is not only darkness; it is a different operating environment. Add hunger, alcohol, or a glowing screen and the system becomes more reactive, more absolute, more willing to gamble the future for immediate relief. This is why many lives contain the same scene on repeat: the midnight argument that never resolves, the late-night message that never helps, the nighttime purchase that feels smart until morning, the 2 a.m. spiral that turns tomorrow into punishment.

Protocol means building rules that respect state timing. A clean protocol is simple: do not treat late-night intensity as truth. Treat it as a state signal. If something still feels true after sleep, food, and daylight, then it is worth action. If it evaporates after those basics, it was chemistry wearing a mask.

State stacks too. One bad night is survivable. A week of bad nights becomes a different personality. One hard day is survivable. A month of hard days becomes a new baseline. This is how people end up saying, "I don't recognize myself," as if a stranger moved in. No stranger moved in. A taxed state became home.

USABLE CHOICE = CAPACITY - CURRENT LOAD

The most useful question before any major decision is not, "What do I want?"

A state audit can be blunt: How much sleep has happened in the last three nights? Has the body moved enough to discharge stress chemistry? Has a safe human been spoken to this week?

Storm conditions are not the time to redesign a life. They are the time to stabilize the body, reduce noise, and return to higher signal. That is not weakness. That is maturity.

Maturity is building a life that does not require heroism to function. The ledger is not asking for perfection. It is asking for accuracy. State is the first layer of accuracy.

When state is respected, choices become cheaper. When state is ignored, everything becomes expensive.

The most powerful shift in a human life is learning to say: this is not who you are, this is the state you are in.

State is the chemistry you are standing in. The same person makes different decisions depending on sleep, blood sugar, pain, hormones, and threat. This is not an insult. It is a fact about mammals.

A person who is rested can tolerate ambiguity. A person who is sleep-deprived reads neutrality as hostility. A person who has eaten can delay gratification. A person who is hungry will gamble for relief. Then the hungry person tells a story about "who I am," when it was really "what state I was in."

Moral lectures alone tend to fail. You cannot rely on words without changing conditions; you have to change inputs, build skills, and let the system settle. Once state changes, values become easier to practice. Before state changes, values can collapse into slogans.

Before you interpret behavior, ask the blunt questions: How many hours did I sleep? When did I last eat? How much caffeine or alcohol is in the bloodstream? What pain am I ignoring? How much conflict did I absorb today? How much daylight did I get? This is not obsessive. This is basic debugging.

Small shifts matter because they are the difference between reaction and choice. Water. Protein. A ten-minute walk. A shower. A nap. A hard boundary with your phone at night. None of this is glamorous, which is why people underestimate it. It is the foundation under every higher-level insight.

If you want the Field in one sentence: stop confusing states with identities. Fix the chemistry, then evaluate the person.

Accountability still matters. Chemistry explains behavior; it does not excuse harm. But if you want behavior to change, you start with state because state is upstream of control. This is true in parenting, in leadership, in relationships, and in self-talk. Stabilize the body, lower threat, and the conversation becomes possible. Skip that step and you get performance or explosions.

Do not negotiate your life from a dysregulated state. Hungry, exhausted, and flooded people sign bad contracts. Stabilize first. Then decide. That one order of operations prevents a lot of damage.

5

Hidden Fees: Why Relief Keeps Winning

Relief Is the Fastest Exit

PEOPLE DO NOT DESTROY THEIR LIVES BECAUSE THEY LOVE DESTRUCTION.

They destroy their lives because something inside the life is unbearable, and destruction is the fastest way to change sensation. That is not a moral statement. It is a systems statement. When a nervous system cannot tolerate a state, it will reach for an exit. The exit is not always physical. It can be chemical, digital, sexual, financial, intellectual, or social. The exit can be called a drink, a pill, a binge, a hookup, a shopping cart, a fight, a marathon work session, a gambling app, a scroll trance, a fantasy, or a disappearance.

Coping and Numbing Do Different Jobs

Different exits. Same function. Relief. The cleanest distinction in this domain is between coping and numbing.

Coping reduces load while preserving contact with reality. It increases capacity. It builds the ability to stay present with discomfort without being consumed.

Numbing reduces contact with reality. It decreases awareness. It buys time by turning down sensation.

Both coping and numbing can look similar on the surface. A person takes a walk. That can be coping, or it can be avoidance. Coping has a cost that goes down with practice.

At first it feels expensive. Breathwork feels stupid. Journaling feels slow. A hard conversation feels terrifying. Sleep hygiene feels like deprivation. A walk feels like a waste of time. Then, with repetition, coping becomes cheaper. The nervous system learns. The state shifts faster. The baseline improves. The person builds options.

Numbing has a cost that goes up with repetition. At first it feels cheap. The hit works. The purchase soothes. The scroll empties the mind. The anger gives power. The hookup provides sensation. The work binge produces applause. The binge provides comfort. The gamble provides hope. Then tolerance arrives.

The system adapts. The same dose produces less effect. The person increases intensity to get the same relief. The cost rises: money, time, health, relationships, self-trust, sleep, risk.

Eventually the exit becomes a trap. People call this "addiction" when it is obvious. But the same mechanism exists in subtler forms that society rewards.

Workaholism is a numbing strategy. Achievement can be a sedative. Perfectionism can be a tranquilizer. Rage can be a stimulant.

Being "the reliable one" can be a way to never feel fear. Being "the funny one" can be a way to never be seen.

A system does not care what the exit is called. It cares whether the exit changes state fast. This is why moralizing numbing behaviors is useless.

Moralization increases shame. Shame increases stress. Stress increases the need to numb. The loop tightens. The better move is functional analysis: what is the exit doing? Is it lowering anxiety?

Is it creating certainty? Is it creating belonging? Is it creating sensation? Is it creating sleep? Is it creating dissociation from pain? Is it creating a temporary identity that feels powerful?

RELIEF TRAP = LOWER NOW COST + HIGHER LATER BILL

Shame Makes the Exit More Expensive

Shame is not one thing. Some of it is social enforcement. Some of it is an internalized voice that keeps replaying long after the people are gone. Some of it is protective - it keeps you attached to a group when belonging is survival. In this book, shame is treated as a pressure currency because it changes what you can afford to do. That framing is not meant to trivialize the inner experience; it is meant to make the mechanism legible.

Once the function is named, the next question becomes obvious: what would reduce the need for this exit without demanding heroism? Advice says: "Stop." A nervous system hears: "Stay in pain with no replacement." A functional plan has three layers: reduce the load, widen the Choice Set, and build replacements that work.

Reduce the load means reducing system pressure. System pressure is anything that keeps the system in a chronically taxed state: sleep deprivation, chronic conflict, unsafe housing, isolation, constant noise, financial instability, humiliation, discrimination, unstable work, illness without care, loneliness, ongoing grief, unresolved legal stress, unpredictable schedules, or a relationship that keeps the nervous system on alert.

A person can be sober and still be in the same Field that created the Default. In that situation, the exit will mutate.

People are sometimes "doing everything right" and still feel trapped.

They changed the behavior but did not change the field. The default is loyal to function, not to form.

Widening the Choice Set means increasing stable supports. Stable supports are the opposite of system pressure: consistent sleep opportunities, safe people, predictable routines, access to food, access to care, meaning, rest, physical activity, sunlight, privacy, boundaries, and environments where the nervous system can downshift. This sounds obvious. It is also why many lives stay stuck.

Support is not a vibe. Support is infrastructure. A person living in chaos cannot "heal" through insight alone. The system will keep reaching for numbing because the baseline state is still unbearable. Stabilization is unsexy. It is paying the rent on time.

It is eating real food. It is reducing daily emergencies. It is creating a predictable morning. It is sleeping as much as possible. It is removing the most dangerous inputs. It is going to appointments even when nothing feels hopeful yet.

Stabilization creates slack. Slack creates choice. Replacements are the third layer.

A replacement is not a motivational quote. It is an action that does the same job with lower long-term cost.

If the job is downshifting an anxious body, replacements might include breath, movement, cold water, progressive muscle relaxation, talking to a safe person, or doing something tactile that grounds attention. If the job is sensation in a numb life, replacements might include exercise, dance, creative work, learning, competition, sex with consent and presence, travel, music, or anything that produces intensity without collateral damage.

If the job is escape from shame, replacements might include safe disclosure, structured accountability, and environments where mistakes are not treated as identity. If the job is belonging, replacements might include groups that do not require performance: recovery meetings, sports, faith communities, volunteering, classes, or friendships built around shared activity rather than shared self-destruction.

If the job is control, replacements might include structure: budgets, schedules, checklists, planning, and boundaries that reduce uncertainty. A replacement must be realistic. A person in crisis cannot replace numbing with a two-hour meditation retreat. A single parent cannot replace numbing with "just take more time for yourself" as if time is available. A person in chronic pain cannot replace numbing with "go for a run" as if the body can. Real replacements match the actual constraints of the life. This is where the fine print lens is compassionate without being naïve. A micro-experiment is a small, deliberate change that tests whether relief can be achieved differently.

Instead of numbing at night, delay by ten minutes and walk around the block first.

Instead of scrolling in bed, charge the phone across the room and keep a paper book nearby.

Instead of using a substance alone, call a person first. Instead of buying relief, eat and drink water first, then decide.

Instead of sleeping with someone to feel chosen, text a friend and name the craving as data.

Instead of gambling for hope, write the exact hope down, then build a concrete plan for one piece of it.

Small experiments sound childish. They are not. They are how nervous systems learn. A nervous system updates from outcomes. It does not update from vows. A vow is language. Outcomes are evidence.

Evidence means: the old trigger happened, a different action occurred, and the world did not end. Then that happened again. And again. Until the system believes it.

Recovery, in any domain, is repetitive. Because the nervous system is conservative. It requires repeated proof before it shifts its Default.

Information means: what state preceded the relapse, what system pressure was active, what support was missing, what boundary broke, what fatigue was present, what conflict was unresolved, what loneliness was unmanaged. That information can be used to redesign the Field.

There is also a simple neurological reason numbing feels convincing. The brain learns through reinforcement. When a behavior produces relief, the behavior gets tagged as valuable. Cues associated with that behavior become loaded: a street, a bathroom, a certain hour, a certain song, a certain smell, a certain person, a certain kind of boredom. Then the cue appears, and the body reacts before thought. Craving is not a thought. Craving is a state shift plus a prediction: relief is available.

"Just don't" is weak advice. The cue is already doing work on the system. A stronger strategy is cue management.

Change the route. Change the room. Change the hour. Change the routine that feeds the cue. Remove the objects that make acting automatic. Replace the cue with another cue that leads to a cheaper behavior. Cues can be internal too.

Some people relapse when life improves because improvement is unfamiliar. The system mistakes unfamiliar for unsafe and reaches for the old exit to restore predictability. It is self-stabilization using an old tool. A second reason numbing persists is identity. If a person's social world is organized around the exit, leaving the exit is not only withdrawing from a substance or behavior. It is withdrawing from belonging. A person may not consciously want that cost, but the nervous system will calculate it.

Replacement must include belonging. A person cannot outdiscipline loneliness. Belonging is one of the core regulators of state.

This is also why some people need structured communities to change Defaults: meetings, teams, groups, classrooms, mentors, religion, therapy, coaching, or any place where a new identity is reinforced by repetition.

Stability means the body can tolerate reality without needing to escape it constantly.

That is the whole game. Coping is not virtue. It is engineering. Numbing is not evil. It is often the best available tool in a bad Field. The goal is to make better tools cheaper than the old ones. When that happens, change stops feeling like deprivation. It starts feeling like relief without aftermath.

That is when the exit becomes a door, not a trap. Numbing also thrives on intermittent reinforcement.

The nervous system learns that uncertainty can be paid for with a swipe. This is not a weakness of character. It is a property of learning systems.

It also explains why some people numb through information. Doomscrolling is a numbing behavior. Outrage is a numbing behavior. Conspiracy is a numbing behavior. Political obsession can be a numbing behavior. The goal is not truth; the goal is stimulation.

Stimulation overrides internal pain by making the outside world loud enough to drown the inside world out. A person can spend ten hours "researching" and call it responsibility while using it as anesthesia. The relief paradox sits underneath all numbing. The exit lowers pain now, then increases baseline pain later.

Alcohol lowers anxiety in the moment, then increases anxiety over days. Overspending creates relief, then creates financial threat that keeps the nervous system on alert. Compulsive sex creates sensation, then creates shame, risk, and relational damage that feeds the next craving. Work binges create identity, then create exhaustion that makes the system more brittle. The person feels more pain. Then the person feels more need to exit.

That is not a moral failure. It is a feedback loop. The loop is also why white-knuckling often fails. White-knuckling is removal without redesign. The trigger still hits. The system pressure still exists.

The nervous system is still taxed. The old exit is gone. The system searches for another exit with the same function. It will find one. This is why many people "quit" and then become cruel, rigid, obsessive, or depressed. They removed the sedative without changing the baseline.

The honest goal is not to remove relief. The goal is to change the cost structure so that relief does not require self-destruction. That requires both internal skills and external redesign. Internal skills are state skills: the ability to downshift, to tolerate discomfort, to name the impulse without obeying it, to separate craving from command. External redesign is Field change: fewer cues, more support, fewer emergencies, safer people, predictable routine, less noise, less humiliation, less chronic fear. One without the other is fragile.

Together, they create robustness. A clean way to think about urges is as waves.

An urge rises, peaks, and falls. The nervous system lies and says the urge will rise forever. It will not. It is a wave. The question is whether the person has anything to hold onto while the wave passes.

Delay is not denial. Delay is creating distance between cue and action long enough for the wave to move.

Delay works even when discipline is low because it does not demand purity. It demands interruption. Interruption breaks automaticity. Automaticity is when the exit happens before awareness can vote. A person can train interruption the way an athlete trains reaction time. The training is simple and brutal: notice the cue, name the state, do the replacement, repeat.

This is also why support matters. Support is not someone saying "good job." Support is someone who can hold the nervous system steady long enough for the wave to pass.

Structured community. It can be a faith leader. It can be a family member who is actually safe. It can be a doctor.

Different supports. Same function: co-regulation while the system rewires. Some exits require professional treatment. That is not weakness. That is accuracy. A Default that has become chemically reinforced or medically dangerous is not solved by slogans. Sometimes the safest move is medical support, medication-assisted treatment, detox supervision, inpatient or outpatient care, or a structured program. That is not failure.

That is choosing survival over pride. The Default manual says: do not romanticize suffering. Use the supports that lower risk. Another overlooked dimension is grief. If a person has never learned to feel loss without collapsing, the system will numb. It will numb through work, through sex, through alcohol, through food, through rage, through distraction, through overthinking. The exit is not pleasure. The exit is avoiding the feeling of being hollow.

A person can mislabel grief as "depression," mislabel grief as "laziness," mislabel grief as "I'm broken," and then chase exits for years.

Naming grief reduces the need to escape it. Naming does not solve it. It makes it tolerable enough to process. Processing is the opposite of numbing.

Processing is staying present long enough for the nervous system to metabolize what happened without freezing in it.

That is why coping looks boring. Relief is a clause with interest. The behavior works in the short term, which is why it repeats. The cost shows up later, which is why people pretend the cost is unrelated.

Every numbing strategy is solving a real problem. Alcohol solves social anxiety. Weed solves boredom. Porn solves loneliness. Doomscrolling solves uncertainty by giving it shape. Overworking solves shame by turning it into productivity. The fact that a strategy is costly does not mean it is stupid. It means it is the only lever the person believes they have.

The Field move is to separate regulation from the method. Ask: what is this behavior regulating right now? Fear. Rage. Grief. Emptiness. Self-hatred. Restlessness. Then ask: what is a cheaper way to regulate the same state? Cheaper means: less damage tomorrow.

"Just stop" is childish advice. If you rip away a regulator without replacing it, the system will find a new regulator. Often a worse one. Replacement is not moral. It is mechanical.

Interest is where the trap forms. If relief costs you sleep, sleep loss costs you regulation, low regulation costs you more relief. That loop is compound interest. The way out is not willpower. The way out is interrupting the loop at the cheapest point: environment, state, relationships, and honest naming.

A person is not weak for wanting relief. The mistake is choosing relief that bills the future at predatory rates.

Build a relief ladder. Put your regulators in order from lowest cost to highest: sleep, food, water, movement, talking, music, solitude, creativity, medication, substances, self-destruction. When the urge hits, climb the ladder from the bottom first. Not forever. Just once. The point is to teach the nervous system that relief exists without a loan shark attached to it.

BUILD A RELIEF LADDER

A useful question is: what is the smallest dose of relief that actually works? Most people jump to the strongest drug first: the heaviest numbing, the most dramatic escape. Train yourself to use smaller doses and you keep more of your future. Escalation is how relief turns predatory.

It is boring because it is real. The last piece is dignity. A person cannot build a new Default from self-contempt. Self-contempt is a Field of constant threat. Under constant threat, the system will keep reaching for exits.

A person can want change desperately while secretly believing they do not deserve stability. The nervous system will obey the belief. Dignity is not self-esteem speeches. Dignity is the decision to treat the life as worth protecting even while imperfect. That decision changes behavior. It changes what environments are tolerated. It changes what people are kept close. It changes what risks are taken.

It changes what exits feel acceptable. Coping becomes possible when dignity becomes non-negotiable. The end goal is simple. Relief without aftermath. A system that can tolerate reality. A life where the cheapest exit is not self-destruction. That is what being free actually means. Relief is rarely neutral. It is social.

Many numbing strategies are also secrecy strategies, because they carry stigma. Secrecy trains isolation. Isolation trains more numbing. Shame is the glue that holds the cycle together - not because shame is useful, but because shame makes the self feel unworthy of help. Shame is social pain. When it sticks, it becomes Terms.

Quick test: coping returns you to life; numbing returns you to avoidance. One lowers pain; the other delays the bill.

Shame is the most expensive emotion in the human inventory. Not because it feels bad. Because it distorts behavior while pretending it is moral.

Guilt says: something you did created harm. Guilt can be useful. It points to repair.

Shame says: you are the harm. Shame is not a signal about a behavior. It is a verdict about identity.

A verdict is heavy. Heavy verdicts create heavy strategies. Shame is an ancient technology. It evolved as social pain. In small groups, being excluded could mean death. A nervous system that felt shame was a nervous system that learned to correct fast enough to stay inside protection. That is the original function: keep the organism inside belonging.

The problem is that modern shame does not operate inside small groups with clear feedback. Modern shame operates inside large systems with corrupted feedback. A school can shame a child for being distracted when the child is sleep-deprived and terrified at home. A culture can shame a person for their body, their accent, their family history, their neighborhood, their sexuality, their poverty, their grief, their illness. People pass shame down the way they pass down recipes: through tone, through silence, through what is allowed to be spoken, through what is punished, through what is mocked, through what is ignored. A parent can shame a child without intending to. A friend can shame another friend by laughing at the wrong moment.

A partner can shame a partner by withdrawing love as punishment. Shame does not need screaming. It thrives on subtlety. Because shame is a threat signal, it changes state.

It tightens the chest. It heats the face. It lowers the eyes. It collapses posture. It speeds the mind. It triggers fight, flight, freeze, or fawn.

Shame is not an idea. Once physiology shifts, the Choice Set shrinks. Under shame, the cheapest strategies are protective strategies.

Protective strategies look like hiding, lying, performing, blaming, attacking, disappearing, overexplaining, overworking, perfectionism, or becoming numb.

That is why shame is expensive. It does not correct behavior. It forces survival. A person under shame cannot learn cleanly. Learning requires safety. Safety allows curiosity. Curiosity allows error. Error allows update.

Shame removes curiosity and makes error feel like death. The system stops experimenting and starts repeating. This is why shame creates the exact outcome it claims to hate.

A person ashamed of being "lazy" becomes avoidant. Avoidance looks like laziness. Shame increases.

A person ashamed of their body often hides. Hiding can shrink movement and social contact. Shame increases.

Shame is a self-feeding loop. The loop is powered by secrecy. Secrecy is shame's habitat. Shame loves private. Shame loves dark.

Shame loves isolation. Because in isolation, the nervous system cannot receive corrective evidence. Corrective evidence is simple: you can be known and not destroyed. Without that evidence, the nervous system assumes exposure equals death. It hides. Hiding protects in the short term. It costs in the long term. A hidden life cannot be helped. A hidden Default cannot be redesigned. This is how high-functioning people stay trapped. A person can be successful and still live in shame.

Sometimes the success is the shame strategy. A person becomes exceptional to avoid feeling ordinary. A person becomes indispensable to avoid being abandoned. A person becomes perfect to avoid being criticized. A person becomes funny to avoid being taken seriously. A person becomes loud to avoid being ignored. A person becomes cold to avoid being hurt.

These strategies can produce achievements. They also produce brittleness. Brittleness is when the system looks strong but breaks easily. Because the strategy is not built on stability. It is built on fear. Shame also disguises itself as sophistication. It calls itself standards.

It calls itself discipline. It calls itself "just being real." But the signature is always the same: contempt, especially self-contempt. Self-contempt feels like motivation. It is usually threat chemistry. Threat chemistry can create short bursts of output. It cannot create a durable life. A durable life requires self-trust. Shame corrodes self-trust.

Because shame requires lying to survive. An ashamed nervous system learns to perform instead of to be accurate. It learns to say yes when no is needed. It learns to agree when disagreement is true. It learns to smile when fear is present. It learns to hide needs to avoid being punished. Over time, the person becomes disconnected from their own signals.

That disconnection has a cost. A person who cannot feel their own signals cannot steer.

That is why some people wake up at thirty-five or fifty and say, "I don't know who I am." The person exists. The signals exist. The connection was trained out.

Shame is also why some people become cruel. Shame can flip into contempt for others as a defense. If someone else is "worse," then your own shame quiets for a moment. This is the social engine behind scapegoating. A group under pressure seeks relief. Relief can be created by blaming an outsider. Blame produces cohesion. Cohesion reduces anxiety. The cost is moral collapse. That Default repeats in families and in nations. It also repeats online.

The internet is a shame amplifier. A person can be publicly mocked by strangers for a mistake. That scale is not human. A nervous system was not built to tolerate thousands of eyes. The system either collapses into shame or hardens into cruelty. Either way, the result is less nuance. Shame does not produce nuance. It produces defense.

Defense produces repetition. What dissolves shame?

Not denial. Not "confidence." Not pretending nothing matters.

Shame dissolves when a nervous system receives safe exposure. Safe exposure means being seen in a controlled dose, by a person or group that does not weaponize the truth. This is why the wrong exposure can make shame worse. If someone confesses in the wrong room, and the room punishes, the nervous system learns that exposure is danger. The shame deepens. This is why intelligence is required.

Exposure must be chosen. It must be gradual. It must be safe enough to count as evidence. Evidence means: you told the truth and did not die. You were imperfect and were still kept. You were seen and were still respected. That evidence rewrites the fear model.

A second antidote is precision. Shame is vague. It wants global statements: "I am disgusting. I am broken. I am a failure."

Precision breaks that spell. Precision says: a specific behavior created a specific outcome, and repair is possible. Precision turns identity verdict into an action problem. Action problems have solutions. Identity verdicts create paralysis. The move is to pull shame back down to the ground.

What exactly happened? What exactly was the cost? What exactly needs repair? Who exactly was harmed? What exactly is the next right step? That is not moralizing. That is engineering.

A third antidote is replacement identity. Shame binds identity to image. Image is fragile. It requires constant defense. Replacement identity binds identity to values. Values are sturdier than image.

Values create spine. Spine is what allows exposure. A fourth antidote is boundaries. Shame is often trained by people who benefit from your smallness.

A boss who mocks workers benefits from fear. A partner who shames needs benefits from control. A family system that shames honesty benefits from secrecy.

In those environments, trying to "heal" shame without changing boundaries is like trying to dry off while standing in rain.

Boundaries reduce the rain. The final antidote is service. Shame collapses the self into a spotlight: everything is about your defect. Service pulls attention outward in a clean way.

Not performative service. Real service. Helping a neighbor. Teaching a skill. Showing up for a friend. Being useful in a way that does not require performance. Service gives the nervous system a different identity: contributor, not contamination.

Many recovery communities use service as a core tool. It is not religious. It is neurological. That proof is built through small accurate actions repeated over time. Shame wants secrecy.

The exit is truth, in safe doses, with spine. That is how the hidden tax stops compounding. That is how a person gets their own life back.

Shame also does something subtle: it makes people defend the system that shamed them.

This is not hypocrisy. It is survival. The nervous system learns: alignment with the shaming standard equals safety. Defiance equals danger. People internalize the standard and become its enforcers.

That is how cultures reproduce without anyone needing to "believe" in the cruelty consciously.

Shame is one of the strongest tools of social control because it recruits the victim as guard.

It also explains why shame is often louder in public than in private. Public shame is performance. Performance is protection. A person proves compliance by shaming others.

The psychology is simple: if the crowd is hunting, join the crowd. Joining reduces risk. That is why group cruelty feels normal inside the group. The cost is paid later.

The cost is paid as dead intimacy, dead creativity, dead honesty, and a population trained to lie politely while suffering loudly.

Shame thrives on comparison. Comparison is a natural cognitive function: the brain calibrates by reference points. The problem is scale and distortion. Social media is comparison on steroids. It is highlight reels presented as normal life. It is curated bodies, curated careers, curated relationships, curated happiness. A nervous system will compare its raw footage to someone else's edited trailer and call itself defective.

Performance deepens disconnection. This is why some people are "successful" and still feel like frauds. The life is being lived for the gaze, not for stability. The gaze is never satisfied.

Shame is also classed. Shame attaches to survival. People learn to hide not because they are dishonest, but because honesty has been punished.

Reject shame, and the system finally gets clean information to work with. That is when growth stops being cosmetic. It becomes real.

A simple test for shame is this: does the thought create repair or disappearance?

If it creates repair, it is guilt, responsibility, growth. If it creates disappearance, it is shame, threat, and distortion. Choose repair.

That choice, repeated, builds a nervous system that can be honest without breaking.

That is freedom in practice. Shame survives by pretending it is you. Name it as a state and it becomes negotiable. A named Default is no longer fate. It is a design problem.

Design problems have solutions. Shame is not just a feeling. It is a tax on cognition. It pulls attention inward, shrinks the Choice Set, and makes secrecy feel like safety.

Guilt says: I did something wrong. Shame says: I am wrong. Guilt can lead to repair. Shame usually leads to hiding, lying, numbing, attacking, or performing. Those strategies are not "bad character." They are attempts to escape social death.

Shame also functions as social control. Communities use it to enforce norms when they lack formal power. Families use it when they do not know how to teach. Institutions use it because it is cheaper than care. The hidden fee is that shame does not create skill. It creates compliance or revolt.

Watch what shame does to time. A person ashamed of their body avoids the doctor until the problem is serious. A person ashamed of money avoids checking the account until the overdraft hits. A person ashamed of desire waits until they are desperate, then chooses badly. Shame turns maintenance into crisis.

The Field move is to drag shame into the light without turning it into confession theater. Name it plainly. Tell the truth to one safe person. Make one repair. Do one honest action that contradicts the shame story. Evidence beats shame faster than argument.

A culture that cannot metabolize shame will keep selling relief. A person who can metabolize shame buys their own freedom back.

Shame thrives in secrecy. Privacy is healthy; secrecy is corrosive. The difference is whether the hidden thing is protected for growth or hidden because you believe it makes you unlovable. One truthful conversation can cut a decade of shame because it replaces imagination with reality. Reality is usually less cruel than the shame story.

Shame also loves perfectionism. If you demand flawless performance, every mistake becomes evidence that you are unworthy. That pressure creates hiding, not growth. The way out is ordinary humanity: making mistakes, repairing, staying present, and letting being seen be survivable.

That is the end of shame's authority. Shame is not something you "get over" with a pep talk. It is a currency. When visibility is expensive, secrecy becomes cheap, and the system learns to hide.

Once you see shame as pricing, a larger pattern becomes obvious: what is cheap tends to repeat. Repetition is not a moral flaw. It is a system using what is affordable.

Part II - Recurrence

Repetition is not fate. It is a system that keeps offering the same cheap move until you change the pricing.

For Elena, recurrence returns as responsibility. For Marcus, it returns as overwork. For Rafi, it returns as relief. Different rooms. Same loop.

This Part follows Defaults in motion. Recurrence is what happens when yesterday’s Terms keep pricing today’s moves. A repeat is a signal: what the system is protecting, what it is avoiding paying, and what kind of cost would have to change before the pattern can change.

You are not here to win an argument with yourself. You are here to read the loop accurately enough to edit it.

6

Why Cycles Return

THERE IS A SPECIFIC NAUSEA THAT COMES WHEN YOU REALIZE YOU ARE LIVING IN SYNDICATION: RERUNS OF YOUR OWN LIFE WITH NEW GUEST STARS.

Marcus feels it in the memo he rewrites, Elena in the family emergency that keeps finding her, and Rafi in the midnight pull that still knows his number. Different city. Different partner. Different plan. Same invoice. The costumes change. The pricing does not.

Rafi can stay steady for days and still feel the old loop tug hardest at midnight. Recurrence is not fate. It is pricing.

Much of what returns is not an accident. People call it "falling back." They call it "relapsing." They call it "going backwards." They talk as if recurrence is proof that change was fake. That belief comes from a fantasy model of life: a straight line with a clean arrow. A living system is not a straight line. A living system is a loop with memory.

The human nervous system is built to stay stable under uncertainty. When the future becomes unclear, the safest move is often the move the system has already survived. That is what recurrence is: the system reaching for the most statistically reliable solution in its archive. Recurrence is not a moral failure. It is a form of stability. A Default often persists until the cost of repeating finally exceeds the cost of adapting. Unless something outside the individual forces a change first (a boundary, an institution, a crisis, a commitment). The core variable is cost: energy, threat, predictability, and coherence.

Then the old action executes. Drink. Spend. Text the wrong person. Pick the fight. Freeze. Lie. Overwork.

Hook up. Disappear. Control. Then the outcome arrives. Temporary relief. Temporary certainty. Temporary power. Temporary numbness.

A person can change one surface behavior and still recreate the same logic somewhere else. Drugs become gambling. One overwork cycle becomes the next. One city becomes a new stage for the same inner war. The surface changes. The regulating function stays.

People look at the surface behavior and think they understand. The Default lives deeper: in the function the behavior served, in the state the behavior regulated, and in the Field that made the behavior cheap.

Evidence means: the old trigger happened, you did something different, and the world did not end. It is noise. The system requires repetition. It needs multiple trials. It needs the new outcome to be reliable enough to become cheaper than the old one. It is the same morning routine repeated until the body begins to predict stability. Recurrence often intensifies right before change because the old system fights for relevance. In behavioral science this is sometimes called an extinction burst: when an old behavior stops getting its usual payoff, the system briefly increases the behavior to see if the payoff can be forced back.

A person can do well for weeks and then suddenly feel the craving spike, the irritability spike, the shame spike, the urge to sabotage spike.

Why the Old Solution Still Feels Safer

Return Clauses

In dynamical systems, a return clause is a region a system falls into and tends to return to after disturbance. You can imagine a landscape with valleys. Drop a ball anywhere nearby and it rolls into the same valley.

The valley is not "evil." It is low energy. It is stable. Human behavior has valleys. Under disturbance, systems roll back into their valleys. That is recurrence.

Defaults are built by repetition. Repetition creates efficiency. Efficiency lowers cost. Lower cost makes repetition more likely. They are stored as procedures, not as opinions.

A person can know, logically, that a Default is destroying their life and still execute it under stress. That is not stupidity. That is the difference between declarative knowledge and procedural memory. Declarative knowledge is the story layer: facts, intentions, beliefs. Under stress, the brain shifts control toward older systems that favor speed over nuance. Training means repeated exposure plus new outcomes. Exposure means encountering the trigger without completing the old loop.

A friend group may pressure you back into partying because your sobriety changes their mirror. A workplace may punish your new boundaries because your overwork was subsidizing other people's comfort. The system is not asking what is healthy. It is asking what is stable. Recurrence is the system's attempt to restore the old stable configuration.

Recurrence is also generational. Defaults travel through families like weather. A parent under chronic stress models control, silence, or volatility.

Generational Recurrence

A child learns that as normal. The child becomes an adult and calls it personality. The adult then recreates the same Field.

The Default is not inherited as a story. It is inherited as regulation style. A culture does the same thing. A population under threat centralizes, polarizes, scapegoats, and repeats old conflict scripts. A population under stability diversifies and becomes more tolerant.

Recurrence teaches a blunt rule. You do not break a Default by declaring it broken. Economic advantage does not mean money only. It means cost.

When the nervous system is exhausted, the old exits can look reasonable. Sleep, food, hydration, movement, friction against the old Default, and support are not lifestyle decoration. They are cost engineering. Remove the easy path where you can. Build barriers where you need them. Add people, routines, and structures that help the system hold the line until the new behavior becomes cheaper.

The nervous system changes when the new behavior survives the old trigger enough times that it becomes cheaper than the old one.

This is also why recurrence should be planned for, not feared. The plan includes contingencies. If craving spikes, there is a list. If loneliness hits, there is a call.

If anger rises, there is a walk. If shame floods, there is a room. If money tightens, there is a budget rule. If sleep collapses, there is a reset protocol.

Planning is respect for how systems work. Recurrence ends the same way it began: through evidence. Not through force. Through replaced stability.

That is where Default literacy becomes power. And that is why recurrence, when read correctly, is not discouraging.

It is diagnostic. It shows what still needs support, what still needs redesign, what still needs repetition. Recurrence does not mean you are back at zero. It means the system is still negotiating cost. Change the cost, and the loop breaks. Recurrence is also why people misjudge "starting over." A person moves to a new city and expects a new self. Then the same insecurity, the same attraction to chaos, the same avoidance of stillness shows up in a different neighborhood. The person feels cursed.

A new environment can help by changing cues and costs. But if the internal rules are untouched, the system will rebuild the old valley even in new soil.

Some people repeat romance the way others repeat seasons. Same beginning. Same intensity. Same collapse. Different face. Same story. It is also why certain times create predictable recurrence.

Payday recurrence: the system feels temporary abundance and tries to convert abundance into relief now, because past scarcity trained it to distrust tomorrow. Sunday-night recurrence: the system anticipates Monday threat and tries to numb before the threat arrives. Anniversary recurrence: the calendar hits an old loss and the body reacts before the mind remembers why.

Success recurrence: the system reaches a level it once learned was unsafe, and it sabotages to return to familiar ground.

Human life behaves like this. That is a chain. Break one link and the probabilities change. This is the practical power of naming the sequence.

Breaking the loop earlier is easier. Sleep earlier. Food earlier. Support earlier. Boundaries earlier.

Systems also have inertia: reversing an input does not instantly reverse a trained state. Lowering stress helps, but a baseline learned under threat often needs repeated evidence (over time) to shift.

The system's threshold for safety is still high. The system was trained to expect danger, which means it demands more proof before it relaxes. This is why someone can "have a good life" and still feel unsafe. The environment improved. The internal threshold did not update yet. The person returns to old strategies even when they "shouldn't."

Evidence is built by keeping the system in the new configuration long enough that safety becomes statistically credible. Recurrence can be engineered for good. Habits are recurrence. Rituals are recurrence. Training is recurrence. Stable relationships are recurrence.

A person who wakes up at the same time, eats real food, moves the body, and speaks to one safe person regularly is using recurrence to build stability. The nervous system loves repetition. It is built to learn from it. The question is not whether life will recur. Life will recur. The question is what will recur. A person who understands recurrence stops trying to "never struggle again."

That is fantasy. The person builds a relapse plan for every major Default: what happens when the old valley calls? A relapse plan is not doom. It is respect. It says: the system has a history. The Field will test it. Here is what happens next.

That plan reduces shame. And reducing shame reduces recurrence. Because shame is one of the most powerful triggers. Shame says: you are broken, which means why try. A Default lens says: information arrived, which means redesign. Information is power. A final distinction matters.

A lapse is a moment. A relapse is a return to the old system. A moment does not have to become a system. The difference is what happens next. If the lapse is treated as shame, the nervous system seeks more numbing. If the lapse is treated as data, the plan improves. Recurrence, handled correctly, becomes a teacher instead of a jailer. Then the redesign begins again.

A rerun is a replay you do not notice you are running. The scene changes, the cast changes, the job title changes, but the emotional script stays the same.

People recreate the same argument in different relationships, or chase the same approval in different workplaces. The trigger is rarely the surface event. The trigger is the Default: a tone of voice, a delay, a look, an authority figure, a closed door.

The Field move is to treat reruns like data. When you feel "here we go again," stop and name what is repeating: the cue, the body response, the story, the impulse. That naming interrupts autopilot long enough to choose a different line.

A rerun does not end because you finally get the perfect ending. It ends when you refuse to audition for the role. That refusal can look like leaving, apologizing, setting a boundary, or choosing boredom over drama.

Your life is not a movie you watch. It is a script you can revise once you admit you are holding the pen.

Write the rerun down. Literally. Two lines: the cue and the usual response. Then write one alternative response you can actually do. The paper turns fog into something you can practice against. Practice is how reruns die.

That is what growth really looks like. Consider three different lives. A janitor works nights in a building where people barely make eye contact. The body learns invisibility. On weekends, the nervous system craves proof of existence. The cheapest proof becomes a loud bar, a risky flirtation, a fight that produces adrenaline. Monday arrives with shame and fatigue.

The cycle repeats until the person builds a different form of visibility: a community, a craft, a team, a relationship where being seen is safe. An analyst lives in spreadsheets by day and uncertainty by night. Every mistake feels like exposure. The nervous system manages threat through control and reward. Payday becomes permission to purchase relief. The purchases are not about objects. They are about turning anxiety into certainty. The recurrence breaks when the person builds a cheaper certainty: automation, a plan, and a life where rest is not treated as failure.

A teenager in a crowded home learns to survive by disappearing into a screen. The screen becomes the nervous system's safest room. Years later, intimacy feels like invasion. The person retreats, then feels lonely, then retreats again. The recurrence breaks when the person learns graded contact:

one honest conversation at a time, with boundaries, with repair, with proof that closeness does not require surrender. Different stories. Same mechanics. The Field offers a trigger, the state shifts, the system chooses the cheapest stabilizer. Recurrence ends when something cheaper and healthier is built. That is not inspirational language. That is the engineering of a human life.

A rerun isn't moral failure. It's the brain replaying code that once worked. Treat it like software: find the trigger, patch the loop, rerun the test.

Ride the Wave

Nothing unfolds once. It turns. Cycles are not poetry. They are constraint. Every complex system uses oscillation to distribute load over time.

Expansion consumes resources. Contraction restores them. If a system expands without contracting, it burns itself out. If it contracts without expanding, it stagnates. The human body is a cycle machine. Breath is a cycle. Heartbeats are cycles. Sleeping and waking is a cycle. Hunger and satiety is a cycle. Attention and fatigue is a cycle.

RECURRENCE = FAMILIAR RELIEF + LOW CHOICE SET

Even emotion is cyclical: activation and settling, intensity and integration. A person who demands constant expansion is demanding a body without breath. That worldview cannot work. Modern culture pretends cycles are optional. It treats constant growth as normal. Constant output as virtue.

Constant availability as maturity. Constant positivity as spiritual success. Constant intensity as love. That worldview is incompatible with biology. The nervous system does not run on ideology. It runs on energy.

The same person can be brilliant one month and empty the next. It is why motivation rises and disappears. It is why attention sharpens and then blurs. It is why desire surges and then quiets. These shifts are not moral character. They are oscillation. The mistake is moralizing the trough. People experience contraction and interpret it as regression. They panic. They try to force expansion.

They increase pressure at the exact moment the system is asking for recovery. Pressure increases load. Load deepens the trough. The system responds with numbness, irritability, avoidance, collapse, or a desperate grab for stimulation. Then the person says, "Something is wrong with me." The truth is often simpler. A cycle is doing what cycles do. Homeostasis is the body's tendency to maintain internal stability. Allostasis is the body's ability to change settings to meet demand.

Both create cycles: when demand rises, the body shifts; when demand falls, the body restores. Restoration is not optional. It is repayment. A nervous system can borrow energy for a while. It cannot borrow forever. This is why people can sprint for weeks and then crash hard. The crash is not a surprise. It is the bill. Cycles also explain why breakthroughs are followed by fog. A breakthrough is often an expansion spike: clarity, intensity, momentum.

Frequency: how often the wave turns. Phase: where you are now. Damping: how fast the wave settles after disturbance. These words are mathematics. They are also daily life.

The goal is not to eliminate waves. The goal is to manage amplitude, frequency, and damping so the life stays coherent. The first cycle most people ignore is the day. Circadian rhythms are the body's 24-hour timing system. Light, darkness, meals, activity, and social rhythm cue it. When circadian rhythm is stable, sleep improves, mood stabilizes, hunger regulates, attention sharpens. When circadian rhythm is chaotic, everything gets louder. This is why a week of irregular sleep can make someone anxious, reactive, and impulsive without any "reason." The body is not dramatic. It is timed.

There are also ultradian rhythms: cycles of focus and fatigue within the day. Many people can concentrate deeply for 60 to 90 minutes and then need a short reset. Ignore the reset and the brain begins to degrade: more errors, more irritability, more craving.

Move. Eat. Hydrate. Then return.

This is not softness. It is the way brains work. Cycles exist across longer horizons too. Learning works the same way. The brain encodes during effort and consolidates during rest and sleep.

A person can feel okay and then be hit by a wave of sorrow months later. That is not regression. That is processing.

People who fight grief often numb. Then grief returns louder. People who allow grief in tolerable doses often heal cleaner. This is not poetry. It is load management.

Relationships cycle as well. Two people move toward and away over time. Healthy systems allow the oscillation without panic. Unhealthy systems moralize it. But that belief requires a stable Field.

Understanding cycles turns conflict into design: how much contact, how much solitude, how much structure, how much freedom. Careers cycle too. A person who accepts seasons can build a long career without self-destruction. Cycle literacy also matters for money. Money has cycles: income cycles, expense cycles, market cycles, and job cycles.

A person without margin experiences every downturn as catastrophe. Catastrophe drives panic spending or panic hoarding. Both are cycles driven by threat. Margin is what turns downturn into discomfort instead of collapse.

A system under constant threat cannot rest. Cycle literacy therefore becomes social justice without slogans: build conditions where rest is possible. When uncertainty rises (war, economic shocks, pandemics, political instability) societies tighten. Rules increase. Surveillance increases. Scapegoating increases. Leaders promise certainty. Populations trade freedom for the feeling of safety.

These cycles are not destiny. They are tendencies. They can be moderated by institutions that build slack: reserves, safety nets, stable education, strong public health, fair systems. Slack reduces panic.

Many people attach identity to expansion. They feel alive only when producing, earning, winning, being wanted, being admired, being busy. Then contraction arrives and they feel worthless. Worthlessness is a story. The story is fueled by unfamiliar state.

That is the spine that prevents troughs from becoming collapse. A second planning tool is building recovery into the schedule instead of hoping it happens. Hope is not a plan. A schedule can include Micro-recovery: short breaks, movement, hydration, quiet. It can include macro-recovery: days off, vacations, low-stakes weekends, seasons of lighter load. Without this, recovery will arrive as illness, injury, or breakdown. The body collects payment. A third tool is forecasting.

Forecasting means looking ahead and naming predictable peaks: busy seasons at work, exams, holidays, anniversaries, family events, travel, deadlines. Then the person builds buffers before and after. Buffers are not indulgence. Buffers are damping. A damped system returns to baseline faster after stress. That is resilience. Resilience is not toughness. Resilience is recovery speed. A fourth tool is rhythm matching. Do hard things at high-signal times. Do administrative things at low-signal times.

When Reruns Become History

How to Read a Life in Cycles

Elena notices that the same week keeps arriving in new clothing: Monday begins with one request she cannot absorb, Wednesday becomes catch-up, Friday becomes triage, and by Sunday she is mistaking depletion for character. Cycle literacy begins there. Put vulnerable conversations where both bodies are resourced. Do creative work when attention is sharp. Rest before the system begs. Acceptance is part of the same discipline: contraction is not failure; it is part of the cycle.

The simplest move in the middle of a low is to stop adding extra punishment. Stop telling a story that the low means failure. Treat the low as data. What is the body asking for? Sleep? Food? Movement? Sunlight?

Social safety? Silence? Reduced stimulation? A boundary? An end to overcommitment? Often the answer is basic. Basic answers are powerful because they are real. This is also why cycles are linked to dignity.

A person with dignity allows the body to be human. A person without dignity tries to force the body into a machine. Machines do not need sleep. Bodies do. Machines do not grieve. Bodies do. Machines do not have seasons. Bodies do. A person who respects cycles does not shrink.

They become durable. They become the kind of person who can hold a long project, a long love, a long career, a long life. The cycle is not your enemy. The cycle is the rule. When the rule is respected, energy returns. When the rule is ignored, the body collects payment.

Eventually. Cycle literacy is the ability to ride what repeats without panicking. That is a form of freedom. Cycles are also why forcing constant intensity creates dependency. Many people try to override cycles with stimulants, screens, caffeine, adrenaline, or social drama. They force expansion when the body is asking for contraction.

Then they use depressants, alcohol, scrolling, food, or sleep debt to force contraction when the body is asking for integration. The cycle becomes artificial: spike and crash, spike and crash. Artificial cycles have higher amplitude and lower control. That is why some lives feel like whiplash. The solution is not "balance" as a slogan. Damping is what reduces amplitude after disturbance.

In a body, damping comes from basics: consistent sleep timing, consistent meals, movement, sunlight, reduced late-night stimulation, reduced chemical volatility, and stable social contact. In a mind, damping comes from meaning and structure: knowing what matters, having routines, having boundaries, having fewer emergencies. In a relationship, damping comes from repair and predictability: conflict that resolves, affection that is consistent, agreements that are kept.

A damped system does not avoid stress. It returns faster. Cycles also show up in creativity. Creative work has phases: capture, incubation, execution, revision.

Incubation looks like "doing nothing." It is not nothing. It is the nervous system integrating, combining, letting the unconscious sort Defaults. People who shame incubation destroy their own creativity. They demand output on a schedule the mind cannot obey. Then they call themselves blocked.

Walking, showering, exercising, and doing repetitive tasks often produce insight. The body is contracting so the mind can reorganize. Parenting exposes cycles brutally. A parent who expects constant patience will feel monstrous. A parent who expects cycles will build supports: nap schedules, co-parenting, childcare, predictable routines, reduced commitments, and repair after rupture. That is the difference between guilt that repairs and shame that collapses. Cycles also mismatch between people. One person is a morning system. Another is a night system. One person needs solitude to restore. Another needs contact.

One person has a high social battery. Another has a low one. One person works in bursts. Another works steadily. Mismatch becomes conflict when it is moralized. "Mature people wake early." "Real adults answer texts immediately." "Hard workers never rest."

"Strong people don't need space." These are not truths. They are norms pretending to be physics. The physics is individual variation. The solution is negotiation, not judgment. A system that negotiates cycles becomes stable. A system that moralizes cycles becomes violent. Cycles are also why some people feel "fine" until they are not.

Some people need more sleep in winter. Some people need more movement to stay regulated. Some people need more sunlight exposure.

Some people become more social in summer and more inward in winter. Ignoring seasonal cycles produces unnecessary suffering. Seasonal planning is not indulgence. It is adaptation. The core lesson is that a life is not built by one heroic push. It is built by repeated cycles of effort and recovery.

Recovery is not the reward for effort. Recovery is the condition that makes future effort possible. People who understand this stop treating rest as something to "earn." They treat rest as part of the system. That shift changes everything. It turns cycles from enemies into allies. It turns troughs into maintenance instead of collapse.

Forecasting the Wave

It turns peaks into productive seasons instead of manic self-destruction. Cycle literacy is also humility: admitting that the body has rules and living inside them. The point is not romance. It is forecast. A practical cycle map can be blunt. Ask three questions: What personal cycles always show up? What external cycles always show up? What usually makes the trough worse or the recovery cleaner?

Design looks like this: reduce commitments before the peak, increase sleep before the peak, schedule support during the peak, postpone difficult conversations during the peak, and plan recovery after the peak. Review does not require a diary of emotions. It requires honest data: what helped, what hurt, what was missing, what was unrealistic.

That data turns the next cycle into an experiment instead of a surprise. People who never review keep repeating the same collapse and calling it bad luck. A reviewed cycle becomes manageable. Not perfect.

Manageable. That is the difference between a life that breaks every year and a life that gets stronger every year. Same body. Different relationship to rhythm.

Cycles also provide a strange comfort. This does not mean pain is imaginary. It means pain has timing. Timing is Leverage.

They wait. They rest. They stabilize. They keep small promises. They let the wave turn. Then, when the high returns, they use it well. They do not waste it on panic.

They build with it. That is the adult relationship to a cycle: respect it, forecast it, and use it. That is how time becomes an ally instead of a threat.

A cycle is a feedback system. Something increases, it creates pressure, the system reacts, and the reaction changes the next round. Once you see the loop, you stop mistaking it for mood.

This matters because cycles create illusions. In the up phase, you believe you are finally fixed. In the down phase, you believe you are doomed. Neither is true. You are cycling.

Healthy cycles build capacity: work and rest, stress and recovery, output and reflection. Unhealthy cycles consume capacity: sprint and crash, numb and panic, overspend and shame, isolate and crave.

The Field question is always: what keeps the loop going? Is it a reward? A fear? A shortage? A social Field? If you change the input or the reward, the cycle changes. If you only shame yourself, the cycle strengthens.

Most people make permanent decisions in temporary phases. They quit jobs in a crash, marry in a high, text the ex at 2 a.m., or declare their life ruined on a bad Tuesday. A simple rule protects you: do not sign major contracts at the peak or the trough. Wait for baseline, then decide. That one delay breaks a lot of cycles.

Cycles also show up in groups: families repeat addictions, nations repeat wars, companies repeat scandals. Individuals get recruited into these loops and call it "normal life." Once you recognize the cycle, you can stop volunteering to be a character in it.

Cycles become prisons when a person mistakes them for personality. Once a cycle is mapped, the calendar stops being destiny and becomes Leverage: predictable windows where different choices can be made. Cycles exist in bodies and in societies. The mechanics repeat at every scale.

Cycles compound quietly: sleep debt, interest, resentment. If the cost grows while you're "not thinking about it," you're in a cycle. Break it by changing the input, not by arguing with the output.

People tell history as if it were a chain of heroic decisions and moral turning points. That story is flattering. It is also incomplete. What drives historical repetition is not only ignorance. It is structure. Scarcity, abundance, density, disease, technology, power, coordination, threat. These forces act on populations the way stress acts on a nervous system.

When pressure rises, systems tighten. When pressure falls, systems loosen. When uncertainty increases, systems centralize. When stability returns, systems diversify.

That is not politics first. The most useful way to think about history is as feedback. Small-scale life had faster feedback. Hunger followed bad planning.

Cold followed lack of shelter. Social conflict had immediate consequences inside small groups. Behavior was corrected quickly because consequence was close.

Defaults still existed, but the environment forced resolution because denial was expensive. As scale increases, feedback delays increase. Trade networks widen. Institutions strengthen. Knowledge circulates unevenly. Power moves through layers. Resources are extracted far from the people consuming them. Harm is displaced onto outsiders. Consequence becomes remote.

When consequence is remote, prediction replaces perception. Prediction is necessary. It is also dangerous. Prediction is how myths are born. A myth is a prediction presented as certainty. Certainty reduces anxiety. Anxiety reduction feels like truth. That is why myths are attractive under pressure.

This is also why propaganda works. Propaganda is not magic. It is regulation. It offers a story that reduces uncertainty. Under threat, people accept stories that restore coherence even if the stories distort reality. That is a nervous system property scaled up. This is why societies repeat the same conflicts under new Names. The names change.

The constraints stay. Consider scarcity. When resources feel scarce, systems become competitive. People hoard. Groups polarize. Trust declines.

Leaders promise control. Outsiders become targets. When resources feel abundant, systems can tolerate ambiguity. Cooperation rises. Exploration increases. Empathy becomes cheaper because survival feels less threatened. Scarcity is not only food.

It can be housing. It can be jobs. It can be attention. It can be status. It can be safety. It can be meaning. Scarcity of meaning is one of the most underrated historical forces. A population with no shared meaning becomes vulnerable to any story that offers purpose, even violent purpose. Consider disease. Epidemics are not only medical events. They are social stress tests.

Consider inequality. When inequality rises, trust declines. People stop believing rules are fair. Cooperation becomes harder. Crime can rise. Populist anger rises.

War is a coordination solution under extreme threat. It centralizes decision-making, simplifies narratives, and creates clear in-group and out-group categories.

War also produces technological acceleration and trauma that feeds future conflict. The loop repeats because the conditions that produce war (scarcity, fear, competition, ideology, territorial disputes, humiliation) repeat. History loops. Because constraints are durable.

They store learned solutions: laws, norms, procedures, education systems, scientific methods, financial systems.

Institutional decay is dangerous. It forces individuals to act as if the world is less predictable. Less predictability increases threat. Threat increases repetition. This is the same logic as the individual level. The core variable is not intelligence.

It is feedback plus structure. The difference between prehistoric time, the Renaissance, and today is not raw cognitive ability. It is scale, abstraction, and the quality of feedback loops.

Default literacy is a form of peace. Not because it fixes the world. Because it removes the illusion that chaos is random. Randomness exists. Once structure is visible, Leverage appears. Leverage does not mean controlling history.

This is how history is interrupted. Not by pretending the loop will stop on its own. Not all of them. Not quickly. Not without cost. But enough to matter.

A thermostat is negative feedback: when temperature rises above a set point, the heater turns off. When it drops below, the heater turns on.

HISTORY = REPEATED DEFAULTS UNDER STABLE CONSTRAINTS

Systems often change slowly until they don't. A system can absorb stress for years, storing tension quietly. Then one additional stress crosses a threshold and the system tips. People call that "out of nowhere." It was not out of nowhere. It was accumulated load.

The nervous system does the same thing. A person absorbs disrespect for years, then one comment breaks them. The comment was not magical. It was the final unit of load. History has tipping points because systems have thresholds. Thresholds are where small causes create large effects. This is why simplistic explanations of history are seductive.

A simplistic story says one leader caused everything, or one invention caused everything. Reality is usually multiple interacting loops plus a threshold. That is less cinematic. It is more accurate. Feedback delay is another reason loops repeat. A policy decision can take years to show consequences. A financial incentive can create harm decades later. A child neglected today can become an adult struggling tomorrow. A city underinvesting in infrastructure can pay for it in a crisis later.

Delayed feedback creates the illusion that behavior has no cost. Then people overdo it. Overdoing creates overshoot. Overshoot creates correction. Correction often overshoots the other way. That is how cycles form.

That means "history" is not only repetition. It is oscillation around constraints. Centralization and decentralization are one example. Under threat, systems centralize because coordination feels safer. Under stability, systems decentralize because autonomy feels tolerable. Then centralization produces rigidity, corruption, and resentment.

Resentment fuels decentralizing movements. Decentralization produces fragmentation and inefficiency. Inefficiency fuels a demand for central control again. That loop repeats in different costumes across centuries. This is not cynicism. It is the predictable behavior of large systems with limited trust.

Trust is one of the hidden constraints. High-trust societies can coordinate without coercion. Low-trust societies need more coercion to coordinate. Coercion creates resentment. Resentment reduces trust. Then the system becomes more coercive to hold itself together. That is another loop.

Trust takes a long time to build and a short time to break. History often looks like slow construction and fast collapse. Information is another constraint. People like to believe the "information age" solved ignorance. It did not. It changed the problem. Information abundance creates attention scarcity. Attention scarcity creates vulnerability to manipulation.

A person cannot process infinite signals, which means the nervous system uses shortcuts: identity, tribe, authority, emotion, repetition.

Ranking systems can amplify this by feeding what increases engagement: outrage, fear, tribal conflict, certainty, humiliation.

Information exposure conditions threat perception and attention; repeated inputs can raise or lower baseline arousal and behavior. Profit can be created by dysregulation. Dysregulation becomes a business model.

This has social consequences. A population kept in chronic arousal tends to lose planning horizon: less patience, more reactivity, and more appetite for simple villains. Economics is another constraint category. Markets can create prosperity. They can also create bubbles.

A bubble is another loop: optimism increases prices, rising prices increase optimism, and reality is ignored until a trigger breaks the confidence and the loop reverses.

Group behavior becomes a feedback loop. Moral panics are cultural bubbles. Outrage rises, group identity hardens, punishments intensify, and nuance disappears. Then fatigue arrives, the panic dissipates, and the same society acts surprised at its own excess. The loop repeats because threat chemistry is addictive and because public shaming creates quick cohesion.

That can be done in a community: building trust, building mutual aid, building transparency, building real consequences for harm.

History becomes personal at that level. Those lessons accumulate. That is how a society becomes what it becomes. Feeding can be attention, money, time, compliance, silence, laughter, outrage, or loyalty.

Loops with feedback can evolve. That is the difference between fate and design. History also repeats because humans learn through stories, and stories compress reality. Compression is necessary. No mind can hold full complexity.

Identity then filters perception. Evidence that contradicts identity is rejected. Evidence that supports identity is amplified. That is another feedback loop: story shapes perception, perception shapes story. This is why nations can repeat the same errors while believing they are rational. This is why institutions can repeat the same harm while calling it policy. This is why families can repeat the same cruelty while calling it tradition. Narrative can be medicine. It can also be a sedative.

A sedative story is any story that reduces discomfort by denying complexity. Blame one group and anxiety drops. Believe in a simple hero and uncertainty drops. Believe the past was perfect or the future is guaranteed and fear drops. Dropping fear feels good, which means the story spreads. Then the cost arrives because reality does not obey the story.

Reality obeys constraints. Progress is not a permanent state. It is maintenance. It requires institutions that keep feedback clean and consequences connected. It requires education that teaches how systems actually behave. It requires leaders who can stay regulated under pressure.

It requires citizens who can tolerate uncertainty without reaching for scapegoats. When those conditions weaken, progress can reverse. Reversal is not shocking when history is clear as cycles plus constraints. It is expected. This is also why generational forgetting is dangerous. When a generation does not personally remember a disaster, the nervous system's threat model fades. Complacency rises.

Slack is spent. Institutions decay. Then the old disaster becomes possible again. This is not pessimism. It is Default. A person who understands this does not become paranoid. They become disciplined about feedback. They measure.

They check incentives. They build redundancy. They insist on repair. They refuse the comfort of stories that require lying. That is how history is handled without being swallowed by it. Because the goal is not to predict every event.

The goal is to understand the forces that make events repeat. When those forces are visible, the future stops feeling like roulette. It becomes a Field with rules. Rules can be used. That is the final promise of Default literacy: not control, but Leverage. When Leverage is used with dignity, fewer people suffer, and the same tragedies stop recycling under new slogans.

7

Place Shapes Your Days

ELENA KNOWS THAT ONE BLOCK CAN CHANGE WHAT HER BODY EXPECTS FROM THE NEXT TEN MINUTES. MARCUS KNOWS IT IN THE COMMUTE THAT DRAINS JUDGMENT BEFORE THE FIRST MEETING. RAFI KNOWS IT IN THE CORNERS THAT SELL RELIEF AND IN THE ROUTES THAT MAKE HIM VISIBLE.

Place is not scenery. It is a pricing engine: distance, noise, safety, transit, access, and whether the body can move through the day without paying with vigilance.

What a Place Teaches the Body

Place is not scenery. It is the pressure system around the body.

People talk about "mindset" as if life is a private project happening in isolation. That is fantasy. Every nervous system runs inside a location: a block, a building, a climate, a culture, a jurisdiction, a price level. Place decides what is easy, what is expensive, what is dangerous, what is normal, and what is even imaginable. This is not poetic. It is mechanics.

A decision is never just a decision. It is a cost calculation under constraint. The same person, with the same values and the same intelligence, will choose differently when the Field changes. Not because character vanished, but because the options moved and the prices changed. Place is one of the largest price-setters. In one neighborhood, walking outside is a regulation tool.

Movement is built into the day. In another, walking outside is a risk calculation. The body learns to stay inside. In one city, groceries are ten minutes away. In another, groceries require two buses, an hour, and a tolerance for humiliation at the register. In one town, sleep is protected by silence. In another, sleep is something fought for through sirens, thin walls, and night shifts. The nervous system does not debate these conditions. It adapts.

Adaptation is not consent. A child does not choose the air, the noise, the crowding, the language, the pace, the threat level, the weather, the policing, the school quality, the commute, the availability of care, or the local definition of "normal." Those inputs arrive first. The body updates second. Identity arrives last, as a story pasted over a calibration.

That story becomes pride or shame depending on whether the environment rewarded the calibration. Place makes "personality" look stable. A person raised in a tight, crowded space learns speed, reading faces, and moving around other bodies. A person raised in a wide, quiet space learns patience, privacy, and distance. A person raised in a place where danger is common learns early detection, fast escalation, and quick exits. A person raised where danger is rare can afford slower interpretation.

Neither is morally superior. Both are the body doing math. Place is also memory. Not memory as nostalgia, but memory as prediction. The nervous system predicts the next five seconds by using the last ten years. Place writes the last ten years. It writes what footsteps mean, what silence means, what a stranger means, what a car idling outside means, what a knock at the door means, what a raised voice means.

Relocation can feel like a second birth. The same stimulus carries different meaning across different places. A city person hears quiet and thinks something is wrong. A rural person hears constant noise and feels hunted. A person from a strict culture walks into a casual culture and interprets it as disrespect. A person from a casual culture walks into a strict culture and interprets it as coldness. Place is the first education.

There is the micro-place: the room, the bed, the light, the smell, the corner where the body finally unclenches. There is the meso-place: the building, the hallway, the block, the route home, the corner store, the nearest park, the nearest clinic, the nearest subway station, the nearest safe bathroom. Then there is the macro-place: the city, the State, the country, the climate, the economy, the language, the laws. Most people talk as if only the macro matters. That is how small violence hides. A person can live in a "good city" and still be trapped in a bad room. A person can live in a "bad neighborhood" and still build one square meter of safety that changes everything. A person can have a stable apartment and still have an unstable stairwell. A person can have a stable building and still have an unstable street. Freedom is often a micro-place first. The simplest example is sleep.

Sleep is not just willpower. Sleep is a location: light level, noise level, temperature, safety, and timing. A person who cannot sleep because of external conditions is not "undisciplined." The body is refusing to power down in a Field that does not feel safe. Health is also place. Air quality is place.

Access to food is place. Sunlight is place. Walkability is place. Stress is place. Even "genetics" expresses differently under different environments. Biology is not a fixed verdict; it is a set of probabilities interacting with inputs.

The idea of equal opportunity is often a slogan, not a description. Opportunities are distributed unevenly across space. That distribution has consequences.

When people judge each other without accounting for place, cruelty looks like wisdom. Place also determines social density. Density changes behavior. In high density, your nervous system is forced to ignore more. It must become efficient. It must triage.

It must develop filters. Those filters can look like "coldness," "selfishness," or "confidence," depending on who is watching. In low density, your nervous system can afford detail. It can afford longer conversations, longer silences, slower pacing. That can look like "warmth," "slowness," or "lack of ambition," depending on who is watching. Place is also a set of incentives.

Every place rewards certain traits and punishes others. A place where status is currency will punish quiet competence and reward performance. A place where conformity is safety will punish difference and reward obedience. A place where creativity is valued will reward risk and tolerate failure. A place where failure is fatal will punish experimentation and reward caution. People call these Defaults "culture." Culture is not floating above place. Culture is what a population learns under repeated constraints.

Different neighborhoods inside the same city can feel like different countries. Different food, different pacing, different language, different rules for eye contact, different rules for masculinity, different rules for softness, different expectations for who belongs outside at night. The body learns those rules before the mind can explain them. A person who moves across these borders inside the same city can feel the nervous system shift street by street. That is not sensitivity. That is accurate detection of Field change. Place is also a story machine. Places generate myths about themselves: "this is the land of opportunity," "this is the dangerous part," "this is where real people live," "this is where people come to become someone." Those myths are not neutral. They pressure identity. They tell a person what role to play to belong.

A person who refuses the local myth will pay. Sometimes that payment is loneliness. Sometimes it is exclusion. Sometimes it is violence. Sometimes it is quiet economic punishment.

These are not romantic statements. They are observed behavior. The Default is simple: Place sets the baseline. The baseline sets the nervous system. The nervous system sets the choices. The choices set the outcomes.

The outcomes set the story. The story then hides the baseline. As an accounting. Stop lying like that.

The environment is doing work on the body every day. Call it what it is. Naming place does not require moving. Moving is not always possible. It is sometimes dangerous, sometimes unaffordable, sometimes impossible because of family obligations, legal status, health, or simple reality. The first intervention is smaller:

Stop treating place as invisible. Place also sets your distance from everything that keeps a life stable. A person can be "responsible" and still lose the week to distance: two buses to work, a long walk to childcare, a pharmacy that closes early, a clinic that requires a day off, a bank that requires standing in line, a landlord who requires a printed form, a government office that requires another office. None of that is character. It is friction. Friction is a tax. Some people pay that tax every day and then get told they should have had more "bandwidth." The cruelty of that word is hidden inside its metaphor. Bandwidth is not moral. Bandwidth is capacity under load. Load is distributed unevenly across space.

Transportation is destiny more often than talent. If a place forces three hours of commuting a day, it is stealing years.

It cares about what is available. Place also sets how many systems are watching you. Surveillance is not only cameras. Surveillance is landlords, neighbors, managers, police, gatekeepers, gossip networks, social media, religious leaders, immigration enforcement, school administrators, and the unspoken rules of who is allowed to be messy.

In some places, a person can fail privately and rebuild. In other places, one visible mistake becomes a permanent identity.

It becomes record, rumor, and restriction. It becomes a reduction of Choice Set. A place that does not allow private error produces either perfectionism or rebellion. Both are expensive.

Place also sets the intensity of comparison. In some environments, comparison is local and human. In others, comparison is constant and industrial. A person living inside a high-status corridor will be fed a daily reminder of what other people have: bodies, partners, apartments, clothing, vacations, degrees, followers, connections.

A person raised in a place where tenderness is mocked will struggle to receive care. A person raised where anger is dangerous will struggle to express it. A person raised where ambition is punished will learn to hide talent. A person raised where stillness is impossible will learn to seek intensity. None of this is fate.

It is training. Place also has seasons, even when the weather is stable. Economic cycles, school cycles, political cycles, migration cycles, tourist seasons, harvest seasons, storm seasons, policing seasons. A place has rhythms. The body learns them and anticipates them, sometimes without awareness. Timing lives inside place.

A person can move "up" economically and still feel hunted. The nervous system may have escaped one place, but it is still predicting based on the old rhythm. The body hears a small crisis and prepares for the big one that used to follow. The person calls it anxiety. It is not irrational. It is old environment logic running on new terrain.

Place is also the availability of exits. An exit is a bus schedule. A friend with a couch. A shelter bed. A scholarship. A clinic.

A library. A supportive adult. A safe public space. A job market that hires. A legal system that believes you. A community that does not punish you for starting over.

Place begins big. Change begins small. And small changes are still place. Place also decides how your identity will be priced.

The same body is read differently in different places. A person can be invisible in one neighborhood and hyper-visible in the next. A person can be safe in one city and unsafe in another, not because the body changed, but because the social rules changed. Gender expression, skin tone, accent, religion, clothing, age, disability, queerness, class markers. These are not only private traits. They are signals interpreted by the Field. Interpretation becomes consequence.

It is not mystical. It is measurable enough to be felt. And it is felt enough to be named. A person does not have to become bitter to become accurate.

DAILY BEHAVIOR = ROUTE + ROOM + RHYTHM

It prices safety, time, health, education, and possibility. The same person with the same habits can get different outcomes because the ground under them is different.

Think of two families with the same income. One lives near reliable transit, clean parks, decent schools, and a grocery store. The other lives where transit is unreliable, food is expensive, noise is constant, and services are far. The second family spends more time and stress for the same basic tasks. That stress is a hidden rent.

Place also shapes who you can become. Some places reward curiosity. Some punish it. Some places are dense with mentors, jobs, and social mobility. Some are dense with surveillance, scarcity, and exit costs. People call the difference "ambition." Place is doing a lot of that work.

The Field question is not "Where should everyone live?" It is: what does this place charge, and who is paying? If the price is constant danger, constant commute, constant bureaucracy, you are not just tired. You are correctly responding to cost.

Place is already forcing the issue in many regions. Climate change is turning some places into risk markets: heat, flood, smoke, insurance, migration. Place becomes more obviously a term when those risks show up as recurring costs and constraints.

It creates confusion. Confusion makes people fight themselves for pressures that were never personal. Confusion makes people worship willpower while ignoring friction. Confusion keeps the Default running. Accurate diagnosis reduces wasted effort; naming the real constraint is often the lowest-cost first move. That is the first advantage. A person cannot redesign a city alone, but a person can redesign exposure inside the city.

A person cannot redesign a country alone, but a person can redesign which rooms and streets become daily life. A person cannot redesign a whole culture, but a person can redesign the circle of people whose norms become internal law. This is not aesthetic. It is survival. The Field is not only inside the mind. It is also the ground. And until the ground is acknowledged, "free will" will keep feeling like a lie.

Reading the Ground

The built environment regulates behavior by altering exposure to noise, threat, distance, delay, and access, which shifts baseline stress and feasible options. This is not metaphorical.

It senses through rules and walls. It responds through doors and locks. It punishes through distance and noise. It rewards through access and comfort. It trains behavior through friction and convenience. People talk about "self-control" as if the environment is not constantly controlling the body. That is backwards.

It still works. The Field begins with Terms. If the door does not lock, the nervous system does not relax. If the walls are thin, the nervous system stays half-awake.

A school with metal detectors teaches: you are a threat, you will be treated as a threat, you should behave like someone in custody.

These lessons become internal law. That is why built environments create culture. Environmental psychology calls these "affordances": the actions a space makes easy or hard. A staircase affords movement. An elevator affords avoidance. A park affords slow social contact. A highway affords separation. A corner store affords impulse. A library affords quiet attention. A streetlight affords safety. A broken streetlight affords predation.

Start with the smallest unit: the room. A room tells the body whether it is allowed to stop. This is not aesthetic advice. It is physiology. A person trying to break a Default while living inside the exact Terms that created the Default is attempting a miracle. Sometimes the miracle happens.

More often, the Default wins, and the person blames the self. Stop that. Design is Leverage. A room can become a regulator. Not perfect. Not forever. Enough.

Its layout predicts conflict or calm. A home with no privacy forces constant contact. Constant contact increases friction. Friction becomes either suppression or explosion. Both are Defaults. A home with only one bathroom creates daily competition and shame. A home where every conversation can be overheard trains secrecy. A home where the kitchen is stressed trains eating Defaults that mirror stress: rushing, hoarding, hiding, binging, numbing.

A home where money is discussed only through panic trains the body to treat every bill as threat. A home where affection is rare trains The body to mistake intensity for love. These Defaults survive relocation because they are not in the walls alone. They are in the body. But the walls can keep feeding them. This is why changing the home environment matters even when "the problem is internal." Internal change needs external support.

Then scale up again: the block. The block teaches regulation through micro-signals. Are there trees? Are there sidewalks? Are there streetlights? Are there safe crossings? Are there places to sit? Are there children outside? Is there a pharmacy? Is there a clinic?

Is there a grocery store with actual food? Is there a bodega with only sugar, cigarettes, and alcohol? Is there a library? Is there a park? Is there a constant police presence? Is there constant speeding traffic? Is there constant construction noise? These are not "urban planning details." These are daily inputs to the nervous system.

They decide what the body learns about the world: welcoming, indifferent, hostile. Then scale up again: the route. A route is a ritual. People underestimate how much life is route. The route to work. The route to school. The route to the store. The route home at night. Routes are repeated. Repetition becomes baseline.

PLACE ALTERS YOUR BODY

WHY DESIGN IS NEVER NEUTRAL

Marcus feels the city in his shoulders before he has words for it. The same city can produce different people. Two routes can feel like two worlds. The built world also determines who meets whom. Streets and transit systems are social algorithms. A place with walkable streets produces casual social contact: the nod, the hello, the small conversation that tells the nervous system it belongs. A place built around cars produces isolation: no third places, no casual contact, only planned meetings or accidental conflict. When people say "community is gone," that is often a design observation, not a moral one. When a city removes public space, community becomes something you must purchase: a bar, a gym, a subscription, a ticket, an event.

That is consumption wearing a social mask. The built world also decides how a population handles stress.

Environmental health research shows that noise exposure, poor housing conditions, and chronically misaligned light schedules measurably alter sleep, cognitive performance, cardiovascular risk, and stress physiology.

A city with green space gives the nervous system an off-ramp. A city with only concrete gives the nervous system only acceleration. Chronic adaptation is expensive. The technical term is allostatic load: the wear And tear of running stress physiology too long. The label is not the point. The point is that bodies pay. Then those bodies get blamed for paying.

The built world also shapes addiction. This is not about morality. It is exposure. A person living on a block with a liquor store on every corner is not dealing with the same trigger environment as a person who has to drive twenty minutes to buy alcohol. A person living in a place where fentanyl is visible on the sidewalk is not dealing with the same exposure as a person who only hears about it on the news. Outcome becomes story.

The built world also shapes discipline. A person who wants to exercise but lives in a place where going outside is unsafe is not "lazy." A person who wants to cook but lives with a broken stove is not "undisciplined." A person who wants to read but lives in constant noise is not "unfocused." A person who wants to recover but lives in a house where chaos is constant is not "uncommitted." Shame says: something is wrong with you. Strategy says: what is the environment doing, and what can be redesigned?

Other layers can be changed by the individual: the room, the schedule, the route, the circle, the phone, the nightly ritual, the exposure profile.

When the built world refuses dignity, people adapt by hardening or numbing. Hardening looks like aggression. Numbing looks like apathy. Both are the same attempt: reduce pain.

Disorder justifies more neglect. Breaking dynamics requires interventions at multiple scales. Zoom out. Density creates a specific kind of pressure. But the principle stays the same: The world you walk through every day is training your nervous system.

If you want to change the Default, change the training. If the city cannot be changed yet, start with the square meter.

That means a "No Loitering" sign. That means a bench designed so no one can lie down. That means a public bathroom that requires a code, because even relief becomes something you must earn. Hostile Terms are the built world admitting what it believes: that certain bodies are problems to be moved, not people to be supported. That belief does not stay in the street. It enters the body of everyone who sees it. Some learn fear.

Some learn contempt. Some learn that the world will not hold them if they fall. This is how spaces teach shame without speaking. The built world also teaches power. Look at who gets to enter without being questioned. A courthouse, a hospital, a police station, an immigration office, a welfare office: these are buildings, but they are also nervous system events. The body reads cues: fluorescent light, long hallways, hard benches, silence, cameras, metal detectors, uniforms, forms, numbers.

A school with overcrowded hallways trains aggression, because space is constantly invaded. Learning is not only intelligence. Learning is safety. A nervous system in fight-or-flight does not absorb algebra. It absorbs threat. Teachers know this intuitively. Students know it in their bones.

Policy often pretends it is not true. Workplaces are Terms. A workplace that never allows you to sit trains the body to accept pain as normal. A workplace that schedules unpredictably trains the body to live in readiness, never fully off duty. A workplace that punishes bathroom breaks trains the body to treat basic needs as weakness. A workplace that demands constant smiling trains the body to hide anger until it becomes illness. These are not "job preferences." They are chronic inputs. And chronic inputs become chronic states.

Then there is the Terms of consumption. Modern environments are often built to make spending frictionless. Checkout becomes one click. Food becomes delivery. Entertainment becomes infinite scroll. Pleasure becomes instant.

The body learns: discomfort can be erased immediately, without movement, without conversation, without patience. That training matters. It reshapes the cost curve of coping. The cheapest coping becomes the Default coping. Then, when a person tries to choose slower regulation (sleep, exercise, relationships, craft, prayer, therapy, recovery) the nervous system experiences it as expensive, because it is. That does not mean the person is weak. It means the environment made the shortcut cheap.

Design is policy. Now return to the smallest layer again. A person living in a harmful environment cannot wait for policy to become kind. The fastest leverage is micro-design: reduce exposure to constant noise where possible; create one predictable morning cue that signals safety; create one predictable night cue that signals shutdown; place the most dangerous temptations farther away and harder to access; place the most stabilizing tools closer and easier to reach. Build one third place that does not cost money: a park bench, a library, a church, a community center, a quiet café with one tea, a stoop, a gym at off-peak hours, or a friend's kitchen. This is not aesthetic. It is engineering. A nervous system is an engineer under pressure. It will take the cheapest path to relief.

In a crowded home, boundaries are scarce. When boundaries are scarce, bodies collide. Collision creates irritation. Irritation creates either distance or violence. Then people call it "relationship problems," ignoring that the relationship is happening inside a pressure cooker. In a home with no private space, a teenager has nowhere to develop a self that is not watched. That produces two outcomes: compliance or secret life. Both are survival strategies. In a home with no predictable quiet, love becomes reactive. The nervous system cannot stay soft when it is always bracing.

When public space is generous, people learn coexistence. They learn minor conflict without catastrophe. They learn that strangers can share space without violence. They learn that the world can hold difference. When public space is absent, people only meet in private and commercial spaces. Private spaces separate. Commercial spaces rank.

Both reduce contact across difference. Then a society becomes more brittle. Brittleness is what people mistake for "division." Division is often a design outcome. Even sidewalks are political. If a child cannot walk safely to school, the child learns dependence early. If an elder cannot walk safely to a store, the elder learns isolation early. If a disabled person cannot move through a city without humiliation, the city teaches: you are not considered.

That lesson becomes a Default of withdrawal. Withdrawal looks like apathy. It is often exclusion. Resilience is an environment that allows recovery.

The built world is not background. It is part of the Field the body encounters every day.

And what you bump into every day eventually becomes who you are. One more practical truth: The built world can be mapped. A person can walk through daily life and mark where the body tightens, where breathing gets shallow, where anger rises, where cravings spike, where attention collapses, where calm appears. Those reactions are not random. They are location-linked predictions. This is how the environment becomes legible. Once legible, it becomes negotiable: a different route, a different time of day, a different seat, a different store, a different room, a different boundary. Small geography changes produce large nervous system changes.

The built world is a set of Defaults turned into concrete. Stairs invite movement. Sidewalks invite walking. Parks invite meeting. Fast food on every corner invites a certain diet. Lack of third spaces invites isolation. The architecture is not neutral.

Design shapes behavior because it shapes friction. If the healthy option requires three buses and an hour, it is not really an option. If the harmful option is open 24/7 and marketed like love, it will win. People call this "choices." It is a rigged menu.

The same person can feel disciplined in one setting and "lazy" in another. Put that person in a walkable neighborhood with a routine and they stabilize. Put them in a car-only environment with constant noise and they fray. The body is responding to friction and reward.

The Field move is to ask: what is the Default here? What does the room, the street, the building, and the schedule make easy? What does it make hard? Then you redesign at the smallest scale you can: your desk, your kitchen, your route, your commute, your bedroom.

Sellable myth: you can out-motivate bad design. Reality: design eats motivation for breakfast. When you change design, you change outcomes without heroics.

A good life is not only a mindset. It is a layout. If you cannot redesign the city, redesign your smallest zone. Remove friction from good behaviors and add friction to the ones that steal life. Put water where your hand reaches. Put the phone farther away. Choose routes with daylight. Choose a grocery that makes real food easier. These are not hacks. They are micro-infrastructure. Micro-infrastructure scales into character.

Politics shows up in your living room. Zoning decides your noise. Transit decides your time. Food systems decide your diet. Design is policy made physical. You can work on yourself all day, but you still live inside a layout someone chose.

Cities as Compression Machines

A city is a compression machine. It compresses bodies into space. It compresses time into schedules. It compresses identity into signals.

It compresses opportunity into competition. It compresses chaos into a daily hum that the nervous system learns to ignore until it can't. Cities do not create human nature. They amplify it.

Density increases contact rates. Contact rates increase influence. Influence increases contagion: ideas, slang, violence, fashion, addiction, ambition, fear, innovation. That contagion is not mystical. It is network math. More nodes. More edges. Faster spread. This is why cities produce culture at speed. It is also why cities produce exhaustion at speed.

They increase system pressure. Choice Set is the set of actions that feel possible. System pressure is the cost of existing inside the Field.

In a city, the menu of possible lives is larger: different careers, different subcultures, different relationships, different communities, different cuisines, different forms of art, different paths out of origin.

Signal becomes survival. The cost is subtle: a person can forget how to be without performing. Then silence feels like death. A city also changes what "alone" means.

In rural environments, alone is physical. You can be far from other bodies. In cities, alone is psychological. You can be surrounded and still unseen. The nervous system experiences that as a different kind of threat. Social isolation in high density can feel more humiliating than isolation in low density because the evidence is constant: bodies everywhere, connection nowhere.

Cities produce loneliness that looks like nightlife. It looks like bars, parties, endless scrolling, constant plans, constant movement. Movement becomes anesthesia. A city is also a time machine.

A city runs on external clocks: transit schedules, appointments, deliveries, deadlines, shifts, sirens, notifications. The nervous system is trained to respond quickly. Quick response becomes competence.

Competence becomes identity. Then the person leaves the city for a week and cannot slow down. The body is still sprinting.

Recent United Nations urbanization estimates place megacities such as Jakarta, Dhaka, and Tokyo among the world's largest urban concentrations. Each is its own Field: different climate, different language, different density, different law, different inequality, different religious systems, different infrastructures, different historical traumas. The point is not the ranking. The point is the mechanism: scale changes behavior. In a mega-city, individual life is shaped by systems no one can see: supply chains, water access, sewage systems, electricity grids, policing networks, job markets, housing markets, informal economies, migration flows.

It is Field structure. Cities are where the Default becomes obvious because the contrast is constant. The same block can contain a luxury building with a doorman and a shelter line around the corner. The same subway car can contain a banker, a student, a janitor, a nurse, a tourist, an addict, a child, a person returning from night shift, a person returning from a funeral.

One can treat stress as a temporary season. One lives in stress as climate. This is why urban arguments often fail.

Food becomes opportunistic. Movement becomes either compulsive or absent. Relationships become transactional. The phone becomes constant. Work becomes identity. The body starts living as if it is always on call.

Then the person calls it adulthood. It is not adulthood. It is adaptation to a Field that never stops. Cities also have a particular moral illusion: Because there are many options, people assume outcomes are purely choice. That is a lie told by density. Density hides constraint by offering distraction.

Machines require operating instructions. Density is one instruction. Borders are another, because borders decide who the machine is allowed to feed. Cities have always been bargains. The bargain is simple: Give up space. Get access.

Access is jobs, hospitals, schools, culture, strangers, and escape routes from origin. Space is privacy, quiet, and the ability to live without being watched. Every city forces a version of this trade. People who thrive in cities are often the ones whose nervous systems can tolerate the trade without tipping into chronic activation. People who struggle are often not weak. They are mismatched.

In a city, time becomes contractual: shifts, appointments, deadlines, deliveries, rents, fees, penalties, notifications. Contract time is not evil. It is cost. Contract time makes life predictable In a town, your presence can be felt. In a city, your absence is often unnoticed. That anonymity can be freedom for people escaping judgment. It can also be brutal for people needing recognition. Recognition is not ego.

Recognition is co-regulation. A nervous system calms when it is seen by someone safe. A city can make "someone safe" hard to find because interactions become brief, transactional, and guarded. Then people mistake guarding for maturity. Guarding is sometimes necessary. It becomes a problem when it becomes permanent. Cities also produce specialization. In a dense economy, people can survive by doing one narrow task well.

Power expresses itself spatially. Who has trees and who has heat islands. Who has parks and who has broken glass. Who has silence and who has sirens.

Who has clean subways and who has late buses. Who has safe sidewalks and who has highways cutting through neighborhoods. Who has hospitals and who has clinics that close.

$$\text{BUILT FORM} = \text{DESIGN} \times \text{EXPOSURE} \times \text{REPEAT}$$

Who has grocery stores and who has corner stores selling sugar and shame. Those differences are not random. History does not disappear. It becomes layout. This is why urban inequality feels so personal.

It is visible every day. Visible inequality produces two psychological outcomes: All four are understandable. Structure requires strategy. There is also a particular city phenomenon: the "always available life."

A city can offer a 24-hour version of almost everything: food, sex, drugs, parties, work, entertainment, people. For some nervous systems, this feels like liberation. For others, it feels like being hunted. Availability makes the brain's reward system louder. The reward system does not care about morals.

It cares about novelty, anticipation, and relief. This is why cities can accelerate addiction.

Not because cities are evil. Because availability lowers friction. Lower friction increases repetition. Repetition builds grooves. Grooves become identity. Cities can also accelerate recovery for the same reason. Recovery is also repetition.

If a city offers access to meetings, therapists, gyms, libraries, supportive communities, and meaningful work, the same density that spreads harm can spread healing. Density is an amplifier. Amplifiers do not choose the signal. You choose the signal you keep returning to. Returning is training. Training becomes self. Now return to attention.

A city competes for it. Every stimulus is asking the brain: look here. The brain learns to scan. Scanning is a stress behavior. It keeps you safe. It also keeps you shallow.

A city person can become excellent at quick judgments and terrible at deep thought, not because intelligence dropped, but because deep thought requires long stretches of uninterrupted attention. Those stretches are rare.

Building Refuge in Density

Certain people become "urban monks" without meaning to. They build strict rules: no phone on the train, early mornings, consistent sleep, one neighborhood, one gym, one grocery store, one café, one park, one route, one circle. Not only economic. Nervous system wealth.

A person can live in a city for a decade and never feel at home. Home is the ability to move through the environment without constant bracing. That requires familiarity, community, and control. Now the practical conclusion:

Coordinate by choosing fewer neighborhoods and learning them well; choosing fewer people and treating them as nervous-system resources rather than entertainment; and making sleep, daylight, food, and quiet more consistent than the city will do for you on its own.

A city makes you visible to systems, not to people. Data knows you before neighbors do: cameras, cards, apps, payroll systems, and rent portals. A person who wants to live in a city without losing the self must protect contact the way money is protected: deliberately, repeatedly, without apology.

The price of attention rises with density. Ads, sirens, screens, crowds, scarcity, and novelty all compete for your nervous system. If you do not set boundaries, the city will set them for you through exhaustion.

At the same time, cities can be the fastest way to expand a Choice Set. Jobs cluster. Skills cluster. Communities cluster. If you are trying to change your life, density can be Leverage. If you do not drown in it.

The Field move is to treat the city like a tool, not a deity. Build routines that protect your body: sleep, food, daylight, quiet. Build routes that reduce friction. Build relationships that regulate, not destabilize. Without that, the city becomes a constant emergency.

Different cities charge different taxes. Some charge money. Some charge time. Some charge safety. Some charge loneliness. A person should choose a city the way they choose a job: by total cost, not by fantasy.

Cities contain many sub-cities. One neighborhood rewards ambition. Another rewards numbness. One rewards family. Another rewards nightlife. The strategic move is to build a refuge: a few blocks, a few people, a few routines that keep you regulated inside the density.

Without refuge, density becomes chaos. With refuge, density becomes Leverage. Attention is the hidden currency of city life. If you spend it everywhere, you have none left for yourself. Choose what you notice. Choose where you walk. Choose what you ignore. Otherwise, the city will rent your mind out to whoever pays for billboards and feeds.

Borders are the lines that decide who gets to cross. In a world of dense opportunity, borders are the gates. Cities create their own physics: density, speed, and constant choice. But the city is also a political object drawn on paper. What counts as a neighborhood, who gets services, where enforcement concentrates, where people can build. These are map decisions that become lived reality. Maps and borders are fictions with real consequences.

In cities, attention is a commodity sold by the minute.

A boundary isn't rudeness; it's your rent. The city speeds you up; your nervous system still bills you at human rates.

8

Borders and the Price of Movement

BORDERS ARE NOT A SIDE ISSUE IN THIS MODEL. THEY ARE ACCESS SYSTEMS. THEY DETERMINE WHICH RULES APPLY, WHICH INSTITUTIONS GOVERN YOU, AND WHICH ADMINISTRATIVE BURDENS YOU MUST CLEAR WHEN LIFE GOES WRONG.

Maps and Migration

Elena holds the paperwork long enough for the paper to feel heavier than its weight. Marcus crosses some borders with an ID, a booking code, and the right language already in his mouth. Rafi knows the smaller borders too: the clubs, clinics, waiting rooms, and checkout counters where one look can decide whether the next hour gets easier or harder. A line on a map can change your entire life. That line is not physical.

Elena knows the stakes before she can name them cleanly. One missed form can mean fewer jobs she is allowed to take, more explaining at every counter, more waiting, more proof, less future. Paperwork is not clerical when one error can shrink a whole year.

It is enforced. Enforcement makes fiction real. A border decides which laws apply to your body, which language controls your paperwork, which currency buys your food, which police can touch you, which courts can judge you, which schools can teach you, which hospitals can treat you, which jobs can hire you, which benefits can catch you when you fall.

A person can walk ten minutes in one direction and gain rights. A person can walk ten minutes in another direction and become illegal. That is not philosophy. That is the Field in ink.

Modern people love to pretend that borders are natural. They are not. Borders are agreements backed by force. Agreements change. Force remains.

It does not care what you deserve. This is one of the most under-discussed forms of constraint because it is easier to talk about mindset than to talk about systems that can arrest you.

A person who does not understand jurisdiction will keep blaming the self for realities that are legal, not personal. Maps also operate inside a country. A state line can change your taxes, your labor protections, your reproductive rights, your access to health care, your school quality, your landlord's power, your minimum wage, your ability to vote, your exposure to guns, your likelihood of being stopped, your ability to unionize, your ability to be evicted, your access to public benefits, your ability to drive without fear.

Describing mechanics is not moral abdication. It is the opposite. If you want to reduce harm, you have to see what is actually enforcing harm. Neutral language here is a tool, not a posture. It lets you trace the Field without turning the analysis into a team sport.

A person who moves from one state to another can feel like a new species not because the body changed, but because the rules changed.

"Just move" is sometimes good advice and sometimes a cruel joke. Moving is expensive. Moving also changes the legal Field in ways that can save a life or ruin one. Here is the scale of the machine, just inside one country. Recent U.S. Census estimates continue to place states such as California, Texas, Florida, and New York in the tens of millions. That is tens of millions of nervous systems living under slightly different rule sets, price levels, infrastructures, and cultural codes. The map decides. Maps also decide who is counted.

Counting is power. If a government counts you, it can tax you, track you, draft you, police you, offer you benefits, deny you benefits, or ignore you strategically. If a government does not count you, you can be exploited more easily because your suffering is invisible in the paperwork that justifies decisions.

An ID card is not only convenience. It is access to the future. Bank accounts, leases, employment, travel, schooling, healthcare, insurance, voting, marriage, divorce, custody, retirement, and inheritance are all tied to paper identity. A person without stable documentation lives in a permanently shrinking Choice Set. Even simple tasks become high-risk. Every interaction becomes an audition for legitimacy. That stress is not a personality issue. It is structural threat. Maps also create social myths. A border is not only a barrier. It is a story generator.

Migration research describes this load as acculturative stress: a measurable interaction between cultural adaptation demands, loss of support, language strain, and psychological health.

Language enclaves are borders. Even gentrification is a border moving, not only a neighborhood changing. A new population arrives with different price tolerance and different norms. The Field shifts. The original population is pushed outward or forced to adapt. Adaptation looks like displacement, resentment, hustle, or collapse. Again: mechanics.

Maps also shape identity through belonging. Citizenship is a powerful nervous system regulator. A passport is a permission slip for the future. It reduces background threat. It reduces the amount of energy spent on legitimacy. A person without that permission lives in a constant low-grade emergency.

Emergency changes behavior. Emergency increases recurrence. Emergency shrinks horizons. Emergency makes long-term planning feel like arrogance. This is why financial advice, wellness advice, and motivational advice often fail. They assume the reader lives in a stable jurisdiction.

Many people do not. Now consider the private version of the map: the address. An address is not only where you sleep. An address is the key to services. No address, no mailbox. No mailbox, no bills. No bills, no proof.

No proof, no bank. No bank, no rent. No rent, no stability. Instability becomes the story of "bad decisions." Bad decisions are often the story of unstable addresses. The map writes the loop. This does not mean responsibility disappears.

It means responsibility must be accurate. A person can only take responsibility for what is inside control. Jurisdiction is rarely fully inside control, but it can sometimes be chosen. Choosing jurisdiction is a form of strategy. That strategy is not glamorous. It is paperwork. It is reading fine print. It is understanding local rules. It is understanding what a place will punish and what it will ignore.

It is choosing where to build a life based on the rules of the game, not only the beauty of the scenery. This is not cynical. It is adult. Adult means: the world contains systems, and those systems do not care about your feelings. A person who refuses to learn the systems will pay in confusion. Maps are systems. A border is a system edge. System edges create pressure. Pressure produces behavior. Behavior becomes moralized. Moralization hides the edge.

Stop moralizing the edge. Read it. A person who reads the map gains one advantage: Predictability. Predictability reduces fear. Reduced fear expands Choice Set. Expanded Choice Set is the beginning of freedom. Maps also decide which mistakes are survivable. A teenager can be reckless anywhere. The difference is what the system does next. In a place with robust schools, healthcare, and second chances, recklessness becomes a story: a suspension, a program, a mentor, a warning, a lesson.

In some jurisdictions, the government is experienced as a service: roads work, offices answer, forms are simple, police are predictable, courts move, schools function. In other jurisdictions, the government is experienced as extraction: fees, fines, delays, humiliation, arbitrary enforcement, broken infrastructure, and constant paperwork that never resolves.

People raised under extraction learn a specific posture toward authority: distrust, avoidance, performance, bracing. People raised under service learn a different posture: expectation, complaint, confidence, entitlement. Then these groups meet and misunderstand each other as if they are debating values. They are debating histories of governance.

What Paperwork Does to the Nervous System

A person with money and citizenship can treat paperwork as annoying. A person without money and without legal stability experiences paperwork as threat, because one mistake can trigger a cascade: loss of benefits, loss of housing, loss of custody, loss of work authorization, deportation, arrest.

Under that kind of threat, even opening mail spikes the nervous system. Then outsiders call the person irresponsible for ignoring mail. The Field made mail dangerous. Maps also decide which credentials count.

A person can cross a border with a degree and become unqualified overnight. A nurse becomes an assistant. An engineer becomes a driver. A teacher becomes a cleaner. The skill did not disappear. The paperwork changed. That reality creates a specific kind of grief: being competent and treated as incompetent. Grief under pressure becomes bitterness or numbness. Again, not personality. Field.

A person living inside each system will behave differently because the cost of being seen is different. Help is a local ecosystem: availability, stigma, price, confidentiality, legal risk. Maps also contain "soft borders." A soft border is not guarded with guns. It is guarded with friction. Application fees. Background checks. Credit scores.

Security deposits. Required references. Required documentation. Required proof of employment. Required proof of income. Required proof of residence. Required proof of stability. These requirements look reasonable in isolation. Together, they become a wall.

A person trying to rebuild after collapse hits this wall repeatedly and then starts to believe the story: "Restart is not allowed." That is often accurate. The map was not built for restarting. Restarting requires either privilege, community support, or an informal economy. A person without any of these becomes stuck. Stuck people then get moralized. Maps also create "hard borders" inside the body. A person who has been stopped, searched, detained, or threatened often develops a permanent physiological response to uniforms, sirens, or official language. The body becomes trained to anticipate danger from institutions. That training does not disappear because someone says "not all cops" or "not all systems." The body learned from experience.

Even language works like a border. If official language is not yours, every form becomes a test. Every phone call becomes a risk. Every medical appointment becomes a vulnerability. Every legal interaction becomes exposure. Then outsiders ask why the person is "not integrating," ignoring that integration requires a nervous system that is not constantly bracing.

"Troubled student," the system begins to treat the label as essence. Doors close. Exits shrink. The person starts behaving like someone whose exits shrank, because exits did shrink. Then observers claim the label was accurate. This is how bureaucracy manufactures proof. The most important thing to understand is this: Changing jurisdictions is like changing operating systems. The same actions can produce different results. The same inputs can be rewarded or punished differently. The same error can be corrected or multiplied.

Some people "turn their life around" after moving. The person did not become magically virtuous. The operating system changed. That does not erase personal responsibility.

It explains why responsibility finally had room to work. A person who wants to build a stable life must think like a strategist, not like a motivational speaker. Strategy begins with asking: Where are the traps?

Those questions sound cold. They are compassionate. They prevent people from confusing morality with physics. Physics does not negotiate.

A person who has crossed many boundaries often becomes fluent in code-switching: shifting voice, posture, vocabulary, and facial expression depending on the room. Outsiders sometimes call that fake.

Maps are stories with consequences. A border is a line that changes what you are allowed to do with the same body. On one side you can work, marry, travel, vote, own property. On the other side you may be detained, deported, or erased.

"Freedom" is not a vibe. It is documentation, enforcement, and belonging. A passport is not paper. It is access to systems. It is the difference between a problem you can solve and a problem you must endure.

People forget that legal fictions rule material life. Money is a fiction. Corporations are fictions. Citizenship is a fiction. They work because enforcement makes them real. When enforcement changes, the map changes.

The Field move is to stop treating the map as nature. Laws can be amended. Borders shift. Rights expand and contract. What feels permanent is often policy plus habit.

This also applies inside a country. Zip codes act like borders. School districts act like borders. Policing zones act like borders. The map is layered, and each layer has its own fees.

Do not confuse "complicated" with "inevitable." Many systems become complicated because complexity protects incumbents and reduces accountability. The more you learn the map, the less magical it feels. The less magical it feels, the more you can move inside it without begging.

If you have ever wondered why you feel powerless, ask if you are standing in a system you have never read. Literacy turns fear into strategy.

When the map changes for you (when you move, willingly or not) the Field has to be relearned from the ground up. Maps define belonging, and belonging determines movement. When the map says "not here," people move. Or are forced to. Migration is not only travel. It is a nervous system shift.

Crossing Fields with different rules means relearning what is safe, what is allowed, and what is affordable while the old Invoice is still on the table.

A person can change countries and still wake up with the old Field in the body. A person can change neighborhoods and still flinch at the old sounds. A person can change languages and still think in the old rhythms. Place moves faster than biology.

Migration is both promise and pain. People talk about moving as if it were a clean reset. It is not. A move changes the external variables: climate, law, language, price, safety, opportunity, social norms. But the internal variables (stress physiology, attachment Defaults, coping loops, shame scripts, reward pathways) do not move at the same speed. A person can leave a war zone and still live in war. It is memory.

There is the obvious load: paperwork, travel, logistics, money, housing, jobs. There is also the hidden load: translation, decoding social rules, being observed, performing competence, managing shame, managing loneliness, managing identity fracture. Identity fracture is real.

A person is also a set of roles that were validated by the old Field: child, sibling, neighbor, worker, friend, elder, leader, troublemaker, golden child, scapegoat, provider, rescuer.

Migration Is a Nervous System Event

Migration also changes time. Jet lag is the trivial version. The deeper version is rhythm mismatch.

A culture has a rhythm: how quickly people speak, how directly they say no, how long people sit together, how late dinner happens, how early work starts, how strict punctuality is, how loud public space is, how much eye contact is expected, how much touch is expected. A person migrating into a new rhythm experiences constant micro-stress because every interaction requires calculation. The nervous system has to ask: what is the correct move here? When that question is asked all day, the body spends energy. Then the person goes home and collapses. The collapse looks like depression.

It can be depression. It can also be exhaustion from translation. Language intensifies this. People become smaller in a language they cannot fully access.

Humor disappears. Confidence disappears. Nuance disappears. The person can sound less intelligent than the person is. That misperception is humiliating. Humiliation under pressure produces either silence or aggression.

Migration can also be a cure. Not for everything. For certain Defaults, it can be decisive. A person trapped in an environment that constantly triggers recurrence can break the loop by leaving the trigger Field. A person trapped in a culture that punishes difference can recover selfhood by moving into a culture that tolerates it. A person trapped in a small economy can expand Choice Set by moving into a larger one.

A person can move and keep the same internal loop: same relationships, different faces; same addiction, different substance; same shame, different language; same self-attack, different scenery. The correct frame is this: Migration changes the Field. Repetitions are what update the nervous system. The first months after a move are critical because the nervous system is plastic under novelty. Novelty increases attention. Attention increases learning. Learning can build new loops fast. Or it can lock in fear fast.

This is the migration paradox: You left to find something new. Your body tries to rebuild what is old. Both are true. Integration is the art of choosing what to keep and what to release. That art is not abstract. It is daily practice. A person integrates by building anchors. Anchors are small consistencies that tell the body: this place is real, and you can live here. A morning walk on the same route.

A weekly call with one safe person. A meal cooked the same way each week. A place of worship, if faith is real. A gym, if movement is real. A community group, if community is real. A ritual that does not depend on perfect circumstances. Anchors do not erase grief. They make grief survivable. Because grief without anchor becomes drift. Drift is dangerous in a new Field. Drift invites predatory systems: exploitative jobs, exploitative landlords, exploitative partners, exploitative substances.

MOVEMENT COST = DISTANCE + DOCUMENTATION + DELAY + THREAT

They have roles, scripts, and equilibrium points. When one person leaves, the system loses a stabilizer, even if the stabilizer was unhealthy.

A person who wants to migrate and still evolve must anticipate this. Anticipation is not coldness. It is prevention. Migration also forces negotiation with class codes. A person can move into a higher-status environment and discover that skill is not the only currency. Accent, vocabulary, posture, clothing, references, manners, and assumptions about what is "normal" become signals. These signals decide how others treat you. That treatment feeds back into identity.

Migration also produces a specific grief that outsiders rarely understand. It is the grief of becoming an expert at survival in one world and suddenly becoming a beginner again. The grief is the losing of perceived dominance over a process as new reality is lower tiered.

Beginners are clumsy. Clumsiness is humiliating. Humiliation under pressure often produces either grandiosity or withdrawal. Grandiosity says: this is beneath me. Withdrawal says: this is not for me. Both protect dignity. Neither builds a life. A person migrating must tolerate becoming an amateur without turning it into shame.

This is a psychological skill more than a logistical one. Children experience this differently. Children adapt faster to language and social codes, but they pay in identity confusion. They can become neither fully from origin nor fully from the new Field. They can become split between worlds: neither fully protected by origin nor fully at home in the new Field. This is not ingratitude. It is reality colliding with a narrative.

The narrative of return is one of the strongest myths in human life. The truth is harsher: You cannot go back to an old Field and be the same organism. You changed. The Field changed. Even if the buildings are identical, the time is not.

Migration also used to require separation. Now it often does not. A phone collapses distance.

These are migrations too. They are crossings of social borders. They produce the same withdrawal, grief, and identity recalibration at smaller scale. The body prefers known suffering over unknown possibility when load is high.

The brave part is tolerating the unknown long enough for it to become home. What makes that possible is not romance but infrastructure: community, health, legal status, language, and time.

They are not side topics. They are the climate inside which most modern Defaults either harden or loosen. Migration tends to move through phases, whether a person names them or not. First is shock. Shock is not always dramatic. It can be quiet disorientation: the wrong foods, the wrong smells, the wrong social distances, the wrong humor, the wrong tone, the wrong silence.

The body stays slightly tense because prediction fails all day. Second is defense. Defense is the attempt to recreate the old world inside the new one: only speaking the old language, only eating the old foods, only socializing with people from origin, only watching old media, only trusting familiar cues. Defense is not failure. Defense is the nervous system buying time. Third is synthesis.

Synthesis is choosing what stays and what goes: keeping the parts of origin that are true, releasing the parts that were only survival, adopting parts of the new Field that increase freedom without erasing identity.

A person who wants migration to be healing must treat the first year as a training period, not a verdict.

A place rarely feels like home on day ten. A nervous system does not grant trust on schedule. Trust is earned by repetition without catastrophe. That is the same rule that governs every Default change here. The Field changes first. The body tests. The body tests again.

The body tests again. Then, slowly, the new Field becomes real. Then, slowly, the new life becomes possible. Migration proves a final point: A person is not only an interior self. A person is a moving system interacting with other systems. When the interaction changes, the person changes. That truth can be used. Not to erase responsibility.

To aim responsibility at the right target. Aim at the variables that actually move behavior. Aim at the Field. That is how migration becomes strategy instead of trauma. Change the environment (rules, safety, access, cues, enforcement) and you change what repeats; over time that changes trajectory. Money is the most common form of system pressure in modern life. Money does not only buy comfort. Money buys time, safety, and the ability to make mistakes without permanent consequence. Under constraint, slack (time, money, safety buffer) is what makes mistake-tolerant change possible.

Migration is a clause you sign when the old Field becomes unlivable. Sometimes that unlivability is war or famine. Sometimes it is economics. Sometimes it is a family system that will not let you grow.

When you move, you do not just move your body. You move your nervous system. You lose routines, language shortcuts, status, and micro-support you did not realize was holding you up. That loss looks like "I'm not myself." It is your system recalibrating.

Migration also reveals how much identity is context. Cross-cultural transitions change competence, safety, and adjustment costs even when the person remains the same.

The Field move is to plan for the hidden costs: loneliness, bureaucracy, accent tax, credential translation, culture shock, grief. Those are not personal weaknesses. They are predictable.

Migration can be liberation, but it is not free. It trades one set of constraints for another. The adult move is to choose knowingly, not romantically.

A move becomes survivable when you build anchors fast. One regular place. One regular route. One person you can call. One ritual that stays the same. Grief for what you lost can coexist with commitment to what you are building. Assimilation is not the goal. Integration is: keeping what is good, adapting what is necessary, and refusing to disappear.

Moving does not erase who you were. It edits what is possible. Give yourself time to become fluent in the new terms.

9

Pressure: Money, Attention, and Scarcity

MONEY AND ATTENTION BELONG IN THE SAME CHAPTER BECAUSE BOTH ARE SCARCITY ENGINES. ONE NARROWS THE MATERIAL MENU. THE OTHER NARROWS THE MENTAL MENU. TOGETHER THEY DETERMINE HOW MUCH FUTURE THE NERVOUS SYSTEM CAN AFFORD TO HOLD.

The Scarcity Loop

Elena checks her balance before she opens her email. There is enough for rent if nothing else happens. Nothing else is exactly what never happens. Her brother needs new cleats. Her mother needs money sent to an uncle. The train card refills today. The body tightens before the spreadsheet does. Under volatility, immediacy can become rational. Small tasks relieve uncertainty. Strategic work delays relief. The recurrence is not moral failure. It is reinforcement under scarcity. Money is not a personality test. Under scarcity, money becomes weather.

Multiple studies suggest that poverty itself can tax cognitive function.

It determines which moves are safe, which moves are risky, which moves are possible, and which moves are fantasy. It sets the temperature of the nervous system because it sets the baseline threat: shelter, food, healthcare, transportation, childcare, time. When money is stable, the nervous system can afford long horizons. When money is unstable, the nervous system collapses into the present.

This is not moral failure. It is scarcity math. Scarcity shrinks the future.

Not because the future is gone, but because the body cannot invest in what it cannot trust.

A person who is one bill away from crisis does not plan the same way as a person who has buffer. Buffer is not arrogance. Buffer is nervous system safety.

The same advice lands differently depending on income. "Be patient" lands as wisdom for someone with buffer. Margin is the word underneath everything. Margin is the distance between life and collapse.

Promises are lies. Systems do not help. Relief must be taken when it is available.

This calibration produces behaviors that look irresponsible to outsiders: impulsive spending, avoidance of bills, avoidance of banks, avoidance of budgeting, avoidance of planning, avoidance of saving.

Virtue is not the full story. Money buys trust. Two people can be given the same financial information and interpret it as two different languages because their nervous systems are living in different climates. Money also shapes attention. A person under financial pressure spends mental bandwidth on constant micro-decisions: which bill first, which day to pay, which late fee to accept, which item to skip, which debt collector to ignore, which family request to refuse, which friend to disappoint, which job to keep, which shift to take, which ride to pay for, which meal to skip. Cognitive load reduces capacity for long-term thinking, learning, and self-regulation.

Then society judges the person for being short-term. Again: cruelty disguised as logic. Money also creates feedback loops.

Debt pulls future money into the present. Interest charges rent on time. Late fees charge rent on mistakes. Penalties charge rent on being human.

The poor often pay more for the same life: overdraft fees, payday loans, high-interest credit, towing fees, court fees, application fees, security deposits, required insurance, and required childcare for work.

These are all costs of entry. They are gates. Now add compounding. Compounding is simple math with violent long-term effects.

A small advantage early becomes a huge difference later. This is why inheritance matters more than motivation. This is why early debt is so destructive. This is why the phrase "start young" is both true and cruel.

True because time amplifies outcomes. Cruel because the people who most need time often spend their early years surviving. Survival consumes time. Now connect this to identity.

Every person has a money role in the family system. Some become the Saver: hoarding safety, fearing collapse, monitoring every dollar, never relaxing.

Some become the Spender: taking relief when possible, proving that life contains pleasure, numbing stress through consumption. Some become the Rescuer: paying other people's emergencies, carrying family survival, using money to buy love and loyalty. Some become the Avoider: refusing to look, refusing to plan, living in denial until the system forces confrontation.

Some become the Performer: using money to signal worth, buying status to reduce shame.

Some become the Ghost: earning but disappearing, hiding resources because resources attract demands.

These roles are not identities. It is fear. Money roles become stable because they regulate. A Saver regulates anxiety by controlling.

A Spender regulates pain by feeling alive. A Rescuer regulates shame by being needed. An Avoider regulates overwhelm by not seeing. A Performer regulates insecurity by signaling.

Physiology wins. If the nervous system is using spending to regulate, a spreadsheet will not overpower it. The role must be replaced with a new form of stability. This is the rule underneath recurrence, addiction, and money: A Default persists until the cost of repeating exceeds the cost of adapting.

Money Defaults are no different. Now zoom out again. Different places teach different money scripts: In some cultures, money is openly discussed, planned, and taught. In others, money is taboo, hidden, and weaponized. In some families, money is safety. In others, money is shame. In some communities, money is collective: shared resources, shared childcare, shared housing, shared emergencies. In others, money is solitary: individual success, individual failure, individual blame. Each script produces different nervous system outputs.

Then society treats one script as “responsible” and another as “immature,” ignoring that the scripts were trained by real conditions. Money is also relational. Money changes power between people. The person who pays often controls the Terms. The person who owes often performs. The person who earns less often shrinks.

The person who earns more often pretends money is irrelevant while benefiting from it. Ignoring money does not remove its power. It just makes the power covert. Covert power produces resentment. Resentment produces conflict. Conflict produces recurrence.

This is why couples break not only over money itself, but over what money represents: safety, control, freedom, respect, burden. Money is the language of constraint. This is also why workplaces shape identity deeply. Wages are not only income. They are permission. They decide where you can live, what you can eat, how you can sleep, who you can date, what you can tolerate, what you can leave. A person with low wages cannot afford certain Moral choices. Not because the person is immoral, but because the penalties are fatal.

"Just quit" is not always advice. It is sometimes a fantasy. Now the Leverage.

Money becomes survivable when it is treated like a system, not like a test of worth.

When Scarcity Shrinks Time

What buffer buys is room to think. Systems can be redesigned. Not perfectly. Enough. The first redesign is margin.

Margin is the goal before wealth. A person who has margin thinks differently. The second redesign is automation. A nervous system under load cannot rely on constant discipline.

Discipline fails when stress spikes. Automation protects you from yourself. Automatic transfers. Automatic bill pay.

Separate accounts. Separate cards. Separate roles. Automation is not laziness.

It is intelligence about human limitation. The third redesign is fixed cost reduction. Fixed costs are the parts of life that must be paid regardless of mood: rent, transportation, debt, subscriptions, childcare. High fixed costs create chronic threat because they leave no room for error. Reducing fixed costs increases margin. Margin increases calm. Calm increases planning. Planning increases freedom. The loop is real.

The fourth redesign is environment. Money habits are location-linked. A person living in a consumption theater will spend more. A person surrounded by expensive friends will spend more. A person living in a place where every social interaction costs money will spend more. A person living in a place with free third spaces and cheap rituals will Spend less without feeling deprived. This is why money is place. Not only math. If money is the weather, then environment is climate control.

Now the final truth: Money does not guarantee happiness. Money guarantees options. Options reduce panic. Reduced panic is the foundation for almost every other change described here.

A person cannot meditate out of eviction. A person cannot journal out of hunger. A person cannot self-love out of a medical bill that destroys the future. Those statements are not pessimism. They are respect for reality.

The Field includes money because money is one of the most powerful forces shaping human behavior in modern life. Money also distorts perception of time. When money is tight, time becomes urgent. Everything becomes "now" because penalties arrive quickly. Rent is due now.

Late fee starts now. Shutoff starts now. Collections starts now. Food is needed now. Work shift is needed now. Urgency becomes the default nervous system state.

That state makes certain behaviors rational: Taking the shift even if the body is breaking. Taking the ride even if it is expensive. Taking the loan even if it is predatory. Taking the quick pleasure even if it ruins next week. Because next week is not guaranteed in the body's accounting. This is why lectures about "delayed gratification" often sound like insults. Delaying gratification assumes the future is stable enough to hold the delayed reward.

If the future is unstable, delay is just loss. A person who wants to help people under scarcity must stabilize the future, not shame the present. This is also why certain financial systems feel like psychological warfare. Late fees punish disorganization. But disorganization is often a symptom of overload. Overload is often a symptom of scarcity.

That means late fees punish scarcity with more scarcity. Interest does the same. Interest is not only a financial concept. It is a time concept. Interest is a tax on needing help. If a person must borrow to survive, the person pays for survival twice: once in the present and again in the future.

This is why debt can feel like a moral stain even when it began as simple need. The stain is manufactured by the structure. Then there is the hidden money stress that rarely gets named: Unpredictability. A person can survive low income better than unpredictable income, because predictability allows planning. Unpredictability produces chronic vigilance: checking schedules, checking balances, checking accounts, anticipating mistakes, bracing for overdraft, bracing for a call from a manager, bracing for a change in rent. Chronic vigilance is allostatic load. Again: the label is not the point. The point is that financial systems can keep the body in survival physiology even when nothing dramatic is happening.

Now return to compounding, because it is the math engine behind inequality. A simple principle rules modern finance: Growth compounds. So does decay. A person with savings earns interest, dividends, or asset appreciation. A person with debt pays interest, fees, and penalties. The difference is not a straight line. It curves. This is why moralizing "bad choices" is often a luxury belief. The platform is often inherited, not earned.

Inheritance is compounding in its purest form. Not only money. Knowledge. Contacts. Confidence. A stable address. A stable credit history. A stable identity.

These are invisible inheritances that operate like money. They expand Choice Set. Then the person who inherited them calls the outcome merit. Merit exists. So does inheritance. Pretending only one exists is propaganda. Money also shapes what kind of person you can afford to be. Generosity is easier with margin.

Patience is easier with margin. Healthy food is easier with margin. Therapy is easier with margin. Rest is easier with margin. Saying no is easier with margin. Leaving is easier with margin.

This is why money is tied to freedom more than happiness. Freedom is not the ability to buy luxury. Freedom is the ability to refuse exploitation. That is the moral core of money, stripped of ideology. Now look at status. Status is an economic system pretending to be taste.

People buy status when they do not feel safe. Status says: look at me, do not discard me. In some environments, status is the only protection available. In a workplace Where people are disposable, looking valuable is a survival strategy. In a social group where belonging is conditional, looking impressive is protection. In a culture that worships money, looking rich is a form of begging: please treat me like a human.

Status spending is not always vanity. It is sometimes self-defense. But defense can become addiction. Because status produces a quick hit of relief.

Relief can become dependency. Dependency becomes a loop.

Money and addiction rhyme: both are systems of relief under pressure.

Now consider the most brutal money fact of modern life: housing, transportation, childcare, and healthcare are baseline requirements for calm.

$$\text{SCARCITY PRESSURE} = \text{NEED} \div \text{BUFFER}$$

When they are priced out, the person is forced into unstable substitutes: crowded housing, unstable roommates, long commutes, unsafe cars, predatory childcare, skipping care, skipping sleep. Then the person is judged for being unstable. Again: cruelty disguised as common sense. Navigation begins with clear accounting. Clear accounting is not obsessive. It is grounding. Grounding is what ends panic.

A person cannot solve money perfectly. A person can reduce panic. Reducing panic changes behavior. Behavior changes outcome. Outcome changes story. Story changes identity. This is the upward version of the same loop that traps people.

The final truth is simple and unsentimental: Money is not everything. Money is everywhere. Money must be clear as structure, not as shame. That is how money becomes a tool instead of a cage. Money becomes a stabilizer when it is treated as engineering. Engineering starts with inputs and outputs, not with self-judgment. If income is unstable, the first goal is not perfect budgeting. The first goal is smoothing. Smoothing is making the system less volatile: predictable bills, predictable pay, predictable savings, predictable minimum survival costs. Volatility drives panic. Panic drives short-term decisions.

Short-term decisions increase volatility. That is the loop. Smoothing breaks it. This is why an emergency fund matters even when it is small. An emergency fund is not wealth. It is insulation. Insulation reduces temperature swings.

Temperature swings are what crack systems. In money, the crack looks like debt. The emergency fund also does something psychological: It proves that the future exists. That proof is a nervous system drug in the best sense. It calms. Calm allows planning. Planning allows better choices. Better choices create more calm.

Track what is actually happening. Automate what must happen. Reduce the fixed costs that threaten you. Build margin before you chase luxury.

Avoid systems that monetize your mistakes. Choose banking, housing, and transportation that reduce volatility, even if the status signal is lower. Predictability does. Finally, understand that money is also social.

A person can sabotage stability by staying inside a group where every hangout costs money, every gift is expected, every appearance is judged, and every "no" is punished.

That group is a Field. Fields train behavior. If a social Field punishes stability, it will keep you unstable. This is why some financial change requires social change.

Not because friends are evil. Because environments have prices. Money is one of the most visible prices. Pay attention.

Paying attention is the first step toward agency. The second pressure is attention itself: what you consume, what it trains the nervous system to predict, and how it steals tomorrow's bandwidth to soothe today's panic.

Information and Attention

Before his feet hit the floor, Marcus has already opened the phone. Ten minutes becomes forty. By breakfast his body has paid for three arguments, two disasters, and a status contest nobody invited him to.

He has not left the apartment, but his nervous system is already living inside four unrelated emergencies. Attention works like money: once it is spent badly early, the rest of the day gets narrower.

Train the Forecast, Don't Rent It Out

Information is conditioning input. What you repeat becomes what you predict. What you predict becomes how you behave.

A person can live in a materially stable life and still feel hunted because the feed is training the body to expect threat, humiliation, catastrophe, and comparison on command.

Many systems compete for attention because attention is monetizable. Fear is sticky. Outrage is sticky. Comparison is sticky. High-arousal content is not always false. It is often just priced to keep you open, reactive, and available.

Prediction is the operating issue. A forecasting machine trained on spikes starts seeing spikes everywhere. That is how neutral life begins to feel like danger.

PREDICTION = INPUTS YOU REPEAT MOST

This is why information hygiene is not etiquette. It is state management. Protect the first and last hour of the day. Limit high-arousal media when the body is already thin. Choose fewer sources and read them more slowly. Prefer primary documents, direct observation, and real conversation over algorithmic weather.

Talk to actual people often enough that the social world can recalibrate the digital one. A feed is not a neighborhood. A comment section is not a community.

Notice effect, not branding. Do you feel clearer or more scattered? More capable or more helpless? More grounded or more inflamed? The body is often a better lie detector than ideology.

Attention is a budget.

You can spend it deliberately or let companies spend it for you.

The next chapter moves from input to interpretation. Once the system is flooded, the real question becomes: what are you reading as signal, and what are you hallucinating out of noise?

PART III - POWER

Here, the Field scales. Terms are not only personal; they are produced and enforced by institutions.

Marcus is easiest to see here, but Elena and Rafi live under these systems too: paperwork, schedule, enforcement, permission, price.

Power is the capacity to lower your own prices, raise someone else's, or externalize the cost entirely. If you want a larger Choice Set, learn where enforcement lives and how incentives get baked into procedure.

10

Reading Signal in Noise

ELENA READS THE ROOM, MARCUS READS THE EMAIL, AND RAFI READS THE SILENCE. HUMAN JUDGMENT IS NOISY: PEOPLE GIVEN THE SAME INFORMATION OFTEN REACH DIFFERENT CONCLUSIONS.

That variability is the gift. It is also the trap. A nervous system survives by predicting what comes next, then adjusting the body and behavior to match. When prediction is good, life feels navigable. When prediction is bad, life feels haunted - by anxiety, by superstition, by paranoia, by the constant sense that something is happening just out of frame.

The Field is not only the pressures outside a person. It is also the internal interpreter. Two people can stand in the same room, hear the same sentence, watch the same event, and walk away with different realities. The difference is not intelligence. It is calibration: what the system decides is signal and what it dismisses as noise.

Signal is what repeats with consequence. Noise is what happens without stable meaning. Most suffering that looks like "bad choices" is a signal problem.

The system misreads the environment, misreads the body, misreads other people, then makes the wrong move with complete confidence.

SIGNAL = REPEATED PATTERN - RANDOM VARIATION

Overfitting and Underfitting

There are two classic failures. The first is overfitting: treating noise as signal. It is superstition, conspiracy, magical thinking, and the constant hunt for hidden meaning. It is the mind stapling a story onto coincidence because uncertainty feels like danger. The second is underfitting: treating signal as noise. It is denial, minimization, numbness, and the refusal to update. It is the mind ignoring repeated evidence because the cost of the truth feels too high.

Both failures are attempts to regulate pain. Overfitting is the brain paying any price for a map. Underfitting is the brain paying any price to keep the old map.

In a stable environment, these errors are manageable. The world corrects them. A superstition fails often enough to be discarded. A denial breaks often enough to become obvious. In an unstable environment - high stress, high volatility, high humiliation - error becomes a lifestyle. The world does not correct it. The world reinforces it.

A person who is hungry, exhausted, and threatened does not interpret like a rested person with margin. Under chronic load, the mind narrows. It becomes hyper-attentive to threat, and threat is noisy.

A face, a tone, a pause, a headline, a glance - everything becomes a potential signal. The system would rather be wrong than surprised. It would rather see a tiger that is not there than miss a tiger that is.

That is not weakness. That is design. The Field rewards whatever keeps the body intact. The problem is that modern life produces threat without clarity.

The nervous system receives alarms without targets. Bills arrive without warning. Rent rises without explanation. Work schedules shift. Relationships rupture in silence. Phones vibrate with crisis. Social status moves like weather. The body learns a simple rule: certainty is safety. The mind starts manufacturing certainty the only way it can - by turning randomness into narrative.

A person sees Defaults everywhere: the number on a clock, the timing of a message, a stranger's look, the way a friend didn't laugh, the way a partner paused before answering. The story arrives instantly: It means something. It means the worst. That person might even be right sometimes. The Field does contain hidden structure. People do lie. Institutions do exploit. Groups do coordinate. The danger is not that hidden structure exists.

The danger is that the mind stops distinguishing between structure and projection. When that happens, the world becomes a slot machine. A slot machine trains the brain with intermittent reinforcement: occasional wins inside mostly losses. That schedule is addictive because it turns attention into a hunting behavior. The nervous system stays activated because the next pull might matter. Many modern lives function on that schedule. A person scrolls, checks, refreshes, waits, and interprets.

The reward is not information. The reward is relief. The reward is a moment where the mind says: Now it makes sense. This is why "being logical" is not a solution. Logic is a tool, not a state. Logic requires enough regulation to tolerate uncertainty long enough to test Reality. Under load, the system does not want truth. It wants the fastest story that reduces distress.

A person who feels unsafe will prefer a wrong certainty to a true ambiguity. That is how propaganda works. That is how cults work. That is how shame works. That is how abusive relationships work. The system is offered a narrative with clear villains and clear rules. It is offered belonging in exchange for surrendering complexity. It is offered relief in exchange for accuracy.

HEAT IS NOT PROOF

The Field does not ask a person to be accurate. It asks a person to adapt. A person who has a real Default, real instability, real exploitation, real mismatch, can trace it across time and contexts. The details change, but the shape repeats. The body reacts in the same way. The outcomes rhyme. The same types of situations produce the same type of pain.

Invented Default is dramatic but inconsistent. It spikes and collapses. It relies on one interpretation. It cannot survive new evidence. It cannot tolerate alternative explanations. It requires constant vigilance to maintain.

Heat can be fear, anger, disgust, humiliation, certainty, righteousness. Heat is useful as a signal - because emotion often points to something important. Heat is dangerous as proof because emotion can be generated by imagination, trauma memory, and social contagion. A person who grew up with volatility is trained to read volatility as normal. Calm feels suspicious. Silence feels like danger.

Stability feels like the prelude to a fall. That person becomes a high-performance Default reader in chaotic environments. In calm environments, the same skill becomes miscalibration. The system searches for danger because it expects it. It interprets neutrality as threat. It treats ambiguous cues as evidence. This is how a childhood becomes an adult reality without anyone choosing it.

The Field teaches the model. The model recreates the Field. Calibration is not a personality trait. It is a state. It is the brain's best guess based on recent evidence. This is why two people can read the same message and hear two different sentences.

One person reads: "Busy. Talk later." Another reads: "Abandonment is happening." The words are the same. The model is different. The second person's nervous System is not reacting to the message. It is reacting to a lifetime of messages that ended in abandonment.

The Field is not only current. It is cumulative. A signal problem can also run in the other direction. Some people ignore signal because they were trained to. In a household where emotion was punished, a child learns to suppress internal feedback. In a culture where suffering is normalized, a person learns to call pain "life." In a job where complaints are labeled weakness, a worker learns to keep the alarm silent.

Underfitting becomes a virtue. The system says: Do not make a fuss. Do not notice. Do not update. Then the body pays. Underfitting is what allows a person to stay in a harmful relationship for years because "it isn't that bad." It is what allows a person to keep working a schedule that destroys sleep because "that's adulthood." It is what allows a person to keep drinking, scrolling, spending, and numbing because "everyone does it."

Underfitting turns slow damage into background noise. It is the silence before collapse. The Field does not collapse a person with one event. It collapses a person with the accumulation of ignored signal. The most dangerous sentence in the book is: "It's fine."

Both are versions of the same injury: the inability to stay open long enough to test reality without falling apart. Better testing begins with humility. This is where shame becomes a cognitive toxin. Shame does not only hurt. Shame distorts perception. Shame makes the mind defend itself instead of seeing. Shame forces the model to protect the ego, not the body.

A person who is ashamed cannot ask, "What is true?" without hearing, "What is wrong with me?" Both are attempts to avoid the hardest sentence: "Not sure yet." A person who can say "Not sure yet" is not weak. That person has a nervous system with enough safety to hold uncertainty. That capacity is rare in a high-pressure Field. It must be built. It must be protected. It must be practiced.

Default testing is not academic. It is survival. Testing patterns against repeated evidence is one defense against manipulation in high-pressure informational environments.

Test the Pattern Before the Story

Default testing asks simple questions: Does the body respond the same way every time? Does the Default survive new information? Can the Default be explained without requiring a villain? This is why small experiments are powerful. A person does not need a perfect theory. A person needs a test. Change one variable. Keep the rest stable.

Watch the outcome. The Field is full of variables that can be changed: sleep, food, exposure, inputs, location, relationships, schedule, substances, information diet, movement, boundaries. A person who cannot change big variables can still change small ones. A small variable is not small if it moves the nervous system. A ten-minute walk is not small if it changes the state enough to stop a spiral. A night of sleep is not small if it prevents a crash. A muted notification is not small if it breaks an addiction loop.

Triage creates stories. Stories create certainty. Certainty blocks learning. This is why people defend bad Defaults. Bad Defaults are predictable.

Predictability feels like safety. A person would rather live in a familiar hell than an unfamiliar freedom, because unfamiliar freedom requires the risk of being wrong.

The Field does not reward being right. It rewards being stable. A stable lie can outcompete an unstable truth.

The Field is not mystical. It is not moral. It is not personal. It is pressure, repetition, reinforcement, and constraint.

Reading it well is the first form of freedom a person can afford. The next form is understanding scale because scale changes what a Default even is. A signal problem shows up in everyday places that look ordinary. These interpretations are not "in someone's head." They are the head doing its job with incomplete data. The danger is that the interpretation becomes a conclusion instead of a hypothesis. A sensation becomes a verdict. A moment becomes a prophecy.

A nervous system can generate convincing evidence for a false story. Stress changes vision. It changes hearing. It changes memory. It Changes the meaning of faces. Under threat, a person over-remembers danger and under-remembers safety. The mind highlights every insult and ignores every neutral interaction.

That is not lying. That is attention being rationed. This is why people argue about what "really happened" and both feel honest. Two nervous systems are not retrieving the same file. They are rebuilding the same scene with different lighting. The Field amplifies this.

In a high-noise environment, the inputs are not only uncertain; they are adversarial. Platforms compete for attention by manufacturing urgency. News cycles reward outrage. Social status systems reward certainty. The loudest claims travel farthest. The brain is fed a diet of edge cases: rare crimes, extreme opinions, catastrophic predictions, and then trained to treat those edge cases as base reality. That person becomes a well-trained consumer of fear.

A mind can become sophisticated inside a distorted world. It can learn to anticipate the next outrage, the next betrayal, the next humiliation. It can become accurate in the wrong universe. Facts are content. Calibration is context. Context includes sleep, hormones, safety, belonging, and the ability to tolerate ambiguity without dissociating. A person can read the best argument in the world and still be trapped because the body cannot metabolize the uncertainty that comes with changing a belief.

Belief change is not only intellectual. It is physiological. It threatens identity. It threatens relationships. It threatens belonging. The nervous system reads that threat as survival threat, because in many lives it is. A person who changes the story can lose the tribe. That is why denial is sticky.

Overfitting and underfitting also hide inside the obsession with "root causes." The mind wants one cause because one cause is controllable. One cause creates the fantasy of a clean fix. But most real Defaults are multi-causal. They are bundles of variables that travel together: poverty and stress and sleep loss and food quality and neighborhood noise and family instability and school quality and exposure to violence and access to care.

The Field is rarely one lever. It is a board of levers. Some are locked. Some are reachable. Some are disguised as moral issues.

This is how misreading Default becomes a life philosophy. Everything becomes a betrayal story. Or everything becomes a personal failure story. Both stories reduce a complex system into a single explanation that can be emotionally managed.

A model can be technically true and practically useless if it produces no Leverage. This is why Default testing is less about certainty and more about consequence. A person does not need to "prove" a feeling in court.

This is also why some people become addicted to interpretation itself. Interpretation provides motion without change. It provides drama without cost. It keeps the system busy. It prevents the quiet moment where the body might notice what is actually wrong.

Interpretation Can Become a Sedative

A person can spend years diagnosing motives, decoding texts, analyzing childhoods, and naming disorders, while never changing the variable that would shift the outcome: leaving, sleeping, eating, boundary-setting, detoxing inputs, seeking care, choosing different rooms. Analysis can become a sedative. It can be an elegant way to avoid action.

Underfitting can hide inside "positivity" the same way overfitting hides inside paranoia. A person who cannot tolerate conflict will call every red flag "misunderstanding." A person who cannot tolerate loss will call every consequence "temporary." A person who cannot tolerate uncertainty will call every ambiguity "a sign." Different costumes. Same injury: the inability to stay with reality as it is.

Signal reading is also distorted by status. Status changes what a person is allowed to notice. High-status people can treat danger as theoretical because the Field cushions them. Low-status people treat danger as immediate because the Field punishes them fast. One person thinks risk is a mindset. Another person knows risk is a landlord. When two people with different cushions talk about "reality," they are often talking about different Default Engines.

Signal reading becomes more accurate when it becomes more specific. Specificity is a form of respect for reality. A vague story is easy to defend. A specific model can be tested.

Specificity sounds like this: Not "People always leave." Instead: "When there is conflict, the body goes into freeze, communication collapses, and the relationship becomes unsafe." Not "Money ruins everything."

Instead: "When rent consumes most income, sleep shortens, attention narrows, and risk-taking increases."

Not "The world is falling apart." Instead: "When a person's information diet is catastrophe-heavy, the nervous system stays activated and long-term planning collapses." Specificity moves a person from doom to design. Design begins with signal. That is why this matters. Misreading Default is not only a mental error. It is a life error. It changes who gets trusted, what gets pursued, what gets avoided, and what gets repeated.

A person who reads signal well does not become perfect. That person becomes steerable.

And steerability becomes the difference between a life that happens to someone and a life that can be shaped.

Signal is what matters. Noise is everything else. Most people live in noise and call it reality.

One bad story can outweigh a hundred boring facts because stories feel like evidence. This is why people overestimate rare dangers and underestimate common ones. It is also why fear spreads faster than accuracy.

Basic statistical thinking is not elitist; it is self-defense. Ask: compared to what? How often? In what sample? What is the base rate? What would I predict if I had no story, only numbers?

Noise also comes from your own state. When you are anxious, neutral data looks threatening. When you are infatuated, red flags look like charm. When you are ashamed, opportunity looks like a trap. Signal and state interact.

The Field move is to slow down and re-measure. Talk to multiple people. Look for Defaults over time, not spikes. Notice incentives: who benefits if you believe this? Incentive is a form of signal.

One way to cut noise is to ask: what would I bet on? Betting forces you to quantify confidence. It exposes when you are repeating a story you like instead of tracking reality. Humility is not weakness here. It is accuracy. Accurate people change faster because they are not defending ego. They are updating models.

When you do not know the base rate, you cannot evaluate risk. You become vulnerable to whoever tells the best story. Ask boring questions: how many cases, out of how many people, over what time period? Boring questions are how you get free from manipulation.

Signal work is slow. That slowness is why it protects you. The fastest stories are usually selling something.

Scale is the next lesson, because scale determines what signal even looks like. Noise can look like signal when you're tired. That's why big decisions made at 2 a.m. are usually just fatigue speaking in complete sentences.

11

When Systems Scale

MARCUS FEELS SCALE AT WORK, ELENA FEELS IT IN PAPERWORK, AND RAFI FEELS IT IN THE DISTANCE BETWEEN ONE ROOM AND A SYSTEM. SCALE IS WHERE PERSONAL PRESSURE BECOMES ORGANIZED FORCE.

INSTITUTIONAL MISALIGNMENT

Throughput is rewarded. Nuance costs time. Metrics stabilize around speed. No one intends harm. Incentives shape recurrence. When metrics change, patterns change.

Scale changes everything without announcing itself. Institutional economics makes a blunt point: institutions are the rules of the game, and scale changes how those rules land.

A person thinks the problem is personality. The problem is often scale. The same nervous system behaves differently in a group of five than in a crowd of five thousand. The same values behave differently in a family than in a corporation. The same morality behaves differently in a village than in a megacity.

Scale does not only increase the number of people. It changes the feedback loop. Small systems correct themselves through proximity. You see the consequence. You feel the consequence. You cannot outsource accountability to an abstraction. A lie spreads only as far as the liar can carry it. A reputation is not branding. It is memory.

Large systems correct themselves through friction, delay, and bureaucracy. Consequences arrive late or never. A person can harm thousands without meeting one face. A person can be harmed by thousands without knowing one name. In large systems, responsibility becomes statistical. The Field becomes impersonal.

This is why modern life can feel surreal. The brain evolved to track small systems: kin networks, local threats, familiar faces, immediate exchange. Modern life is built from massive systems: supply chains, platforms, markets, bureaucracies, legal codes, surveillance, and algorithmic ranking. The nervous system is trying to act like a village creature in a planetary machine.

Scale Changes the Feedback Loop

Scale is the invisible variable behind the sentence, 'It doesn't make sense anymore.' From above, scale can look clean. From below, it often feels brutal.

Density Raises the Price of Stability

Density is scale with proximity. Density concentrates pressure. Density makes the Field louder.

In low density, the Field is quieter. Mistakes dissipate. Conflict can be avoided by distance. Identity has fewer mirrors. A person can be unknown, which can feel like freedom. A person can also be trapped, which can feel like suffocation. In high density, the Field is loud.

Mistakes echo. Conflict follows because there is nowhere to disappear. Identity is constantly reflected back by strangers, ads, competition, noise, speed. A person can reinvent, because nobody knows the past. A person can also become a nervous system on fire, because everything is friction. Neither is morally superior.

Scale is not background. Scale is a force.

Scale can build miracles. It can also build hells with clean paperwork. Most people do not experience 'the country' or 'the economy' directly. They experience rent, commute, waiting rooms, crowded trains, school rules, shift schedules, and the constant sensation of being measured. That is scale becoming daily life.

In a dense city, opportunity is high because networks are close. Talent can collide. Ideas can spread. Services can cluster. Romance can be available. Culture can be invented in real time.

In the same dense city, stress is high because friction is constant. Space is scarce. Attention is scarce. Calm is scarce. Privacy is scarce. The nervous system is asked to regulate itself inside an environment that is engineered to stimulate. Impatience teaches extraction: from other people, from the body, from time.

Scale also changes how violence works. In small systems, violence is often personal. It is relational. It is visible. In large systems, violence can be procedural. It can be hidden inside policy, pricing, and paperwork. It can be distributed so widely that no single person feels responsible, yet many people suffer. A person who is denied housing is not punched in the face.

That person is still harmed. A person who is denied care is not assaulted in an alley. That person is still harmed. Scale turns harm into administration.

Inside that fog, people do things they would never do in a small room. Scale also changes what honesty costs. In small systems, honesty can cost a relationship. In large systems, honesty can cost employability. A person who is known in a small system can be protected by reputation.

A person who is unknown in a large system is protected by paperwork. This is why identities change with scale.

In small systems, identity is sticky. A person is remembered as the child, the sibling, the troublemaker, the genius, the failure.

Reinvention is hard because memory is everywhere. In large systems, identity is fluid. A person can be a stranger in a week. Reinvention is possible because memory is thin. That can be liberation. It can also be loneliness. It can also be predation, because anonymity allows some people to live without consequence. Scale produces anonymity.

Scale also changes the meaning of trust. In a small system, trust is personal: this person has shown up. In a large system, trust is institutional: this credential, office, or process is supposed to mean something.

When institutions lose legitimacy, people retreat to smaller maps: tribes, families, subcultures, conspiracies, charismatic figures. That move is not always rational. It is often regulatory.

It is also violent to biology. Bodies do not evolve for the quarter. Bodies evolve for the day and the season. When scheduled time becomes absolute, the body becomes a malfunctioning machine in a machine world. Sleep becomes optional. Meals become irregular. Touch becomes rare. Movement becomes constrained. The nervous system becomes uncalibrated.

Advice often fails because advice that works at one scale fails at another. 'Just talk to the landlord.' 'Just switch jobs.' 'Just go for a walk.' Those moves may be available in one Field and impossible in another.

It concentrates pressure where demand is high and control is low. It concentrates pressure where people have to compete for the same limited resources: housing, attention, safety, status, healthcare, and time. This is why population density is not neutral. Density is a force multiplier for everything here: weather, money, information, addiction, shame, and social belonging. Density changes exposure. It changes temptation. It changes the cost of being different.

A person who understands scale stops asking, 'What is wrong with me?' and starts asking, 'What is this Field doing to a nervous system?' That shift reduces shame and returns some bandwidth.

Scale belongs here because money and information are not only personal pressures. They are industrial and platform pressures shaping millions in parallel, from the scale of the body and household to the workplace, neighborhood, city, country, internet, and planet.

Each scale has its own feedback loop, its own currencies, its own rules. Conflict often happens when a person tries to solve a large-scale problem with a small-scale tool, or a small-scale problem with a large-scale tool. The tool does not match the scale, which means the Default persists. Scale also changes what "responsibility" means. In a small system, responsibility is literal: a person can clean the mess. In a large system, responsibility becomes collective, then dissolves.

Everyone contributes a small amount of harm, which means no one feels guilty. Everyone benefits a small amount, which means no one feels grateful. The emotional circuitry that governs moral behavior - guilt, pride, shame, empathy - was not built for diffuse causality. A person may feel moral outrage toward a system, but moral outrage is a small-system emotion. Outrage wants a face. Outrage wants a villain. Large systems often have no single villain. They have incentives. They have metrics.

They have feedback loops that reward certain outputs regardless of anyone's intentions. This is why the phrase "They don't care" often feels true. It might even be true on the level of individuals. But the deeper truth is that large systems cannot care in the way a person cares. They do not have a nervous system. They have a budget and a rule set. Their "care" is whatever keeps the system stable.

Scale also changes the experience of safety. In small systems, safety comes from known people: family, neighbors, community. In large systems, safety often comes from infrastructure: streetlights, emergency services, building codes, public health measures. Infrastructure can be protective, but it is also impersonal. When infrastructure fails, the feeling of betrayal is intense, because a person trusted an abstraction. That betrayal pushes people back into small systems - sometimes healthy, sometimes predatory.

A healthy small system provides shelter, accountability, and shared reality. Both feel safer than being alone inside a failing large system. Scale is also why loneliness can exist in a crowd. Loneliness is not the absence of people. It is the absence of attunement. High density can produce thousands of interactions with almost no attunement.

The brain gets social friction without social nourishment. It gets faces without care. It gets bodies without touch. That mismatch is exhausting. It creates a hunger that people often try to fill with consumption: food, sex, substances, attention, shopping, scrolling. A dense Field offers endless stimulation as a substitute for connection. The nervous system eventually notices.

At large scale, attention becomes an economy. Platforms trade it. Brands buy it. People compete for it as a proxy for status and survival.

Public conversation becomes extreme under scale. A calm voice is drowned out by a screaming one.

A measured claim is drowned out by a certain one. A complex model is drowned out by a simple enemy. Scale amplifies the wrong signals. A person living inside that amplification can become distorted without noticing. The mind begins to treat visibility as truth. It begins to treat engagement as value. It begins to treat repetition as evidence.

Those are all scale errors: confusing the outputs of attention markets with the structure of reality. Scale also creates a new kind of border. Some borders are geographic. Others are algorithmic. A person's feed becomes a country. A person's subculture becomes a neighborhood. A person can live in the same city as someone else and never share a reality because their informational neighborhoods do not overlap.

Build Smaller Stable Units

Large populations create large markets for attention.

Scale is why cities create genius and madness in the same blocks. Scale is why the same person can feel like a hero in one environment and a failure in another.

Scale is why advice becomes ideological: it is often advice that works in one scale disguised as universal truth.

A person who learns scale stops arguing about personality and starts asking about structure. That shift is not only analytical. It is compassionate. It makes it possible to see that many "bad people" are simply people shaped by a punishing Field, and many "good people" are simply people protected by a cushioned one. The Field is not a courtroom. It is a map. Scale is one of its main dimensions. The next dimension is the machinery that makes scale operate: institutions.

There is also a human limit under every discussion of scale: beyond a certain point, people become roles, then numbers. Compassion becomes abstract. The mind protects itself through compression.

Compression is efficient. It is also where dehumanization begins. This is why large systems need constant counter-pressure from art, storytelling, and moral education. Those are not luxuries. They are re-humanizing technologies.

It is also a sensory environment that programs nervous systems. It trains attention, speed, suspicion, improvisation, and appetite. It trains people to become small-scale strategists inside a large-scale machine. That training is why cities are magnetic.

It is also why they are exhausting. Scale is not destiny. But it is never neutral. It is the force that makes the rest of the Field louder or quieter.

Scale changes everything. A behavior that works in a family can fail in a city. A rule that works in a small town can collapse in a nation. The geometry changes when the number of moving parts changes.

At small scale, trust can be personal. At large scale, trust becomes institutional. If the institution fails, people fall back to tribes, and the system becomes unstable.

Scale also explains why modern life feels crowded. When too many people compete for the same limited resource - housing, healthcare, attention, jobs - the lines get longer. That is not just inconvenience. It is stress exposure.

Queueing is a simple example. If a clinic can see 20 patients a day and 30 show up, the wait time explodes. People then blame the staff or the patients. The real problem is capacity versus demand.

The Field move is to stop demanding small-scale solutions for large-scale problems. 'Be kinder' is not enough. You need design, capacity, policy, and feedback mechanisms that can hold the load.

Scale is why the future feels uncertain. We are running planet-sized experiments with climate, data, and energy. The outcomes will not be evenly distributed.

At large scale, "good intentions" are not enough. You need procedures that work even when people are tired, biased, or selfish. Checklists, redundancy, audits, feedback loops - boring things that prevent catastrophe. That is why serious societies invest in systems, not slogans. Compassion without design collapses under load.

At scale, small errors become disasters. A 1% failure rate is tolerable in a room and catastrophic in a nation. That is why systems need safeguards that feel excessive. The safeguard is not pessimism. It is math.

When you feel overwhelmed, check scale. You may be trying to solve a systems problem with a personal mood.

Institutions are what translate that force into rules. At scale, incentives beat intentions. Ten good people can't outvote a bad rule repeated a million times.

When a system scales, small harms become mass harms. That's why design details are ethics.

An institution is memory that can punish. When a society becomes too large to run on face-to-face trust, it builds storage. It writes rules. It creates categories. It invents procedures.

It turns judgment into policy. It turns people into cases. Institutions are the external nervous system of scale. They sense by collecting data. They decide by applying rules.

They act by distributing resources or withholding them. They do not need to hate a person to harm a person. They only need a form that does not include that person's reality. This is why institutions feel cold. Coldness is not always cruelty. It is often compression.

A large system cannot hold the full texture of every life. It reduces. It simplifies. It creates "eligible" and "ineligible," "approved" and "denied," "employee" and "contractor," "citizen" and "non-citizen," "insured" and "uninsured," "creditworthy" and "risky." A category is a gate. A gate is power.

Most people imagine power as a person. Power is usually a process. A process is a set of rules that keeps running even when the people inside it change.

Arguing with an institution can feel like arguing with weather. The individual behind the counter might be kind. The system can still deny. The system can still punish. The system can still force a person into a narrower life. Institutions do not merely respond to reality. They produce reality. A school does not only teach content.

It teaches what counts as intelligence and what counts as failure. It teaches timing. It teaches compliance. It teaches how a body is expected to behave in a room. It teaches a child which emotions are acceptable and which are dangerous. A court does not only apply law. It teaches which stories are believed and which stories are irrelevant. It teaches what happens when power meets language.

A bank does not only store money. It teaches a person what the future costs. It teaches who is allowed to borrow time and who is forced to pay interest just to exist.

Institutions are not neutral. Neutrality is an aesthetic. Institutions have incentives. Incentives are the engine underneath policy. A system ignores what it cannot measure. A system punishes what threatens its stability.

Many institutions are allergic to complexity. Complexity is expensive. Complexity slows processing. Complexity requires judgment. Judgment creates inconsistency. Inconsistency creates liability.

Liability creates fear. Fear creates rigidity. Rigid systems create suffering. This is not a conspiracy. It is a workflow. A person experiences it as: "Nobody is listening."

The template is the real authority. This is why documentation becomes a second body. In a large system, a person's paper-self often matters more than the flesh-self. A person can be sick, but if the paper-self is not coded correctly, the system treats the person as healthy. A person can be safe, but if the paper-self says "risk," the system treats the person as dangerous. A person can be competent, but if the paper-self lacks a credential, the system treats the person as unqualified. Leverage can be used for care or control. Institutions also create time. They create deadlines, waiting periods, probation, eligibility windows, grace periods, penalties, and renewal cycles. They slice life into administrative units. They convert human time into institutional time.

A person's body collapses in months and waits for specialist care for a year. This mismatch is not accidental. It is the result of scale meeting scarcity. Institutions manage scarcity by rationing. Rationing is always painful.

The pain is often disguised as procedure. Because that is how the institution touches a life.

Institutions also outsource moral responsibility. A person inside them can say, 'That's policy,' and feel innocent. Sometimes that person is trapped too. The worker has metrics, quotas, scripts, and risk management. The worker is inside a Field as well.

That is not just frustrating. It is a nervous system injury. It teaches helplessness. It teaches rage. It teaches dissociation. Some people respond by overfitting: seeing institutions as monsters everywhere.

Some respond by underfitting: accepting institutional harm as "just life." Both responses reduce a complex reality. Institutions can be protective. They can also be predatory. Often, they are both at once. A public hospital can save a life and dehumanize a patient in the same hour.

A school can protect a child and break a child in the same year. A welfare program can feed a family and humiliate a parent in the same hour. That is not a paradox. It is care delivered through scarcity and rules.

Mystification is what keeps people trapped. If the system is opaque, the person blames the self or an invisible enemy. Either way, the structure remains untouched.

Institutional literacy starts with blunt questions: What does this institution measure? What risks is it trying to avoid? What happens when an exception is requested? What time horizon does it actually care about?

A person's credit score, medical record, criminal record, academic record, employment record, immigration record - these are data bodies that follow someone across rooms. They determine which doors open and which doors stay locked. This is not only external. Over time, people internalize institutional categories. A child becomes "gifted" and builds an identity that collapses under failure. A teenager becomes "trouble" and learns to live inside the label. An adult becomes "patient" and starts speaking in symptoms.

A worker becomes "low performer" and starts moving like someone who is watched. Identity is often a reflection of what institutions call a person. That reflection can become a trap. Institutions are also where the private becomes public. An institution asks for proof: proof of income, proof of residence, proof of diagnosis, proof of relationship, proof of need. Proof requires exposure. Exposure requires vulnerability. Vulnerability in a punishing Field feels like danger, which means people lie or hide.

Then the institution punishes dishonesty. The cycle hardens. The system becomes more suspicious. People become more defensive. This is how institutions generate the very behavior they claim to manage. A rigid system produces rule-breakers. The Field is always feedback. There is no life outside institutions. Even the people who "opt out" rely on infrastructure: roads, currency, supply chains, laws, markets, and the invisible work of others. The question is not whether institutions will exist.

The question is whether a person understands how they shape behavior and how they enter the body.

Because the institution does not only run on paper. A person can feel this most clearly at the edges of life - when something goes wrong and help is needed. A parent loses a job and applies for assistance. The form asks for documents that require time to retrieve. Time is scarce because the parent is now hunting for work and managing the household. The system is designed to prevent fraud, which means it treats the applicant as a potential liar. The applicant is treated like a potential liar at the exact moment the applicant is most destabilized. The stress response rises. The ability to organize paperwork drops.

A deadline is missed. The application is denied. The institution calls it noncompliance. The nervous system experiences it as abandonment. A patient shows up in pain. The patient does not have the language for the pain. The patient has learned to be polite, or learned to be dramatic, or learned to minimize. The institution reads tone as data, even though tone is a survival strategy. The system wants measurable symptoms. The patient offers a story.

The clinician has limited time and a risk-managed protocol. The story is compressed into a code. The code triggers a treatment path. The path might help. The path might miss the real problem. Either way, the patient learns a lesson: pain must be translated into institutional language to be believed. A teenager enters a school that is designed for compliance. The teen is restless, bright, traumatized, bored, or sleep deprived. The institution calls it behavior.

Behavior triggers discipline. Discipline triggers removal. Removal triggers failure. Failure becomes identity. The teen is not only learning math or history. The teen is learning what kind of person the system thinks exists.

These are not personal tragedies alone. They are Default outputs. They are what happens when scarce resources meet rule-based rationing. One of the most overlooked variables in institutional harm is discretion.

Many modern institutions remove discretion to appear fair and to avoid liability. Scripts replace judgment. Metrics replace conversation.

Automated decisions replace human attention. This increases speed and consistency. It also increases misfit, because human lives do not arrive in standardized shapes. A person can meet a worker who wants to help and still be denied because the system removed the worker's ability to help. That removal turns both sides into enemies. The system remains intact.

This is one reason institutions produce hostility even when no one wakes up wanting to be cruel. People inside institutions often operate under threat as well: threat of losing a job, threat of being audited, threat of being sued, threat of being punished for making an exception. That threat narrows discretion. It pushes workers into defensive behavior. Defensive behavior looks like coldness. Coldness looks like contempt. Contempt triggers rage. Rage confirms the institution's suspicion. Feedback again.

Institutions also shape what counts as proof. Many forms of proof are least available to the people who need help most. That is not always a bug. It is often what happens when systems are designed around the lives of the already stable.

The result is another pressure in the Field: poverty becomes not only a lack of money but a lack of administrative survivability. The poor pay a paper tax in time, stress, and humiliation.

The middle class pays it too, just less often. The wealthy often outsource it.

Technology amplifies institutional power. It speeds decision-making and extends reach. It also lets one wrong code, one bad record, or one frozen assumption follow a person everywhere.

Institutions should be read like weather. Not because they are mysterious, but because they are systemic. Weather is not personal. It is still life-altering. A person who respects weather prepares.

A person who denies weather gets hurt. Institutional literacy is preparation.

Preparation begins by accepting that institutions respond to inputs, not pain. They often cannot process pain at scale without translation. That does not make them innocent. It does explain why begging a system to behave like a loved one usually ends in heartbreak.

Procedure Is Not Care

A loved one can listen. An institution can process. Processing is not listening.

Institutions also create their own cultures. Two agencies with the same policy can feel completely different because culture changes how policy is applied. One office looks for reasons to approve. Another looks for reasons to deny. One workplace values human judgment. Another values compliance.

One clinic treats a patient as a person. Another treats a patient as a case. A person who recognizes culture can avoid unnecessary shame. If an office is hostile, it is not proof of personal failure. It is a feature of that local Field. This is why "choice" inside institutions is often geographic. Different neighborhoods, different offices, different schools, different hospitals - same system, different micro-climate.

Scale creates the macro rules. Culture creates the micro experience. The Field is always both. This is also why institutions can be sites of real liberation. A fair court can protect someone from abuse. A good school can change a family's trajectory. A competent clinic can treat pain that has been dismissed for years. A strong union can turn exploitation into stability.

A social program can buffer a child long enough to grow. Institutions can be the difference between a life surviving and a life collapsing.

The point is not to demonize them. The point is to see them clearly. Clarity allows strategy.

A person aligned with reality learns to present a case in the language an institution can hear: clear timeline, relevant documentation, correct office, written record, and, when possible, an advocate.

The truth is often simpler than shame allows: you are in a system designed for someone else. That separation protects dignity. Dignity protects state. State protects cognition. Cognition protects options.

This is the ladder that institutions often break - and the ladder a person must rebuild by hand.

INSTITUTIONS ARE MEMORY AT SCALE

Institutions are where scale becomes real. Institutions are collective memory. They are how a society repeats behavior without needing every person to reinvent the wheel. Schools, hospitals, courts, banks, employers, and agencies are the second nervous system.

When institutions work, they make life boring in a good way. You can plan. You can rely. When institutions fail, life becomes improvisation, and improvisation is expensive.

Institutions also shape morality. People assume morals come from inside. A lot of morality comes from what systems reward. If an institution rewards lying, lying spreads. If it rewards repair, repair spreads. Incentives are ethics in disguise.

The Field move is to read institutions the way you read a person: by behavior over time, not by mission statement. What happens when you make a request? What happens when you complain? What happens when you are inconvenient?

Paperwork is not neutral. It is a gate. A form can be a wall for someone who is exhausted, disabled, undocumented, or working three jobs. The hidden fee is time and humiliation.

If you want to change the Terms for many people at once, you do not start with motivational posters. You change institutions.

Adults who live inside institutions learn to keep receipts: names, dates, reference numbers, copies, screenshots, written summaries. Not because they are petty. Because memory does not beat bureaucracy.

People who grew up in functional institutions rarely notice them. People who did not notice them because dysfunction was constant. Institutional failure teaches helplessness. Institutional competence teaches agency. When you fix institutions, you change psychology at scale.

Institutions can be redesigned. Cynicism is understandable. It is not a plan. Structure is a plan.

Work is where institutions enter the day. A person can feel the institution most intensely in the minutes before going to work, in the way a day is scheduled, in the way a paycheck is routed, in the way an ID card determines access. The institution is not only a building. It is a rhythm imposed on time. That imposed rhythm becomes the invisible Terms of adulthood. It dictates when sleep is possible, when food is eaten, which relationships can be maintained, which neighborhoods are reachable, and how much silence a person gets. Work is not a moral issue or a motivational issue. It is a Field that converts time into survival.

An institution is yesterday's decision laminated. If you cannot change the institution, change your exposure: where you opt in, where you buffer, and where you exit.

12

Work: Selling Hours, Buying Identity

By 11:40 p.m., Marcus has revised the same memo three times and is still scared to hit send.

The partner has not asked for a fourth pass. The firm's real instruction is older and less precise: do not become legible as replaceable. Marcus stays. The billing clock keeps translating fear into proof. Elena knows the unpaid version of the same arithmetic at home. Rafi knows the after-hours version, when relief starts looking like the only real shift change.

From the outside, this looks like ambition. From inside the Field, it is a schedule, a hierarchy, and a prestige system that turns exhaustion into evidence of seriousness.

What the Job Buys and Burns

Work is where biology meets economics. Demand-control research makes the point: the same job becomes a different life depending on how much control you have inside it.

A person can have the best psychology in the world and still unravel under a schedule that destroys sleep, a wage that cannot cover housing, and a job that treats the body like a disposable tool. Work is not only an activity. It is a Field: an arrangement of time, authority, incentive, and surveillance that trains behavior. People often talk about work as if it is purely moral: discipline, ambition, laziness, drive. That language hides structure.

Work is one of the main ways the Field enters the day. Research on emotional labor shows how jobs price behavior in hidden currencies.

It decides when someone wakes, how long someone stands, when someone eats, how often someone is touched by other humans, how much sunlight someone gets, how much silence someone gets, how often someone is watched, and what counts as "enough." A nervous system does not experience "career."

A nervous system experiences shifts. A person who works nights lives in a different circadian universe than a person who works mornings. A person who works rotating shifts lives in a universe where time is unstable. A person who works two jobs lives in a universe where recovery is impossible. A person who works from home lives in a universe where boundaries dissolve. A person who has no work lives in a universe where shame and insecurity replace structure.

Each is a different Field. Most advice about productivity and motivation ignores this and blames the self. That is convenient for systems. It makes structural problems look like personal failures. The body does not care about ideology. The body cares about rhythm.

When Work Colonizes the Body

Sleep is rhythm. Work rearranges rhythm.

When rhythm is rearranged against biology, the nervous system pays with allostatic load: chronic stress adaptation that looks like "Normal life" until it becomes illness, depression, addiction, or collapse. This is why a person can feel fine for years and then suddenly break. The body has been paying on credit.

Work Also Names the Self

Work also rearranges identity. Many people are not only paid by work. They are named by work. They are granted status, belonging, and narrative through work. "What do you do?" is not a neutral question in modern life.

It is a sorting mechanism. It decides how much respect a person receives, how much attention they receive, and sometimes how safe they are allowed to feel. That treatment shapes self-perception. It shapes posture. It shapes voice. It shapes risk. It shapes the willingness to speak.

Work becomes a social skin. This is why some people stay in jobs that hollow them out. Leaving is not only losing income. Leaving is losing identity. Work can provide meaning. Work can also steal it. The difference often comes down to autonomy and dignity.

Autonomy is the ability to influence time and method. Dignity is the experience of being treated as human. A job can be physically hard and still feel dignified if autonomy and respect exist. A job can be physically easy and still feel brutal if autonomy is removed and humiliation is constant. Humiliation at work is a direct nervous system injury. Threat narrows cognition.

Narrow cognition increases mistakes. Mistakes invite more humiliation. Feedback again. Work also changes relationships. Schedules decide who a person can love, who a person can see, when a person can parent, and whether a person can maintain friendships. A job that consumes evenings and weekends is not only a job. It is a reconfiguration of social life. It pushes a person into an information diet and a relationship diet that fits the schedule, not the soul. This is why work Defaults often predict addiction Defaults. A person who is isolated, sleep-deprived, and stressed will seek regulation wherever it is available. If the only available regulation is alcohol after a shift, scrolling in bed, nicotine on breaks, sugar in a car, or a drug that creates artificial relief, the nervous system learns quickly.

Work is often the upstream variable behind downstream "bad choices." The Field is always upstream. Work also changes the meaning of time. In many jobs, time is not owned. Time is sold. A person sells hours. The institution then purchases the right to shape those hours.

That purchase is not only economic. It is neurological. It Trains a person to treat their own time as not fully theirs. Over years, this becomes a posture toward life: waiting to live later, waiting for the weekend, waiting for vacation, waiting for retirement. Waiting becomes the Default. This is one reason modern people feel numb. Numbness is the nervous system's response to living as if the present does not matter.

Some people respond by building a second life at night: intense pleasure, intense consumption, intense socializing, intense sex, intense risk. The nervous system tries to reclaim aliveness after hours of compliance. That rebound is not immoral. It is compensation. The compensation can also become a trap. Work then becomes more threatened. Threat increases rebound.

METRICS REPLACE HUMAN MEMORY

Feedback again. Work is also where institutions measure a person. Modern work is increasingly tracked: minutes, clicks, deliveries, calls, tickets, sales, outputs. Measurement can improve fairness when it is aligned with reality. Measurement can also become a form of violence when it reduces a human to a number and then punishes proof of humanity: bathroom breaks, illness, grief, pregnancy, aging, pain.

A system that measures output without measuring load creates suffering. A person is asked to be a machine inside a body. The Field of work often treats limits as defects. A person learns to hide limits.

Hidden limits become collapse. This is not a character flaw. It is a Field effect.

Work also creates class reality. Class is not only income. It is control over time. It is access to rest. It is access to predictable schedules, healthcare, safe neighborhoods, and a future that can be planned. Two people can earn similar money and live in different class realities depending on schedule stability and risk exposure. A nurse with mandatory overtime and a consultant with flexible hours can have very different bodies over ten years even if the pay is similar.

A job that kills imagination is not only tiring. It is existentially corrosive.

A job that keeps a person in chronic threat is not only stressful. It is a Default generator for every problem that comes after: addiction, depression, conflict, illness, despair.

Work is also where dignity can be restored. A good team, a respectful manager, a meaningful craft, a stable schedule, a predictable paycheck, and a fair boundary can turn survival into life. This is why stable work can be healing. Not because work is salvation, but because predictability reduces load. Reduced load allows the nervous system to update. It allows the person to read signal instead of noise.

It allows relationships to function. It allows sleep to return. It allows appetite to normalize. It allows addiction loops to loosen. The Field does not moralize which one it becomes. It follows incentives.

That is why understanding work means understanding power: who sets the schedule, who controls the wage, who defines the metric, who holds the threat. Wage floors and labor protections are Terms with studied effects that vary by setting, enforcement, and labor market conditions.

It is a boundary enforced by the possibility of survival loss. Work is the daily one. Law is the formal boundary: the rules that decide what happens when someone refuses. Work also includes the labor that is rarely counted. Parenting is work. Caring for an elderly parent is work. Managing a household is work. Translating for family members is work. Emotional regulation inside a relationship is work.

In many lives, this unpaid labor is the difference between stability and collapse, yet it is treated as natural, invisible, and expected. When work is invisible, exhaustion is misread as laziness. A person who has been working all day might still be "doing nothing" in the eyes of a system that only pays certain labor. That misrecognition produces shame, conflict, and a distorted self-image. The nervous system learns: effort does not equal value.

Over time, that belief makes people brittle. Work also reorganizes geography. A job decides where a person can live, because housing must be within reach. A job decides commute time, and commute time is a daily extraction of life. A long commute is not only inconvenience. It is a chronic stressor: time pressure, noise, crowding, unpredictability, and the daily message that a person's time is expendable. Commuting is one of the most underrated Default Engines in modern life.

Time is not a side variable. Time is the body's main resource. Work also has an "autonomy gradient." The higher the autonomy, the more the body can self-regulate. Autonomy means control over breaks, control over pace, control over methods, control over communication. The lower the autonomy, the more the body becomes reactive. Reactive bodies seek regulation through fast rewards. This is why low-autonomy jobs often correlate with high rates of burnout, conflict, and self-medication.

It is not because the people are weak. It is because the Field is hard. Modern work increasingly removes autonomy through software.

The boss is no longer a person. The boss is a dashboard. The boss is an algorithm assigning tasks, rating performance, and adjusting pay. The worker is managed by metrics that are not negotiable and often not explainable. An algorithmic boss is a perfect example of scaled power: impersonal, relentless, and unarguable.

WORK PRICE = HOURS + HIERARCHY + IDENTITY COST

A person cannot persuade a dashboard. This changes the psychology of effort. Effort becomes a chase, not a craft. Craft requires pride. Pride requires human recognition. A dashboard does not recognize. It only counts. When a worker's experience is reduced to counting, the worker becomes numb or enraged.

Some people respond by dissociating: doing the work without being present. Some respond by inflaming: staying angry to stay alive. Both are survival strategies in a Field that is too tight. Work also trains what kind of future a person is allowed to imagine. In stable work, the future feels like a line: save money, plan, invest in relationships, pursue goals. In unstable work, the future feels like a cliff: a sudden loss is always possible. The nervous system adapts by shortening time horizon. It becomes harder to do long-term thinking. Long-term thinking requires the belief that tomorrow will be similar enough to be planned.

It is a rational adaptation to a Field where the future is unreliable. A person who is paid weekly, whose schedule changes, whose hours can be cut, whose rent can rise, whose health insurance can disappear, lives Inside a short horizon. It makes sense to take pleasure now. It makes sense to spend now. It makes sense to say yes to the thing that feels good today. The long-term future feels hypothetical. This is not a moral judgment. It is an economic nervous system.

Work also shapes how people relate to authority. A person who is constantly watched learns to perform. A person who is constantly punished learns to hide. A person who is constantly micromanaged learns helplessness or rebellion. A person who is respected learns competence. That training does not stay at work.

Workplaces leak into relationships. A person treated like a child all day may become controlling at home to regain control. A person treated like a machine all day may become emotionally flat at home because there is nothing left. A person humiliated all day may become sharp at home because the nervous system is still in threat.

Work also has "moral spillover." A person in a job that harms others (directly or indirectly) must manage that internal conflict.

Some people numb. Some rationalize. Some become cynical. Some become ideologically rigid to make the harm feel necessary. Some quit. The ones who stay often have to build a story that makes the work tolerable. That story can harden into worldview. The Field uses work to train beliefs. This is one reason culture follows economics. A person's moral language often reflects the demands of the job that keeps them alive.

A person does not only sell time. A person often sells conscience in small increments. None of this means work is evil. It means work is powerful. The modern myth says: "You are what you choose."

Work reveals a harsher truth: "You are what the Field rewards." This is why stable, dignified work is one of the strongest interventions a society can offer. It reduces instability. It reduces shame. It reduces addiction loops. It reduces family conflict.

It reduces crime. It reduces despair. It increases long-horizon thinking. It gives people the ability to be decent. Not as a moral achievement, but as an energetic. Possibility. Decency is easier when the nervous system is not being chased.

Marcus calls it drive until the body starts keeping different books: shallower sleep, shorter temper, a weekend that exists only as recovery from the firm's appetite. That is when ambition stops sounding clean and starts sounding colonized.

This is the unromantic truth behind the phrase "character." This also clarifies why "hustle culture" is so seductive. Hustle offers a story that turns exploitation into virtue. It turns exhaustion into identity. It says: pain is proof. For some people, hustle is a temporary bridge out of poverty. For many, it is a trap that extracts life and calls it ambition.

The field loves hustle because hustle produces output. The body eventually hates hustle because hustle consumes recovery.

13

Law: Force in Formal Language

PROCEDURE IS WHERE FORCE PUTS ON A SUIT.

Elena learns quickly that a neutral form can still carry force. An envelope arrives with a seal, a case number, and a deadline; the idea of law as legitimate force stops being theoretical.

Law as Enforced Language

The language is not yours. The timeline is not yours. Ignore it and the system moves anyway. This is law: force translated into language. Law is a set of rules backed by enforcement. If a rule can be ignored with no consequence, it isn't law. It's suggestion. Law becomes real when someone can be compelled: fined, evicted, sued, restrained, imprisoned, deported, or otherwise forced to comply. This isn't an anti-law statement. It's a clarity statement.

Clarity matters because many people are confused by how quickly "civil" life turns into coercion; the Restatement (Second) of Contracts is blunt about what a contract is: a legally enforceable relationship. A person can think a dispute is personal and then discover it is legal. A person can think housing is a home and then discover it is a contract. A person can think a relationship is private and then discover it is governed by custody, property, and the state.

Marcus knows a softer version from work: the clause in the employment agreement, the HR sentence that looks neutral until liability appears, the signature that seemed routine until it starts dictating what can be said, disclosed, or refused. Procedure becomes personal the moment it starts pricing silence.

The Field is not only emotional and economic. It is legal. Law creates the official boundaries of behavior. It defines who owns what, who owes what, who can move where, who has authority over whom, and what happens when someone refuses. Most people meet law not in philosophy but in friction: a ticket, a court date, a notice, a warrant, a letter, a hearing, an arrest, an order.

The experience is often surreal because it is formalized conflict. The language is different. The pace is different. The consequences are disproportionate to the feeling. A person can lose a life trajectory through one record. A person can lose housing through one missed payment. A person can lose a child through one mistake. A person can lose freedom through one bad night.

Procedural-justice research suggests that compliance is shaped not only by fear of sanction but by whether legal authorities are perceived as fair, legible, and legitimate.

Law concentrates consequence. That is the point. In a large society, law is one of the only ways to coordinate strangers at scale. It can protect people from violence. It can enforce contracts. It can create public safety. It can also legitimize exploitation and punish the vulnerable. It can be a shield and a sword. Often it is both in the same system.

The difference is not the word "law." Enforcement is where the Field becomes physical. A law on a page changes nothing until it is applied. Applied law is a street-level reality: who gets stopped, who gets searched, who gets charged, who gets bailed out, who gets sentenced, who gets fined, who gets forgiven, who gets a second chance, who gets labeled forever.

Justice is a moral ideal. Legality is a procedural reality. Procedures can produce justice. Law is also a literacy test. The system is written in a specialized language. People with knowledge and resources can navigate it. People without them often cannot. This creates a hidden inequality: not only of money, but of comprehension, time, and access to representation.

Administrative-burden research clarifies the same mechanism from another angle: learning costs, compliance costs, and psychological costs reshape who can actually use the rights a legal system claims to provide.

Representation is not just a service. It is Leverage inside a system built of language.

Law can feel like a foreign country. It has its own vocabulary. It has its own rituals. It has its own timelines.

Procedure Is Not the Same as Justice

Records Outlive the Event

It has its own gods: precedent, statute, record. A person who has never been trained in it can still be judged by it. The law also creates records. Records are memory that follows a person. A record is a kind of institutional tattoo. It can outlast the behavior that produced it. It can outlast the person's growth. It can outlast the context. It can freeze someone in a past version of the self and force the future to pay for it.

Records are a form of time control. The Field uses records to keep people in place. A punch ends. A record persists.

Law also shapes intimacy. Marriage, divorce, custody, inheritance, tenancy, property. These are legal structures that determine how love and family are allowed to behave. People often pretend these structures are irrelevant until a crisis arrives. Then the structure becomes the room. The relationship becomes paperwork. A couple can love each other and still be destroyed by legal conflict. A child can be harmed and still be unheard because the story is not legible to the system. This is not because the law is evil.

It is because the law is designed to process certain kinds of evidence and certain kinds of harm. Harm that is slow, psychological, or ambiguous is often hard to translate into the system. The system prefers sharp events, clear dates, clear proof. Many real harms are not like that. The Field of law therefore changes what kinds of harm are visible.

Visibility determines protection. Invisibility determines vulnerability. Law also teaches social behavior. It teaches what a society officially values and officially punishes. But more importantly, it teaches what the society actually enforces. People learn from enforcement, not from rhetoric. When enforcement is consistent, behavior updates. When enforcement is inconsistent, behavior becomes strategic, cynical, or opportunistic. Inconsistent enforcement turns law into gambling.

Gambling is not stability. A society that enforces unpredictably teaches strategic behavior rather than stable trust. Those expectations become culture. The Field closes the loop.

Law is also where violence becomes legitimate. Not all violence is physical. Forced displacement is violence. Forced separation is violence. Forced deprivation is violence. The law authorizes these acts when they meet procedural criteria. The procedure can be followed perfectly and the outcome can still be devastating. This is why law must be treated as a physical force, not as an abstract ideal.

A person living under law is living under a climate. That climate shapes risk-taking. It shapes speech. It shapes what is safe to report and what must be hidden. It shapes who trusts institutions and who avoids them. It shapes who calls for help and who refuses because help might bring punishment. This is one of the tragic outputs of a punitive Field: people stop seeking protection because protection is unsafe. A person who cannot call for help is living in a different universe.

Law also interacts with money in obvious ways. Fines are a tax that hits the poor harder. Bail, fees, and representation are priced gatekeepers. A wealthy person and a poor person can commit the same act and experience different realities because the legal system is not only moral; it is logistical. Logistics depend on resources. Options are what the Fine Print distributes unequally. This is not a conspiracy theory. It is a Field description.

The Field is always: constraints plus incentives plus enforcement. Law provides enforcement. It also provides legitimacy. Legitimacy is powerful because it shapes what people accept as normal. A person will tolerate harm longer when it is legal. A person will tolerate exploitation longer when it is official. A person will tolerate humiliation longer when it is framed as "procedure." Procedural formality can normalize harm by turning coercion into routine and framing outcomes as 'official,' which reduces resistance. A person can be devastated and still be told, calmly, that everything was done correctly. This produces a specific kind of despair: the feeling that reality itself has no appeal.

A society that wants durable stability needs something other than fear. That "something" is often legitimacy: the belief that rules are fair enough to accept even when they hurt. In many lives, that experience is missing. When legitimacy is missing, people build their own boundaries: informal rules, street codes, family codes, gang codes, survival codes. Those codes can be protective. They can also be violent. They exist because the official boundary did not feel safe.

Every system creates and enforces access lines (who can do what, where, and at what cost), formally or informally. If official law fails, unofficial law rises. A person who understands this stops being naive about coercion. Coercion is not an exception. It is a feature of large-scale coordination.

Law is also a theater of time. It takes a fast event and stretches it into months or years. A single fight becomes a long case. A single mistake becomes a long sentence. A single incident becomes a long probation. Time itself becomes punishment. Even when a person is not incarcerated, a case can dominate attention and sleep. It becomes a background threat: a court date, a hearing, a payment, a check-in, a condition. The nervous system lives under anticipation.

Anticipation is one of the strongest stressors. It keeps the body braced. It makes recovery hard.

Legal pressure often shows up as insomnia, irritability, appetite change, and impulsive coping. The body is treating the future as a threat because the future contains enforcement.

A person's relationship to law is often formed early. A child who sees adults treated fairly by institutions learns one model: the system is a resource.

A child who sees adults humiliated or punished learns another: the system is a predator. That model becomes behavior. Some people call the police easily. Others avoid any contact. Some people expect due process. Others expect betrayal. Those expectations are not ideology.

They are memory. The Field teaches legal belief through lived experience. Law is also a set of games. Each game has different rules: criminal, civil, administrative, family, immigration, employment. People who have never had to learn these games often think "law" is one thing. It is not. It is an ecosystem of procedures, and the procedures decide what kind of Leverage exists. The weapon changes, but the structure is consistent: rules plus enforcement plus consequences. Consider eviction. Eviction is not only losing a home.

It is a legal process that can push someone into a cascade: loss of address, loss of stability, loss of sleep, loss of school continuity for children, loss of work performance, loss of social support. The eviction itself is the visible event. The downstream consequences are the real injury. The law makes the injury official. It stamps the record. It follows the person to the next housing search. It turns a crisis into a history.

A person might "fail" at housing in the eyes of the system even if the real failure was affordability. This is how law can punish scarcity as if it is character. Now consider a traffic stop, or any enforcement encounter that turns routine into danger. The nervous system activates before thought finishes.

The body reads threat. The mind narrows. If a person is already living under chronic pressure, the threshold for panic is low. Panic changes speech, posture, and compliance. The system can misread those changes as suspicion. Suspicion increases force. Force increases panic. The loop tightens. Many tragedies are not one person being evil.

They are feedback between fear and authority. This is why the Field of law must be designed with human physiology in mind. A policy that assumes calm compliance is a policy designed for an imaginary nervous system. Real people are tired, traumatized, hungry, intoxicated, mentally ill, scared, embarrassed, and angry. Law meets people at the edges, not at their best.

Laws and policies determine who can access care, who can access reproductive decisions, who can access gender expression, who can access marriage, who can access migration, who can access public space. These are not abstract debates in many lives. They are daily constraints that shape identity, risk, and belonging. A person under bodily constraint does not have "choices."

Law is the official ledger of those costs. A healthy legal Field expands the range of permitted moves for the vulnerable and constrains the predatory. An unhealthy legal Field does the reverse. This is not an ideological claim. It is a functional description. Law can also create surprising care.

Rights are real Leverage. Labor protections can change lives. Anti-discrimination enforcement can expand safety. Protective orders can create breathing room. Child support can keep a household afloat. Bankruptcy can reset a future. A fair judge can interrupt a cycle.

A public defender can prevent a life from being destroyed by a plea made under fear. These are not romantic. They are concrete.

Law is a Field. It can tilt. The tilt is made of incentives, culture, discretion, and enforcement. A person living inside it needs accuracy more than ideology. Accuracy means recognizing a hard truth: law is not only a moral system; it is a survival system.

The nervous system often prefers a harsh order to uncertain disorder. This preference can be exploited. It can also be sincerely felt. Either way, it shapes history. Law is one of the main ways societies attempt to stabilize the Field. When the legal Field is perceived as illegitimate, people stop cooperating. Cooperation collapses. Informal violence rises. The state responds with more enforcement. The cycle accelerates.

Legitimacy is not a philosophical luxury. It is a stability mechanism. A person who understands this can see the Field with less confusion.

The Field is not personal. The Field is not fair. The Field is enforceable. That enforceability is why people bargain, why they comply, why they run, why they hide, and why they sometimes break. Wanting is not free either. Desire is also policed, priced, and punished. That is the next Field.

LAW IN PRACTICE = RULE × ENFORCEMENT × ACCESS

Law is also embedded in places people forget to name as legal: employment contracts, lease agreements, Terms of service, non-disclosure clauses, arbitration agreements, debt Terms, subscription traps, and the quiet rules written into platforms. A person clicks "agree" and enters a micro-legal universe. That universe might never matter. Until it matters completely. Then the person discovers the boundary was set long ago. This is another way scale hides coercion. The coercion is preloaded.

It sits quietly in documents nobody reads because life is already too busy. When the moment arrives, the system says: you Consented. The person feels tricked. The system feels correct. Both are true in different registers. The Field of law is therefore not only courts and police. It is the invisible Terms of everyday agreements.

It is the network of permissions and penalties that decides what happens when money is missing, when a job ends, when a relationship breaks, when a debt is sold, when a platform bans, when a landlord raises rent, when a body becomes sick.

Law is the official story of consequence. A person who wants to understand human behavior cannot ignore it.

Law is a language that turn power into procedure. It decides whose pain counts, whose property counts, and whose body can be moved by force.

People confuse "legal" with "right." Legal means backed by enforcement. Right means morally defensible. Sometimes they overlap. Often they do not. This gap is where people get shocked: they assumed the world was fair because the word "law" sounded clean.

Law also operates through cost. Even when you are correct, you may not be able to afford to be correct. Time off work, legal fees, paperwork, court dates, risk of retaliation. These are hidden barriers. Justice is priced.

The Field move is to treat the law as a system, not a father figure. Learn the rules that apply to you. Document. Get things in writing. Build alliances. Know when to negotiate and when to escalate. This is not paranoia. It is literacy.

At scale, law is how a society decides what violence is allowed. Policing, prisons, borders, and courts are not side issues; they are the infrastructure of enforcement. When enforcement is biased, the map is biased.

Legal terrain keeps expanding into data rights, algorithmic discrimination, and biometric surveillance. People who treat law as background can wake up inside rules they did not read.

Legal literacy is unevenly distributed. And that asymmetry predictably benefits people and organizations that can pay for it. If you ever feel "I didn't know I could do that," you just found the gap. Fill it. Ask questions. Get advice. Document. The system will not volunteer your options. It will charge you for ignorance.

Law shapes behavior by threat of consequence. When enforcement is predictably unequal, legitimacy collapses and people shift from compliance to cynicism and brute power. Legal fairness is not idealism. It is stability infrastructure.

If you cannot enforce it, it is a wish. Treat wishes differently than rights. Enforcement is the hidden verb. Learn who can enforce, when, and at what cost, before you rely on the rule.

PART IV - HUMAN CLAUSES

The Field is not abstract. It touches the body. It touches the people you love. It touches what you fear losing.

Elena is most visible in family, Marcus in closeness, and Rafi in desire and relief - but each of them crosses all four human clauses in different ways.

This Part brings the framework back to the clauses people bleed on: family, relationships, desire, mortality. These are the arenas where Defaults become intimate, shame becomes a tax, and constraint masquerades as personality.

14

Family

ELENA STILL FEELS THE OLD ROLE ARRIVE BEFORE THE FIRST SENTENCE IS FINISHED.

Family is the first Field most people ever live inside. It sets prices on rest, honesty, anger, affection, and need. It teaches what costs you love and what buys you safety. Marcus still feels the old bargain in the reflex to earn calm through usefulness. Rafi still feels it in the assumption that chaos is easier than being fully seen.

Some families enforce Terms through silence. Others through volatility. Others through obligation dressed as virtue. Whatever the style, it produces Defaults: appease, perform, disappear, control, rescue.

As an adult you can leave the house and still be governed by its pricing. The return clause is not nostalgia. It is the nervous system snapping back to the cheapest strategy it learned for keeping connection.

RETURN CLAUSE = OLD THREAT + BELONGING COST

The Family Bargain

A child senses tension, avoidance, strange rules, sudden mood shifts, missing relatives, unexplained rage, unexplained addiction, unexplained money panic. The child learns: certain topics are danger. The child learns to manage the room, hoping the family will finally become safe. The bargain keeps the person striving. The bargain also keeps the person emotionally young, because it treats the family as something that can be earned into health. Sometimes families do heal. Sometimes families do not. Either way, adulthood begins when the bargain is released.

Consider a kitchen table where nothing is said directly. A teenager brings up a college application and the room goes cold. A parent changes the subject. Another parent makes a joke. The message is not "don't apply." The message is: ambition costs connection here. The enforcement is not a rule on paper. It is mood, silence, ridicule, and the sudden withdrawal of warmth. The child learns a cheap move: shrink.

Or a home where love is real but conditional. Affection arrives when you perform and disappears when you need. The child becomes competent early, not because competence is noble, but because competence buys peace. Years later, the adult still cannot rest without guilt. Rest is priced as danger. That is not personality. That is training.

Family also teaches what emotions are allowed. In some homes, anger is permitted but tenderness is punished. In others, tenderness is permitted but anger is punished. In others, both are punished and the only safe move is humor. These are not preferences. They are survival contracts. They become Defaults that fire automatically when closeness rises.

People can be smart, accomplished, and still collapse into an old role the moment they walk through the old door. The Terms are familiar, the enforcement is immediate, and the body chooses the cheapest path back to belonging. The Return Clause is not a theory. It is what happens when the same Field conditions reappear.

Releasing the bargain is painful because it forces a new truth: the past cannot be renegotiated. That truth is not despair. It is the starting point of agency. When the fantasy family dies, the real life can begin. The person can stop living for a reaction and start living for alignment. Alignment does not mean abandoning family. It means refusing to let family anxiety dictate the shape of the future. This is where forgiveness can appear without becoming self-erasure.

Forgiveness is not excusing. Forgiveness is releasing the need for the past to be different so the present can be lived. Grief is not optional if change is real. Without grief, the old strategy remains sacred. A sacred strategy cannot be replaced because it is defended by identity. Grief makes room for new loyalty: loyalty to the life that is possible. A person can honor ancestors without repeating their damage.

The Role You Were Paid to Play

Differentiation Changes the Line

In family systems theory, there is a concept called differentiation: the ability to stay connected without being controlled by the emotional Field of the family. Differentiation is not coldness. It is the ability to remain a self while remaining in relationship. Low differentiation looks like fusion or cut-off. Fusion means a person's feelings and choices are governed by the family's anxiety. Cutoff means escape becomes the only way to be free. Both are understandable. Both are incomplete. Differentiation is the middle move: connection with boundaries. It looks like saying no without explaining for hours.

It looks like telling the truth without trying to win. It looks like changing habits without announcing it as a moral indictment of the family. It looks like earning money without flaunting it as revenge. It looks like choosing a healthy partner even if the family thinks chaos is normal. It looks like building a quiet life even if the family thinks drama is love. Differentiation is hard because it triggers old alarms: rejection, exile, betrayal, abandonment. Those alarms are real to the body, even when the mind knows the family is not a tribe on the edge of starvation. The body is older than the mind.

The work is to teach the body a new truth: connection can survive difference. That is not learned through speeches. It is learned through repeated moments of staying steady while the system reacts. Over time, the family Field adjusts. Sometimes it adjusts with love. Sometimes it adjusts by trying to punish the new behavior. Either way, the person becomes data.

Data changes fields. This is how a chain shifts: one person becomes a stable anomaly long enough that stability becomes imaginable for others.

That is not rebellion for aesthetics. That is a direct investment in the future. A child is not only raised by parents. A child is raised by the Defaults that parents never questioned. When those Defaults are questioned, the child receives a different Field. Transmission happens through ordinary Routines. A child watches how adults apologize, or never apologize. A child watches how adults handle anger, or pretend anger does not exist. A child watches how adults treat money, or treat money like shame. A child watches how adults speak about bodies, about other people, about themselves. A child watches whether love is stable or conditional.

The warning: inherited Defaults will fight for survival. A family system that depends on your role will pressure you back into it. A culture that depends on your compliance will call your boundaries selfish. A friend group that depends on your chaos will feel bored when you get stable. This pressure is not always malicious. It is the Field defending itself.

The promise: the pressure is proof that change is real. A system resists a person who is actually leaving the script. That resistance is not a reason to quit. It is the indicator that the chain is moving. A person does not have to solve the entire family to change the line. The minimum requirement is to stop participating in the most damaging loops. Stop lying for the system. Stop enabling for the system.

Stop sacrificing health for the system. Stop making pain look normal for the system. That refusal is not selfish. It is protective. It is the first act of future-building. Inheritance can be chosen after a point. Models can be adopted. Mentors, books, communities, friendships, partners, teachers. These become voluntary ancestors.

A person can borrow nervous systems from healthier people by spending time near them. That is not dependence. That is learning. Choose sources carefully. Exposure shapes priors. Priors shape choices. Choices shape life. The point is not to escape the past.

The point is to stop being ruled by it. A person cannot change where the line began. A person can change where the line goes next. That is what adulthood is in the Field: not a birthday, not a vibe, but a decision to become the translator between what happened and what happens next. Translation is work. It is also freedom. When the script is translated, it stops being a spell. The line does not need perfection to shift. It needs a single person willing to notice, to tell the truth, and to repeat a better choice until it becomes the new Default.

Family is the first relationship. It is not the last. The same pricing logic appears anywhere closeness exists. Friendships, romance, teams, communities. The next question is not who you love. It is what closeness costs in your Field.

15

Relationships: The Price of Closeness

MARCUS CAN HEAR "WE NEED TO TALK" AS VERDICT, ELENA CAN HEAR NEED AS OBLIGATION, AND RAFI CAN HEAR SILENCE AS REJECTION. RELATIONSHIPS ARE NOT ONLY EMOTIONAL. THEY ARE REGULATORY ECONOMIES.

Relationship Co-Regulation Loop

Elevated stress sharpens tone. Withdrawal produces relief. Relief reinforces withdrawal. By altering timing and framing, escalation weakens. The loop was structural.

Closeness Changes State

Relationships are not only emotional. They are regulatory economies. Other people change your State, and State changes what you can afford.

A relationship is a set of Terms: what is safe to ask for, what gets punished, what earns repair, what triggers exile. Most people call this chemistry. In practice it is enforcement, history, and expectation.

Because relationships change State, they change the entire menu of actions that feel possible. A stable bond can widen your Choice Set. A chaotic bond can shrink it until even basic decency feels unaffordable.

A simple example: one partner says, "We need to talk," and the other partner's body hears, "You are about to lose love." The sentence is short. The physiological cost is not. Heart rate rises. Attention narrows. The person reaches for the cheapest regulator available: defensiveness, jokes, avoidance, a counter-attack, a drink, a scroll. From the outside it looks like immaturity. From the inside it is a body trying to keep connection from collapsing.

Relational conflict often escalates over nothing. It is rarely about the dishes. It is about what the nervous system expects the dishes will prove:

care, respect, safety, status, betrayal. Once the body is priced into threat, even good communication becomes expensive.

A nervous system is not private. It lives in a body, and that body lives among other bodies.

That is not philosophy. That is biology. Humans are social mammals. Safety is not only an internal condition. Safety is also a relational condition. A baby cannot downshift alone. A baby borrows the caregiver's nervous system. Tone, touch, voice, face, rhythm. These are not sentimental details. They are regulators. That borrowing does not stop at infancy.

Adults borrow nervous systems too. A calm person can calm a room. An anxious person can infect a room. A hostile person can tighten a room. A loving person can soften a room. This is why some places feel heavy the moment you enter. The air is not haunted. The nervous systems are.

Co-regulation is the process by which bodies stabilize each other. Dysregulation is the process by which bodies destabilize each other. Most relationship advice fails because it treats relationships as debates between ideas. Many relationships are not debates. They are nervous system interactions.

The content is surface. The state is the driver. When two nervous systems are taxed, they look for relief. Relief can be found through connection, or through control. Connection requires vulnerability. Vulnerability is expensive under threat. Control is cheaper. Control can be created through criticism, interrogation, blame, silence, withdrawal, or dominance. This is why stress turns love into a negotiation.

A person does not become "toxic" out of nowhere. A person becomes protective. Protection can look like toxicity. A Field lens helps separate character from configuration.

Conflict Scripts Become Defaults

It asks: what state are these bodies in, and what Default is the system running? Most couple conflict follows predictable scripts. One common script is pursue and withdraw. One person feels threat and moves toward: questions, demands, intensity, chasing.

The other person feels threat and moves away: silence, shutdown, distraction, leaving. Both are trying to regulate.

Both moves make sense in the body. Both moves can damage the bond. The problem is that the two regulation strategies collide. Threat makes the strategies more extreme. Soon the relationship is not a relationship. It is a loop.

CONFLICT LOOP = TRIGGER + BODY RESPONSE + PROTECTIVE MOVE

Loops are sticky because they become familiar. That is why people often choose partners who recreate early Defaults. The system is not looking for happiness first. It is looking for known terrain. Known terrain allows prediction. Prediction allows survival.

This is why someone can leave a painful relationship and then recreate the same emotional geometry with a new person. The names change. The nervous system stays the same. This is also why some people feel bored in healthy relationships. Healthy can feel unfamiliar. Unfamiliar can feel unsafe.

The body confuses safety with intensity because intensity was the original proof of connection. The person creates intensity to feel alive. That is not romance. That is regulation. The social body logic does not only apply to romance. It applies to families.

Families are shared Fields. A family has roles: the responsible one, the mess, the peacekeeper, the clown, the scapegoat, the star. Roles are Default stabilizers. They keep the system coherent, even when the coherence is unhealthy. If one person changes their role, the family system often pushes back. Not because people are evil, but because the system resists destabilization. This is why people can "do work on themselves" and then feel crazy when they go home. The work changed the internal state. The old Field tries to restore the old Default.

Workplaces are social bodies too. A workplace can run on fear, scarcity, humiliation, and constant urgency. In that environment, people become protective. They gossip, compete, hoard information, Overwork, or detach. A workplace can also run on safety, clarity, and respect. In that environment, people become more creative, more honest, and more collaborative. It is the same species. Different Field. This is why "communication skills" are not enough. Communication skills matter, but Field conditions matter more.

A person cannot communicate calmly when the room punishes calm. A person cannot be honest when honesty is weaponized. A person cannot relax when every mistake is treated as identity. This is why some people think they are broken and then change jobs and suddenly feel sane. The body was reacting accurately to an insane Field. A key implication: relationships are not only emotional. They are regulatory infrastructure. A stable relationship can lower baseline stress and widen the Choice Set.

A chaotic relationship can raise baseline stress and shrink the Choice Set. That changes everything: health, money, parenting, creativity, patience, addiction risk, career stability, and even lifespan. This is why choosing people is a survival decision. The strongest Leverage is not finding perfect people. It is finding regulated people. Regulated means: capable of repair. No one is calm all the time. The real test is repair.

Repair is the ability to return after rupture without punishment, without contempt, without keeping score. Repair is what trains safety. A relationship without repair trains threat. Threat produces Defaults. Defaults repeat. This is where the social body meets time. A relationship is a time series. It is thousands of small moments that teach the nervous system what to expect. Does contact produce warmth or danger? Does honesty produce intimacy or punishment? Does vulnerability produce care or ridicule?

Does conflict resolve or linger as war? Those answers become embodied predictions. A person can say, "This is a safe relationship," and still tense up because the body does not believe the words yet.

The body believes history. What builds co-regulation? First: pacing. A dysregulated conversation cannot be won. It can only be survived.

When state is hot, slow down. Reduce words. Reduce volume. Reduce stakes. Name the state and step back. Pacing is not avoidance. It is preventing damage while regulation is restored. Second: clarity.

Ambiguity is expensive. Clear agreements lower threat. Clarity about money. Clarity about time. Clarity about boundaries. Clarity about expectations. Clarity about what is and is not acceptable. Third: containment.

Containment means conflict has a container: a time limit, a place, a rule set. No screaming. No name-calling. No threats. No bringing up old unrelated wounds as weapons. No arguing when intoxicated.

No arguing in bed if bed is the only place the body ever downshifts. Containment is not control. It is protection of the bond. Fourth: repair rituals. A repair ritual can be simple: acknowledge harm, name what happened, validate the impact, state the next step, and then behave differently. Fifth: chosen proximity. Proximity matters.

This is not mystical. It is nervous system mimicry plus reinforcement. The question becomes: what rooms are shaping you?

A person can read a thousand pages about growth and still be trained daily by a Field of contempt.

Field beats intention. This is why boundaries and environment are not optional. They are the social version of sleep and food. They are basic.

The last truth is blunt: some relationships cannot be regulated from the inside. If someone is committed to chaos, you cannot coregulate them into stability. Co-regulation requires two nervous systems participating. In a one-sided system, the only Leverage is distance. Distance is not cruelty. It is self-preservation. There is no unified theory of human experience that ignores relationships. Because another regulated body is one of the fastest ways to teach a nervous system that the present is different from the past. The social body is the bridge between what you know and what you can actually do when it matters.

When two nervous systems repeat the same loop long enough, it becomes history. And history, in any form, will repeat until the system learns a cheaper way to be safe. Co-regulation is the baseline condition of a social species. Codependence is when regulation requires self-betrayal.

The difference matters. Healthy co-regulation allows two people to influence each other without losing boundaries. Unhealthy coregulation turns boundaries into threats and turns individuality into abandonment. Attachment is the first map of this.

Attachment is the nervous system's early model of what happens when you need something.

Those models become adult Defaults. The adult may not remember the original scenes. The body remembers the original math. That is why two people can love each other and still trigger each other constantly.

They are also colliding models. Closeness triggers threat. Then the second person withdraws. Withdrawal triggers the first person's model: withdrawal equals abandonment.

Defense looks like personality. It is Default. This is why "just communicate" is weak advice. Communication cannot solve two nervous systems that are both in threat chemistry.

Safety comes first. Safety in adult relationships is built through repeated proof, not declarations. Proof looks like: a boundary is respected. A conflict ends in repair. An apology includes behavior change. A promise is kept. A no is tolerated. A need is not mocked. A mistake does not become a weapon.

Proof accumulates slowly. This is why stable relationships feel boring to people trained by chaos. Chaos creates constant novelty. Novelty creates constant signal. Signal feels like aliveness.

Safety can feel quiet. Quiet can feel like emptiness if the nervous system is addicted to intensity. The person starts problems to feel alive. A person might call this "passion." It is often dysregulation. A culture that glorifies chaos calls it romance.

A nervous system that wants peace calls it exhaustion. The social body shows up in micro-moments. A kitchen with constant criticism feels different than a kitchen with humor. These differences are not only emotional. They are regulatory. Regulatory environments determine how much energy a person spends on bracing versus building. A person bracing all day has less energy for patience, for learning, for creativity, for love.

Some people come home and become someone else. They were bracing at work. They collapse at home. The collapse is not laziness. It is recovery. If the home is also hostile, there is no recovery. Then the nervous system starts living in pure defense. Defense becomes Identity.

This is why choosing environments is as important as choosing beliefs. Beliefs can change state. Environment can change baseline. Baselines drive the future.

Co-regulation also explains why certain friends feel like medicine and others feel like poison. Some people bring calm. Some people bring chaos. Some people bring contempt. Some people bring admiration. Some people bring curiosity. Some people bring threat. The body knows. The body feels the cost. Most people ignore the cost and call it loyalty.

Loyalty without cost accounting is how people stay sick. A clean loyalty is loyalty to stability. Stability does not mean comfort at all times. Stability means repair is possible. A person can be intense and still be stable if repair is reliable. A person can be polite and still be unstable if repair is impossible. This is why charisma is not a measure of safety.

Some of the most charming people are the most destabilizing. Charm can be a tool of control. The test is not charm. The test is what happens when you say no. The test is what happens when you disagree. The test is what happens when you have a need. The test is what happens when you are not performing. That is when the nervous system learns what is real. The practical question becomes: what kind of relationships build the future you want?

If the future requires calm, choose people who can downshift. If the future requires courage, choose people who can hold fear without punishing it. This is not elitism. It is survival. Because relationships are the training ground for state. This is not destiny. It is exposure plus learning.

The most underrated skill is learning to leave rooms that make you smaller. Leaving does not always mean ending relationships dramatically. Sometimes it means reducing time. Sometimes it means building distance while staying respectful. Distance is a form of boundary. Boundary is a form of safety. Safety is a precondition for growth. The social body is where personal Defaults become collective. This matters because the Field is not only your internal state.

The Field includes the people you orbit. Orbit is not metaphor. Orbit is structure. Time spent together becomes history. History becomes expectation. Expectation becomes behavior. Behavior reinforces history.

That is the recurrence engine. Time is where social Defaults prove themselves. A person can deny a Default in a single day. Time does not allow denial. Time shows what repeats. That is why relationships are the best laboratory and the most dangerous one. They can stabilize the nervous system faster than any philosophy. The difference is not romance.

Co-regulation is a form of power because one nervous system can raise or lower another's threat load.

A manager sets the nervous system tone of a team. A teacher sets the nervous system tone of a classroom. A parent sets the nervous system tone of a home. A police officer sets the nervous system tone of a street corner. A doctor sets the nervous system tone of a hospital room. A leader who cannot downshift spreads threat. Threat makes people lie, hide, and repeat old Defaults. A leader who can stay regulated under pressure spreads capacity.

Capacity makes people think, speak, and solve. This is also why some people heal rapidly after leaving an environment with unregulated power. A worker leaves a humiliating boss and suddenly sleeps. A student leaves a punitive classroom and suddenly learns.

A child leaves a chaotic home and suddenly relaxes. The social body has a responsibility layer. If you hold power, your state becomes everyone's weather. Not everyone can leave immediately. But everyone can begin to see the regulatory economics of their relationships and environments.

Seeing is the first Leverage. Once seen, choices get cleaner. That is the bridge between insight and change. Because time is where environments either teach safety or teach threat, one day at a time, until the lesson becomes destiny.

Time is the Field where co-regulation becomes recurrence. Building a regulated life is not only choosing one partner or one friend. It is building a small ecosystem: at least one person who calms you, at least one place that feels quiet, at least one practice that downshifts your body, and at least one boundary that protects your time.

That ecosystem becomes the base layer of every other ambition. Love is easier to give when the nervous system does not feel hunted. This is not romantic. The social body is not a side topic. It is the infrastructure that determines whether time becomes growth or time becomes repetition.

If there is no safe person yet, build one deliberately. Choose lows-takes contact first: a class, a team, a support group, volunteering, a consistent barber, a weekly coffee with someone who listens. Stability is trained through repetition. A nervous system learns safety the same way it learned threat: through thousands of small interactions. Start small. Stay consistent. Let time do what time does.

That is how the social body becomes a stabilizer instead of a trigger. A person does not need a large circle. A person needs a small circle that does not require armor. One regulated connection can change the trajectory of a decade. Because it changes what the body expects when it needs something. Expectation is the beginning of every Default.

Attachment is not childhood trivia. It is the Default expectation a nervous system carries into other nervous systems. When that expectation is violated repeatedly, the body learns to anticipate rupture. That anticipation becomes recurrence: the same relationship script replayed in new settings. Recurrence is the basic unit of change.

Humans regulate in groups. Co-regulation is not a therapy term; it is biology. A calm nervous system can lend calm. A dysregulated nervous system can spread dysregulation. This is why rooms change you.

Attachment is the first expectation you inherit. It teaches the body what to expect from closeness: safety, threat, unpredictability, distance. You carry that expectation into friendships, work, romance, parenting, even into how you talk to yourself.

Two adults can hear the same sentence and receive different meanings because their attachment histories are different. "We need to talk" can land as collaboration or catastrophe. "I'm busy" can land as neutral or abandonment. The body responds before the mind explains.

This is also why loneliness is not just sad. Chronic isolation raises threat. Raised threat narrows choice. Narrow choice increases short-term coping. The loop looks like personal failure, but it is often missing social infrastructure.

The modern world adds a new clause: digital co-regulation. People outsource regulation to feeds, group chats, and parasocial relationships. Sometimes it helps. Often it spikes threat, comparison, and performance. The nervous system does not know the difference between a village and a comment section. It only knows signal. If you want to change your Terms, you cannot only change thoughts. You have to change who you are regulated with. Proximity is policy.

Your "people" matter more than your intentions. A friend group can make sobriety feel normal or make it feel like exile. A partner can make rest feel safe or make it feel like betrayal. Choose environments that reward repair, not performance. You become what your nervous system rehearses with others.

Co-regulation can be designed. Put yourself around people who sleep, eat, tell the truth, and repair conflict. Limit time with people who live on chaos and call it "real." This is not superiority. It is nervous-system economics.

Attention is a spotlight with a battery. Every platform tries to rent your battery back to you - one swipe at a time. Most people try to change alone, then act surprised when the same Defaults return. The Field includes the people you orbit. Orbit is not metaphor. Orbit is the pricing environment you rehearse inside. Choose it like your life depends on it, because it does.

16

Desire Under Pressure

RAFI KNOWS THAT DESIRE CAN BE HUNGER, ANESTHESIA, TENDERNESS, PROOF, OR PANIC BEFORE IT EVER BECOMES A STORY. ELENA KNOWS HOW QUICKLY DESIRE CAN COLLIDE WITH OBLIGATION AND LOYALTY. MARCUS KNOWS HOW FAST IT CAN BE PRICED BY STATUS, EXHAUSTION, AND THE NEED TO FEEL CHOSEN WITHOUT EVER SLOWING DOWN.

DESIRE IS DATA, NOT DOCTRINE

Desire is not a belief. Incentive-sensitization research makes this hard to unsee. Desire is a signal. People try to talk about sex as if it is a simple preference: what someone likes, what someone chooses, what someone is. That framing misses the deeper reality. Sexual desire is a state-dependent Default generator. It is shaped by biology, learning, shame, stress, novelty, attachment, culture, and opportunity. It is one of the most honest data streams a nervous system produces - because it often arrives before language, before morality, before identity can explain it.

This is why sex creates so much confusion. A person can believe one story about the self and feel a different reality in the body. A person can love someone and still want someone else. A person can crave touch and not want intimacy.

A person can crave intensity and not want care. A person can crave care and mistake it for lust. The Field turns these signals into narratives: "This means the self is broken." "This means moral failure." "This means the self is unlovable." "This means more is needed." "This means less is allowed." Most of these stories are attempts to control uncertainty. Desire does not like being controlled. Desire is not a moral court.

It is a prediction machine in the body: an anticipatory system that links cues to reward, bonding, safety, status, and regulation. A person cannot separate these cleanly because they co-train each other. Biology matters. Hormones, nervous system arousal, sleep, stress, and health all change desire. A person who is exhausted often wants less.

A person who is stressed sometimes wants more. A person who is lonely can experience desire as hunger. A person who is ashamed can experience desire as compulsive. A person who is depressed can experience desire as absent. These shifts are not proof of character. They are state. Behavior creates identity stories.

Identity stories feed back into state. The loop is tight. Learning matters. The brain learns what gets rewarded. It learns what is paired with relief, with belonging, with novelty, with approval. A person's early experiences of affection, attention, and safety become templates.

Some people learn that touch equals comfort. Some learn that touch equals obligation. Some learn that sex equals love. Some learn that sex equals danger. Some learn that sex is the only time they are valued. Some learn that sex is a currency. Some learn that sex is a performance.

DESIRE LOOP = CUE + STATE + MEANING

Those lessons do not disappear when someone becomes "mature." They become the Field of intimacy. This is why people repeat sexual Defaults they claim to hate. Repetition is not always desire. Repetition is often familiarity.

Familiarity can feel like safety even when it is harmful. A person can be drawn to the same kind of unavailable partner, the same kind of risky situation, the same kind of humiliating dynamic, because the nervous system recognizes the shape. It knows how to survive that shape. The unknown feels more threatening than the known, even when the known is pain. This is not romance. It is conditioning.

Shame Distorts Sexual Signal

Shame is one of the main distorters of sexual signal. Shame says: wanting is dangerous. Wanting is dirty. Wanting is proof of weakness. Wanting is proof of wrongness. Shame makes the body split.

Desire remains. Conscious acceptance disappears. The person then seeks desire in secret, in shadows, in compulsive bursts, in dissociation. The secrecy increases shame. The shame increases compulsion. The loop tightens.

Culture builds that engine on purpose. Controlling desire is one of the oldest tools of social control. If a society can dictate when sex is allowed, with whom, and with what consequences, it can dictate family structure, inheritance, gender roles, and the distribution of power. Sex is therefore rarely "private" in a practical sense. It is private in the bedroom and public in consequences.

The Field of sex is legal, religious, economic, and social. Modern technology changed the boundary system. Platforms did not invent desire, but they changed its availability and its training. A person can now access novelty at industrial scale. Novelty is a powerful Reward signal. It triggers dopamine. It keeps the attention loop alive. It trains the brain to crave the next stimulus. Over time, the nervous system can become less responsive to ordinary intimacy and more responsive to novelty, intensity, and speed. This is not moral failure.

It is neural adaptation to an environment designed for craving. Dating apps also change the economics of desirability. They turn attraction into a market. Markets create competition. Competition increases comparison. Comparison increases insecurity. Insecurity increases performance. Performance reduces authenticity. Reduced authenticity reduces connection. The person becomes lonelier while being more "connected."

The field of modern sex often produces this contradiction: more access, less satisfaction.

More options, less safety. More attention, less intimacy. A person can be desired by many and still feel unseen. The nervous system cares about safe.

RELIEF CAN MASQUERADE AS DESIRE

Some people use sex as regulation. Sex can calm the body. Sex can provide touch. Sex can provide a temporary sense of being chosen. Sex can provide a moment where the mind is quiet. For someone living under pressure, that relief can be one of the few reliable medicines available.

The body learns: this is how to breathe. Then the Field changes. The person starts chasing relief rather than connection. Partners become doses. Novelty becomes a drug. The person might still be kind. The person might still have ethics.

The nervous system is still using sex as a regulator. The cost rises: shame, risk, emptiness, burnout, broken trust, increased loneliness. A person can have a lot of sex and still feel starving. Touch is not the same as attunement. Orgasm is not the same as regulation. Sometimes it is.

Often it is not. There are also people who avoid sex not because they do not want connection, but because sex has been paired with danger or obligation. Avoidance is a survival strategy. It can protect a person. It Can also isolate a person. When avoidance becomes identity, a person might stop being curious about what the body actually wants. The nervous system learns to shut down desire to avoid risk. Over time, the person becomes numb. Numbness feels safe. It also feels like absence.

Again: state, learning, and culture. Desire is not one thing. Some loops are symbolic: power, status, taboo. Some loops are grief loops: the attempt to feel alive when life feels dead. This is why sex cannot be clear by morality alone. Morality asks: is it right? Morality matters. But a deeper question comes first: what is it doing? A person who asks these questions gains Leverage. Leverage does not mean repression. It means choice that is based on signal, not on compulsion or shame.

The Field also includes consent, and consent is where sex becomes ethical. Consent is not only a legal checkbox. It depends on the ability to say no without punishment, intimidation, or coercive pressure. Power matters because distorted power distorts what can be freely refused. The Field of sex therefore cannot be separated from law, money, and status. Those forces shape what is possible to refuse. Freedom is never equally distributed.

Sex is not only personal. Sexual behavior reflects biological arousal systems, relational context, and power. Reducing it to any one frame makes it incomprehensible. A person who wants a coherent life needs to treat desire like data. When desire is clear, it stops being a tyrant. It becomes information: a clue about what the body needs, what the mind fears, what the soul is hungry for.

Sometimes the clue is simple: more sleep, less stress, more connection. Sometimes the clue is painful: a Default of shame, a history of trauma, a mismatch in attachment, a need for repair. Repair is possible. But repair requires honesty, and honesty is hard when desire has been policed for a lifetime. It teaches that a person can want without being ruined by wanting.

Sex reveals something else as well: the shadow of mortality. The drive to merge, to touch, to be alive, to feel chosen - these are often louder because life is temporary. The final constraint is not law. It is death. That is where the Field becomes unavoidable.

Desire also changes with context in ways that surprise people. Many people assume libido is a fixed trait. It is not. It is an output of state plus environment. A person can feel no desire in a life filled with exhaustion, resentment, and constant interruption. Then that same person takes a week away, sleeps, feels safe, and desire returns. Nothing "mystical" happened. The nervous system moved from survival to play.

Sex often requires play. This is one reason modern couples struggle. A household with children, debt, long commutes, and constant digital noise is not a play environment. It is a management environment. People become managers of logistics. The body learns to stay in task mode. Task mode is useful for survival. Task mode is often incompatible with eroticism.

Margin is what money, time, and social support can buy. A person who understands ecology stops blaming the partner as the first explanation. The partner might be part of it. The Field is always part of it too. Long-term relationships also reveal a paradox: safety can reduce novelty. Novelty fuels arousal for many people. Safety fuels attachment and trust. Some couples treat this as a tragedy, as if stability must mean boredom.

The deeper truth is that novelty does not have to mean new bodies. Novelty can be new experiences, new vulnerability, new play, new environments, new ways of seeing. But that kind of novelty requires effort and honesty. It requires turning toward the partner instead of using distraction to avoid discomfort. Avoidance kills intimacy faster than time does. Many people also confuse sexual desire with validation hunger.

Validation hunger is the craving to feel chosen because the nervous system does not believe it is lovable without proof. A person can chase attention, compliments, and sexual availability not because the body is deeply hungry for sex, but because the mind is hungry for confirmation. Confirmation is temporary. The chase continues. This is why some people feel emptier after "success." The event delivered the proof, but the nervous system could not hold it.

The internal model still says: not enough. The next hit is required. The person is not chasing sex. The person is chasing relief from selfdoubt. Relief that depends on other people's attention becomes a cage. Presence is what turns sex from transaction into connection. Fantasy also matters. People often fear fantasy as if fantasy is intention. A mind can imagine many things without wanting to enact them.

Fantasy is sometimes a way the nervous system plays with power and vulnerability in a safe internal space. It can reveal psychological needs: to be seen, to be wanted, to surrender, to control, to be safe, to be transgressive, to be cared for. Treating fantasy as guilt creates shame loops. Treating fantasy as command creates compulsion loops. Fantasy is best treated as information, not orders.

Desire also interacts with identity in complicated ways. Many people want identity to be clean: one label, one script, one stable story. The body is not always clean. The body is sometimes fluid. The body is sometimes contradictory. This does not make a person fake. It makes a person human.

A culture that demands purity turns normal complexity into pathology. Again: a loop. The healthiest approach to sexual identity is often the same as the healthiest approach to any Field: accuracy without cruelty. A person can name what is true without turning it into a weapon against the self. A person can accept the shape of desire without making it a moral identity. "This is what the body responds to" is not the same as "This is who you are allowed to be."

Confusing the two creates suffering. The modern attention economy also sexualizes everything. Ads sell desire. Platforms sell desirability. Filters sell a face that never existed. The Field trains people to treat the self as a product. The product must be optimized: body, Style, photos, persona, status signals.

Optimization increases attention. It can also kill authenticity. A person becomes a brand to survive, then forgets how to be a person.

Being a brand is exhausting. It makes intimacy feel like performance. Performance blocks vulnerability. Vulnerability is where real bonding happens. Bonding is what regulates the nervous system over time. This is why a person can have a "hot" life and still be dysregulated.

Healing is consistency, safety, and repair. Repair is also about grief. Many sexual Defaults are grief Defaults: attempts to out-run loneliness, to out-run aging, to out-run the feeling that time is passing. Some people chase intensity because intensity makes time disappear. It creates a bubble where mortality is not felt. That bubble is temporary. When it pops, the person feels the underlying grief again.

Intensity is a drug against time. Often it is not sex that is missing. It is meaning. Or safety.Or love. Or rest. Or a future. Sex becomes the substitute because it is one of the fastest ways to shift state. Fast state shifts are tempting in a life with chronic pressure. There is also the reality of mismatch. Two people can love each other and have different sexual rhythms. One wants more; one wants less.

This mismatch becomes a power struggle if it becomes moral. One person feels rejected. One person feels demanded. Shame and resentment grow. The relationship becomes a negotiation over proof of love. This is a trap. The healthiest couples treat the mismatch like a Field problem: sleep, stress, resentment, workload, body image, medical issues, trauma history, novelty, connection, and communication.

The mismatch is rarely only libido. It is often the sum of many variables that changed over time. They are often emotional and physiological: to be touched, to be appreciated, to feel safe, to feel free, to feel alive. Sex is one language for those needs. When sex is treated as the only language, the relationship becomes brittle.

Brittle systems break. The Field of sex therefore teaches a broader lesson: a person must learn to separate desire from identity, intimacy from validation, fantasy from action, and pleasure from regulation. Not to become sterile. To become free. Freedom does not mean wanting less.

Love only matters because everything ends. That ending is the final Field: death. Sex also tests communication. Many people can discuss finances, schedules, and politics more easily than sex, because sex carries shame and vulnerability. Silence turns desire into guessing. Guessing turns into resentment. Resentment turns into avoidance or coercion. The Field becomes unsafe.

HONESTY CHANGES THE TERMS

Safety is the prerequisite for erotic honesty. Erotic honesty does not mean bluntness. It means truth without punishment. It means being able to say yes and no without fear.

It means being able to change and still be loved. That ability is rare. When it exists, sex becomes less like a battlefield and more like a shared language. It becomes a place where the nervous system can learn trust again. Trust matters because desire does not exist in a vacuum. Desire exists inside time.

Awareness of mortality changes how people value time and intimacy. Mortality is one of the hidden pressures behind urgency, attachment, and meaning-making.

Desire is data. It is information about the body, the mind, and the environment. People get into trouble when they treat desire as a command or as a shameful secret instead of as information to interpret.

Sex is also social. It carries power, status, risk, attachment, and meaning. That is why it can be freeing and destabilizing in the same hour. The same act can be intimacy for one person and anesthesia for another.

The Field question is not "Is sex good or bad?" The question is: what is sex doing here? Is it connection? Is it proof? Is it bargaining? Is it dissociation? Is it rebellion? Is it a way to feel real for ten minutes?

Consent is the minimum. The deeper clause is honesty. If you cannot be honest about what you want, what you fear, and what you are using sex to avoid, the Field will keep charging you.

Modern life adds new distortions: porn scripts, dating app markets, performance metrics, parasocial fantasy. They can expand possibility, but they can also train the nervous system to chase novelty while losing capacity for closeness.

A person who can read desire as data can choose sex that builds life instead of borrowing life.

Healthy sex is not just pleasure. It is alignment: your body, your values, your safety, and your honesty in the same room. If sex repeatedly leaves you emptier, more ashamed, or more confused, treat that as information, not proof that you are broken. Desire is pointing at a need - for touch, for power, for comfort, for escape. Choose accordingly. Desire also changes with state. Exhaustion, loneliness, alcohol, shame, and novelty can all masquerade as desire. Slow down enough to separate the signal from the distortion. The goal is not purity. The goal is consent, honesty, and outcomes you do not regret. Desire without honesty becomes confusion. Honest desire becomes clarity. That pressure deserves a name.

17

Mortality: The Clause No One Escapes

MARCUS BURIES TIME IN WORK, ELENA IN RESPONSIBILITY, AND RAFI IN RELIEF, BUT MORTALITY KEEPS CHARGING ALL THREE. DEATH IS THE FINAL CONSTRAINT.

Death Is the Final Constraint

Death is the final constraint. Every other Field can be negotiated. Money can increase. Information can change. Location can shift. Relationships can repair. Laws can be appealed. Work can be replaced. Even addiction can be interrupted. But death remains.

It is the boundary that makes every other boundary meaningful. A nervous system knows this even when a mind refuses it. Mortality lives in the background as pressure: urgency, fear, grief, ambition, denial, nostalgia, and the constant hunger to matter.

Many people spend a lifetime trying not to feel death. They treat death as a distant event instead of a present force. They build distractions. They build status. They build schedules. They build pleasures. They build noise. The Field offers endless ways to avoid the silence where mortality can be heard. Avoidance works until it doesn't.

Then death arrives as shock: the loss of a parent, the loss of a friend, the diagnosis, the accident, the aging body, the funeral, the empty room. Suddenly the mind cannot maintain the illusion that time is infinite. The nervous system is forced to update. This update is brutal and necessary. It strips away fake priorities. It clarifies what is real.

GRIEF IS RECALIBRATION

It exposes the ways people have been living as if they will live forever: postponing love, postponing health, postponing honesty, postponing joy, postponing repair. Death turns "later" into a lie. This is why grief can be both devastating and strangely clarifying. Grief is not only sadness. Grief is recalibration. The nervous system is updating the model of reality: the person is gone; the future is different; the world is less safe; the story changed without permission. The body experiences this update as shock: disrupted sleep, disrupted appetite, disrupted concentration, disrupted immune function, disrupted desire. Grief is a full-body event because love is stored in the nervous system, not only in the mind.

A relationship is not only memory. When someone dies, coregulation disappears. The body is left without a familiar stabilizer. The nervous system searches for the missing Default. It expects the person to walk through the door. It expects a text. It expects a voice. That expectation is not stupidity. It is the model persisting until the data is undeniable.

Denial is the first stage because denial is the nervous system buying time to metabolize the update. People often judge grief as if it is a performance: too much, too little, too long, too short. That judgment is itself a Field problem.

Grief is not uniform because love is not uniform, attachment is not uniform, and context is not uniform. A person with a supportive community grieves differently than a person alone. A person with a secure base grieves differently than a person who has been abandoned before. A person who loses someone after a long illness grieves differently than a person who loses someone suddenly. The Field changes the shape.

What stays constant is the function: grief is the cost of bonding in a world where everything ends. Mortality also shapes ethics. A person who believes time is infinite can postpone responsibility forever. A person who feels time is limited starts asking different questions: What matters? What lasts? What will be regretted? What will be forgiven? What will be carried forward?

It also creates tenderness. Fragility changes the meaning of cruelty. Cruelty becomes obscene when the finitude of life is felt. When life is short, wasted pain is intolerable. When death is near, petty status games look ridiculous. When someone has watched a life end, the social theater loses power.

LEGACY ANSWERS TIME

This is one reason older people can become wiser. Not because of age itself, but because proximity to death changes calibration. Mortality also creates the human need for legacy. Legacy is not always ego. Legacy is sometimes the nervous system's attempt to make meaning from finitude. If a life ends, the mind asks: did it matter? The answer is often built through impact: children, art, work, love, mentorship, stories, institutions, and the small ways someone changed others.

Legacy can be beautiful. Legacy can also become a trap when it becomes status: chasing immortality through fame, wealth, or domination. That chase is often death anxiety wearing a suit. A person who cannot accept finitude becomes hungry for control. Control is another form of denial.

This is how death shapes politics, culture, religion, and war. Many collective projects are attempts to outrun mortality: empires, monuments, ideologies, purity systems. They offer the fantasy of permanence. They promise that the individual can dissolve into something bigger and thereby escape disappearance. Religion is one response to death.

So is art. So is family. So is science. So is addiction. So is violence. Different strategies. Same pressure.

The Field does not judge these strategies. It shows their functions. Understanding death also clarifies the idea of "meaning." Meaning is often treated like a personal philosophy. Meaning is also a biological requirement. A nervous system needs a reason to tolerate pain and delay gratification. In a world of suffering and uncertainty, meaning is a stabilizer. It allows endurance.

It creates coherence. Coherence reduces anxiety because it turns chaos into narrative. The danger is that people trade truth for meaning. They adopt stories that reduce fear rather than stories that align with reality. That is understandable. It is also how harmful ideologies become seductive. A story that promises certainty in the face of death is a powerful drug. The body wants certainty.

Death offers none. The mind manufactures it. Signal matters because mortality pressure distorts the model. Mortality pressure can cause overfitting: seeing signs everywhere, believing in fate, believing in conspiracies, believing in cosmic justice that does not exist. Mortality can also cause underfitting: nihilism, numbness, treating life as meaningless because meaning feels fragile. Both are attempts to regulate death anxiety.

A healthier approach is to accept finitude without collapsing into despair or fantasy.

Acceptance is not cheerful. It is precise. Precision creates freedom. Freedom from living for someone else's script.

$$\text{PRECISION} = \text{MORTALITY} + \text{PRIORITY}$$

Freedom from spending a life chasing a status that does not matter at the end. Death also changes the experience of time. Time becomes not only quantity but quality. A long life can be empty. A short life can be full.

Fullness is not constant pleasure. Fullness is precise: being in the day, connected to reality, connected to others, connected to the body.

Presence is hard under pressure. Mortality makes it non-negotiable. Now is where the nervous system learns safety again. Death also makes people notice ancestry. A person realizes that a life is not isolated. It is a link in a chain. Parents shaped children.

Children shape the future. Culture transmits Default. Trauma transmits Default. Wealth transmits Default. Education transmits Default. Neglect transmits Default. Violence transmits Default. Love transmits Default.

The Field is not only personal. It is generational. This is why "being a good ancestor" is not a slogan. It is a design principle. If a life is temporary, the rational move is to reduce unnecessary suffering for the people who come next. That can be done through parenting, through building institutions that are humane, through creating stable relationships, through protecting the environment, through teaching literacy, through mentoring, through art, through simply refusing to pass on the worst Defaults.

This is also how death reframes freedom. Many people imagine freedom as unlimited choice. That is a fantasy. Freedom is always constrained by biology, environment, law, money, and time. Death makes the ultimate constraint explicit: time is limited. Therefore freedom is not the absence of constraint. Freedom is the ability to choose within constraint with awareness and dignity. Awareness is the skill.

A person who lives with awareness and dignity does not need immortality. That person needs coherence. The Field can destroy coherence. It can also create it.

Final claim: human experience is not random. It has structure. The structure can be read. When it is read well, a person stops being buffeted by invisible forces and starts making moves that align with reality. Death does not disappear. But life becomes less wasted. That is as close to freedom as a nervous system gets.

Mortality pressure does not only appear when someone dies. It appears quietly in everyday behavior. It appears in violence: the attempt to dominate finitude by making someone else fear it. Different bodies, different stories, same engine: a nervous system trying not to feel the boundary.

A person can live for decades inside these strategies and still insist death is not relevant. Then a loss arrives and the strategy is exposed. The busy person cannot outwork grief. The status person cannot purchase the missing voice. The perfectionist cannot correct death. The cynic cannot mock the empty chair into fullness. The addict cannot numb forever. The violent person cannot threaten the universe into mercy. Grief is the moment the Field refuses negotiation.

Grief often produces anger. Anger is the nervous system's protest against helplessness. It is energy searching for a target.

Sometimes it targets doctors, fate, God, family, institutions, or the dead person for leaving. Sometimes it targets the self. Anger is not a moral failure. It is a transitional state. It is the body attempting to reassert agency in a situation where agency was removed. The danger is when anger becomes identity and freezes the grief process. Some people build a fortress of anger to avoid the softer emotions underneath: longing, love, fear, tenderness, regret.

Anger is easier than longing because anger feels powerful. Longing feels helpless. But longing is often the real truth. Longing is love that has no place to land. Grief is also not linear because the nervous system does not update in one step. The model shifts in waves. A person might feel "fine" for a few hours and then be hit by collapse. This is not inconsistency. It is integration. The system can only metabolize the update in intervals.

If grief were constant intensity, the body would break. The nervous system protects itself by cycling. People often shame this cycling. "You were okay yesterday." That shame is ignorance. Recovery is rhythmic.

So is loss. Rituals exist for this reason. Funerals, mourning practices, anniversaries, prayers, songs, memorials - these are not decorative traditions. They are nervous system technology. They provide a shared container for the update. They allow a community to witness reality together, which reduces isolation.

They give the body permission to feel what it is feeling without being judged for it. A culture without grief rituals produces private grief. Private grief often turns into pathology because it has no social metabolization. The Field of modern life often isolates grief. People live far from family. Work schedules do not pause. Friends do not know what to say. Digital life continues. The grieving person is asked to "be normal" quickly. The system treats grief like inconvenience.

If grief is suppressed, it leaks into other channels: irritability, numbness, insomnia, panic, substance use, compulsive behavior, sudden relationship ruptures. The body finds a way to process the update. If language and ritual are not available, symptoms become the language. This is why the healthiest thing a society can do is normalize grief as a human state rather than a personal failure. Regret hurts because it points to time that cannot be recovered. That pain can become wisdom if it is used for recalibration instead of self-torture.

Many people decide to become kinder after a loss not because they became saints, but because the loss made cruelty feel like wasted time. A person becomes more willing to apologize. More willing to speak love plainly. More willing to rest. More willing to stop performing. Mortality pressure can soften or harden.

Control is the most common false response to death. After a loss, some people try to control everything: schedules, diets, family members, partners, children. The mind says: if everything is managed, nothing bad will happen. This is understandable. It is also impossible. Control can reduce certain risks. It cannot remove finitude.

When control becomes obsession, it destroys relationships and health. It spreads the death pressure to everyone else. A person who has lost someone often becomes sensitive to this. The nervous system begins to see how much of life is unearned. Health is not guaranteed. Safety is not guaranteed. Time is not guaranteed.

Control stories collapse. A mature relationship with death does not require constant contemplation. It requires occasional honesty. Honest mortality awareness is like good lighting: it reveals what is real without making everything bleak. It makes the priorities visible.

Priorities change when time is limited. Some priorities are revealed as noise: status games, petty resentments, performative arguments, unnecessary cruelty, compulsive consumption.

Other priorities become clear: sleep, health, love, friendship, craft, beauty, honesty, play, quiet.

These priorities are not moral commandments. They are what the nervous system tends to value when survival threat is not being used as a motivational tool.

Death, paradoxically, can make life more humane. It strips away the lies that keep people busy. It makes truth urgent. Death removes permission.

A person who accepts that becomes more willing to act. Action can be small: a phone call, a visit, a boundary, a change in schedule, a health check, a walk, a conversation that has been avoided for years. Small actions become meaningful when the mind stops assuming tomorrow is guaranteed. Mortality also reframes forgiveness. Forgiveness is not forgetting.

Forgiveness is the decision to stop spending limited time feeding hatred. Hatred is sometimes justified. It is also expensive. It consumes attention. It consumes energy. It keeps the nervous system bound to a person or event. Some people choose to keep that bind because hatred feels like justice. Others choose to release it because hatred feels like waste. Both choices have costs.

Death makes the costs visible. This is why a "good life" is often not glamorous. It is coherent. It is aligned. It is made of repeated, ordinary acts of care. It is made of sleep, food, movement, honest relationships, and boundaries that protect dignity. These are not inspirational slogans. They are the infrastructure of a life that can be lived without constant regret.

A person who integrates mortality can become more serious about consequence without becoming joyless. Finite time changes what matters, what gets delayed, and what finally feels worth saying or doing.

Joy Gains Depth at the Edge

This is the last Default to name: joy is not the opposite of death. Joy is what life produces when it is lived inside the boundary with awareness. Joy is the nervous system recognizing a moment of safety, connection, beauty, and meaning - and knowing it is temporary. Temporary makes it precious. Finitude creates meaning. This is why the Field is not a depressing framework. It is a realistic one. It shows how constraint produces shape, how pressure produces Default, and how awareness allows a person to respond instead of react.

Death is the final constraint. But it is also the final teacher. It teaches that time is a currency that cannot be saved. It can only be spent.

A person can spend it unconsciously, in noise. Or spend it consciously, in care. That choice is not absolute. It is moment to moment. It is the closest thing to freedom the Field allows.

Death is the clause nobody likes to read, which is exactly why it runs many lives from the shadows.

When you pretend you are not going to die, you treat time like it is infinite. Infinite time makes procrastination rational. Infinite time makes cowardice easy. Finite time makes priorities obvious.

Death also equalizes and does not equalize. Everyone dies. Not everyone gets the same runway. Poverty, racism, war, addiction, and bad healthcare shorten the timeline. The Field is honest about that without turning it into nihilism.

The mature move is to use death as a calibrator. If this were your last year, what would you stop tolerating? What would you repair? Who would you call? What would you build that outlasts you? These are not sentimental questions. They are engineering questions.

Planning Is Love in Paperwork

Planning is love in paperwork. Wills, beneficiaries, medical directives, honest conversations, funerals that match values - these are ways of removing chaos from grief. People avoid them because they feel morbid. The cost of avoidance is that survivors pay the chaos bill.

The future will add new death clauses: climate disasters, pandemics, AI-accelerated warfare, and also longer life for some. Mortality will remain the same teacher. It will just speak louder.

People think talking about death makes it happen. The opposite is true. Talking about death reduces chaos and lets love show up as action. Write the damn document. Tell the person you love them. Make the repair before the clock forces it. Mortality is not meant to scare you. It is meant to wake you up.

A lot of suffering comes from acting as if there will always be a better time. Finite time changes what should be said, repaired, or documented sooner.

Say the thing. Make the call. Write the note. Let the people in your life know what they mean while you can still prove it with time.

Grief is unavoidable. Chaos is optional. Planning turns grief into something you can carry.

Facing death does not make life grim. It makes it precise. Let it guide you daily.

The final clause doesn't ask for bravery; it asks for precision: what matters, what can wait, who you want beside you, and what you refuse to leave unpaid.

Clarity is not change. Clarity is the moment the Field becomes visible. Change begins when the pricing changes - when the better move becomes affordable on a bad day, not only on a good one.

Part V- Leverage

You cannot control everything. You can control a few levers. This Part is the blueprint and the engineering section.

The final work is concrete: what Elena would need to stop being priced by rescue, what Marcus would need to stop being priced by performance, and what Rafi would need to stop being priced by relief.

These chapters are about editing the architecture: widening the Choice Set, increasing capacity, replacing Defaults, and making the better move usable under pressure.

18

Why Insight Doesn't Rewrite Defaults

ELENA CAN EXPLAIN HER FAMILY ROLE, MARCUS CAN EXPLAIN HIS OVERWORK, AND RAFI CAN EXPLAIN HIS RELIEF LOOP. EXPLANATION IS NOT THE SAME THING AS CHANGE.

Understanding Is Not Updating

Insight is useful. It is not decisive. Research on introspection keeps finding the same limit: people are often poor reporters of the real causes of their own decisions.

A person can understand a Default perfectly and still repeat it. That is not hypocrisy. It is the difference between understanding and updating. Understanding happens in language. Updating happens in the body. Language can describe a fire. Description does not lower the heat.

INSIGHT ≠ REDESIGN

The organism moves first. The story arrives after, making the move feel coherent. A Default is not a thought. It is a cost equation living in nerves, habits, relationships, and environment. Under pressure, the system reaches for what has regulated before.

Cheap does not mean good. It means familiar, fast, and statistically safe. That is why insight rarely breaks recurrence. Insight is a light. Change is construction. Light does not rebuild a house.

Leverage is structural, not magical. It lowers the cost of repeating the better move. It also reminds you that not everyone is starting with the same buffer: cash, time, health, support, and legal safety all shape what is feasible. Find the next feasible edit to the Terms you are actually under.

The body requires evidence. Evidence is what happens when the old trigger appears and the old catastrophe does not, repeatedly, under survivable conditions. That is how models update.

A threat-trained system would rather be wrong than surprised. This is why insight can feel like progress while nothing visible changes.

Relief is not change. Relief is the moment the mind understands the prison bars.

The bars remain. Change begins when they become negotiable. That learning happens through lived exposure, not explanation. Culture prefers the dramatic breakthrough. Living systems change through repeated, non-identical contact with the same old trigger.

The mind wants a clean break because the mind is tired. The body resists clean breaks when they look like threat. This is why people can read better books, listen to better advice, and still stay inside the same loop.

The environment stays the same. The schedule stays the same. The social role stays the same. The substances, inputs, and sleep stay the same. Then the person becomes a librarian of insight and a prisoner of outcome.

Insight Can Become Identity

Insight can also become identity. A person becomes 'the one who understands.' The role provides status, meaning, and the feeling of progress. Then real change threatens the role, because real change is quieter than performance.

The Field uses a blunt rule: if the output remains, the training remains. A system can say anything. What it believes is what it does when pressure rises.

A person can know a job is toxic and still stay because leaving threatens housing. A person can know a relationship is harmful and still stay because distance threatens collapse. Insight does not produce options. It clarifies the absence of options.

Sometimes the missing option is plain: a locked door, a predictable meal, a schedule that stops changing, a friend who answers without charging shame.

Choice Set is the real substrate of change. Once it widens, the system can run experiments. Without it, recurrence often remains cheaper than failure.

REDESIGN = NEW TERMS + REPEATED EVIDENCE

That split matters. A person can be brilliant at declarative learning and still trapped in procedural repetition. Intelligence can become another mask: the ability to name the cage without leaving it.

Immediate relief is a powerful teacher. Delayed consequences are weak ones. That is why a person can slowly wreck a relationship, a body, or a future while still repeating the move that keeps regulation cheap in the moment.

Shame rarely repairs behavior. It usually raises threat. Raised threat narrows time horizon and makes relapse cheaper.

Under high arousal, the body discounts the future. It chooses immediate regulation over long-horizon values. That is not lack of care. It is temporary loss of access to the part of the system that can hold tomorrow in view.

That is why binges, explosions, and compulsions feel inevitable. A calm person remembers calm options. A flooded person remembers flooded ones.

The plan was written in one state and executed in another. The body returned to the archive available in that state.

This is why 'become your best self' advice fails. A human is a stack of states with different priorities. The work is not eliminating states. It is building bridges between them.

Most people try to change at the peak of stress. That is like trying to learn a new language during a house fire. Change is trained on low heat first.

The rehearsal feels small. It is not. It is the first break in the chain. The person who wants to stop disappearing begins by staying for ten more minutes, then by sending one honest message instead of vanishing.

These are not moral gestures. They are state training. The person who wants to stop chasing achievement as regulation does not begin with a blaze of glory. The person begins by building safety elsewhere.

Many ruptures are avoidance disguised as courage. Novelty can feel like freedom. Often it is just a stimulant.

Catastrophe is not a method. It is a cost.

Chronic damage is easier to deny than a single explosion. Denial preserves the Default. The Default then becomes the person's climate. A person says they want peace, but aggression ends humiliation quickly. A person says they want closeness, but distance prevents being judged. A person says they want health, but the job pays the rent. A person says they want stability, but chaos provides stimulation and identity. A person says they want love, but control prevents abandonment.

Until incentive changes, intention becomes decoration. This is why "motivation" is not a plan. Motivation is the temporary emotion that appears when the mind imagines a future. Incentive is the pricing mechanism that decides whether the future is reachable. A system will not travel to a future it cannot afford. This is also why certain people sound "self-sabotaging" when seen from the outside. From the inside, sabotage is often protection.

A person ruins the relationship before the relationship can ruin them. A person quits before being fired. A person insults before being rejected. A person cheats before being left. A person disappears before being asked to show the self. Sabotage is not random. It is a strategy trained under conditions where waiting was expensive. When the strategy persists in a new environment, it becomes tragic. The environment changed. The model did not.

The nervous system survives the past and then lives as if the past is still here.

Insight names the lag. It does not erase it. Erasing it requires the boring work of new evidence.

New evidence is built by repeated contact with the trigger while running a different program. Different does not mean perfect.

Different means non-identical. This is why small differences matter.

A person who used to drink at 7:00 p.m. and now drinks at 9:00 p.m. has already begun to change the loop, because the loop is time-coded. A person who used to rage in person and now leaves the room has already begun to change the loop, because the loop is proximity-coded. A person who used to hide and now sends one honest sentence has already begun to change the loop, because the loop is shame-coded.

Small differences create cracks. Cracks create new routes. Routes become habit. Habit becomes identity. This is not inspiration. It is mechanics.

The deepest danger of insight is that it can turn into cruelty toward the self. Once a person understands, every repetition can feel like failure. Shame then tightens the loop it claims to fix.

The solution is not a slogan about self-forgiveness. It is accurate framing. If recurrence is a bid for stability, then recurrence is a signal: the Field is still too expensive for the new move.

Change the Price, Not the Speech

A person who asks the right question stops wasting energy on moral panic. Insight becomes useful when it locates leverage.

Price is what the nervous system pays in energy, threat, humiliation, isolation, or loss.

Price is what the nervous system pays in energy, threat, humiliation, isolation, or loss. Once price is named, responsibility gets cleaner: not responsibility for what was trained, but for what gets built next.

Trauma does not automatically design the exit. The exit is built with evidence, not with explanation.

Evidence requires repetition. Repetition requires capacity. Capacity requires environment.

The mind loves insight because insight is private. Environment is not. Environment involves money, other people, systems, and time.

Insight is not a substitute for contact. Contact means changing the actual variables that trained the loop: sleep, hunger, money, shame, inputs, relationships, and the calendar.

When the price changes, the behavior changes. When the behavior changes, the identity story catches up. The sequence matters. It is Terms first, story second.

Insight is a flashlight, not a lever.

People can do therapy, read every book, understand every origin story, and still repeat the same behavior. Understanding is upstream of choice, but it is not the same thing as choice. Choice requires capacity. Capacity requires conditions.

If you are sleep-deprived, isolated, broke, and constantly threatened, insight becomes another thing you are supposed to do better. Insight without capacity curdles into self-contempt.

The Field move is to pair insight with a concrete term change. Change the room. Change the routine. Change the relationship. Change the exposure. Change the schedule. Change the script.

This is also why some advice feels fake. "Just think positive" is asking the mind to override the Field. Sometimes the Field wins. The Field often wins. That is not failure. That is reality.

When you respect reality, you stop asking yourself to be superhuman. You build conditions that make the good action cheaper.

Insight stalls when the old behavior is still rewarded: with relief, belonging, attention, or avoidance of conflict. Change the reinforcement and the system finally has reason to learn.

Insight must be followed by friction changes. If the environment makes the old behavior easy and the new behavior hard, the old behavior wins.

Insight is necessary. Term change is decisive.

A smaller, cleaner Choice Set beats a larger chaotic one: fewer options, clearer moves, less regret.

19

Expand the Choice Set

ELENA NEEDS MARGIN, MARCUS NEEDS A WIDER LIFE THAN PERFORMANCE, AND RAFI NEEDS SAFER REGULATORS. CHOICE SET IS THE REAL DEFINITION OF FREEDOM.

Constraints Shrink the Menu

Choice Set is the real definition of freedom. The capabilities approach makes the same point: freedom is the real range of lives you can actually choose.

Freedom is not a slogan about choice. Freedom is the number of realistic moves available under pressure. Most lives do not collapse because people lack desire. Most lives collapse because the menu is too small. A person can be intelligent, moral, educated, motivated, spiritually awake, and still trapped because the Field prices the obvious exits as impossible. This is why insulting someone with "just leave" is not advice. It is ignorance.

Leaving costs money, housing, safety, documentation, childcare, community, and time. Those currencies are not distributed evenly. The Field does not equalize them. It exploits differences. Choice Set is not ideology. It is geometry. In math, a constraint reduces degrees of freedom. In life, a constraint reduces the number of moves that do not produce collapse.

When constraints pile up, the system begins behaving like a cornered animal. The cornered animal is not "bad." The cornered animal is out of options. Most moral arguments are disguised arguments about Choice Set. A person says someone is lazy. The truth is the schedule is impossible. A person says someone is irresponsible. The truth is the margin is zero. A person says someone is dramatic. The truth is the nervous system is living at the edge of capacity. A person says someone is selfish.

The truth is the Field has trained scarcity. A person says someone is addicted. The truth is the body has no other reliable regulator. This does not excuse harm. It explains why harm repeats. Choice Set is built from concrete variables. The main ones are boring and brutal: Time. Money.

Safety. Health. Location. Documentation. Relationships. Skills. Information. Sleep. Remove any one of these and the menu shrinks. Remove three and the menu becomes fantasy. Remove five and the menu becomes a cage.

LEVERAGE = LOWER COST + WIDER MENU

The same "choice" can be easy in one life and impossible in another. The act looks identical from the outside. The internal cost is not. A person with savings can walk away from a toxic boss. A person with no savings negotiates with fear every morning. A person with stable housing can recover from a breakup. A person in unstable housing experiences breakup as a threat to survival. A person with a passport and clean paperwork can leave a collapsing economy. A person without documents is trapped inside jurisdictions that do not care.

These differences are not character. They are Terms. Choice Set also explains why small resources change everything.

An extra hour of sleep is not "self-care." It is a neurological budget. An extra hundred dollars is not "consumerism." It is reduced threat. A door that locks is not "comfort." It is safety. A quiet room is not "Preference."

It is nervous system repair. A predictable schedule is not "discipline." It is the foundation of regulation. A friend who answers is not "nice." It is co-regulation. A doctor who listens is not "luck." It is access to reality.

These are the levers that change behavior without speeches. Modern culture loves to say "mindset matters." Mindset matters when the Field is negotiable. When the Field is not negotiable, mindset becomes denial. Denial is expensive because it forces the body to keep trying strategies that cannot work.

Choice set is the border between responsibility and cruelty. Cruelty demands that a person perform miracles inside constraints.

Responsibility asks: which constraints can be reduced, and what new moves become possible once they are?

Constraint removal is not always personal. Sometimes it is systemic: laws, policies, labor protections, housing markets, discrimination, violence, unequal schools, unequal healthcare. A book cannot fix those. But a person can still increase Choice Set inside the real world by understanding where constraint lives. The first step is identification.

Constraint hides in the places people do not like to name, because naming them reveals how little of life is moral.

Constraint can be inside the body: chronic pain, autoimmune disease, injuries, hormonal instability, depression, anxiety, addiction, sleep disorders. These are not personality. They are load. Load shrinks Choice Set by consuming energy.

Constraint can be inside the calendar: unpredictable shifts, multiple jobs, caretaking, commuting, paperwork, legal battles, immigration processes, court dates, probation check-ins, school meetings, elder care. Time disappears. Choices disappear with it.

Constraint can be inside place: unsafe neighborhoods, lack of transit, food deserts, noise, crowding, environmental toxins, distance from opportunity, policing, isolation. Place shapes the body's baseline.

Constraint can be inside relationships: a controlling partner, a resentful family, a workplace that punishes boundaries, a friend group built on stimulation, a community that weaponizes shame. Social systems enforce roles. Roles shrink options. Constraint can be inside information: constant outrage, constant catastrophe, constant comparison, constant stimulation. Attention is a resource. When it is hijacked, options become invisible. Constraint can be inside meaning: a rigid identity that punishes change, a belief system that turns suffering into virtue, a culture that glorifies exhaustion, a family myth that defines worth as sacrifice.

Buffer Widens What You Can Afford

Meaning can be Terms. Buffer is what absorbs shock so a system does not collapse. This is why talking about "resilience" without talking about buffer is propaganda. Resilience is the ability to absorb shock and still function.

Absorbing shock requires resources. Resources are not equally distributed. Some people are told to be resilient while being denied buffer. That is not a motivational problem. That is a design problem. The Field treats buffer as the central lever because buffer changes the pricing mechanism.

When buffer increases, the system has more room to experiment. When the system has more room to experiment, it can gather evidence.

When evidence accumulates, models update. When models update, identity shifts. Choice Set is the reason a person can "change" in one season and relapse in another. The season changed the Field. The person did not become fake. The constraints returned. The menu shrank. The system reached for what worked. Choice Set is also why advice feels insulting.

Advice is usually offered from a different menu. The person giving the advice is not lying. The person is describing what was possible inside That life. The mistake is assuming the menus are identical. This is why the Field refuses moral language as the primary language. Moral language confuses menus with virtue. It also lets systems off the hook. If every failure is personal, then nothing structural has to change. Choice Set is political without being partisan. It is simply the recognition that constraints are real and enforced. The enforcement can be physical: violence, policing, war, neighborhood threat, domestic abuse.

The enforcement can be economic: rent, debt, medical bills, inflation, layoffs, the cost of food. The enforcement can be bureaucratic: forms, fees, waitlists, language barriers, documentation, background checks. The enforcement can be social: exclusion, shame, reputation, family punishment, community surveillance. Narrowed menu produces predictable behavior. There is another mathematical truth that explains why people misjudge Choice Set: threshold effects.

Many systems do not change linearly. They change after a threshold is crossed. Below the threshold, effort produces little movement. Above the threshold, the same effort produces acceleration. Crossing can be small. It can be one consistent meal. One stable bedtime.

One reliable transit route. One friend who does not drain. One medication that reduces panic. One legal document. One job that stops changing shifts. One neighborhood that is quieter. One skill that increases earnings. One boundary that ends a daily humiliation.

The right intervention often looks "too small" to outsiders. Outsiders do not see the threshold. Choice Set is the hidden reason why some people appear to "turn their life around" quickly once one variable changes. It was not a miracle. The menu widened. The system crossed threshold. New behavior became repeatable. Identity then followed. There is a second reason people misjudge Choice Set: they confuse capacity with pain tolerance. Many people can endure extreme pain. That endurance is mistaken for capacity.

Capacity is not how much pain can be carried. Capacity is how many options remain while pain is carried. A person can carry pain and still have no options. That person will eventually seek relief through whatever is available. That is not weakness. That is economics.

Cheap regulators are not only substances. They include rapid behaviors that quickly reduce uncertainty or create a short burst of power or sensation

These regulators are expensive long-term, but cheap in the moment. Choice Set work is finding regulators that are slightly more expensive in the moment but dramatically cheaper over time: sleep, food, movement, contact, truth, boundaries, skills, savings, structure. This is where constraint removal becomes practical.

There are two primary strategies, and they can be mixed: Subtract constraints. Add buffers. Subtracting constraints means removing what taxes the nervous system. Some taxes are obvious: substances, toxic relationships, unsafe environments. Some taxes are socially rewarded: constant work, constant availability, constant performance, constant stimulation.

Some taxes are invisible: a phone that never stops, a feed that keeps arousal high, a home that has no quiet, a schedule that keeps shifting, a commute that steals sleep, a role that requires masking. Removing these taxes is not a lifestyle choice. It is Choice Set engineering. Adding buffers means stacking small advantages until the menu changes. Buffer stacking is the realistic way most people escape.

Not through one big leap, but through ten small shifts that compound: a little more sleep, a little less debt, a little more skill, a little fewer obligations, a little more honest contact, a little more health, a little more savings, a little less noise, a little less shame, and a little more predictability. None of these alone is a new life. Together they change the price. This is why "discipline" is often mis-defined.

Discipline is not suffering. Discipline is strategic resource allocation. It is spending energy on buffers instead of on displays. It is refusing to waste the scarce currencies on what does not widen the menu. A person can spend ten hours a week on status theater and call it success. A person can spend ten hours a week building a buffer and call it boring. The second person becomes free.

Choice Set also clarifies a painful truth: some environments are not compatible with growth. Growth requires slack. Some systems remove slack as a business model. They keep people exhausted, dependent, ashamed, and reactive because reactive people are easier to manage. If a workplace punishes boundaries, if a relationship punishes truth, if a community punishes divergence, then the menu will remain narrow no matter how much the mind wants to change. This is where leaving becomes not a moral triumph but an engineering requirement. Leaving is often the most expensive buffer. That is why many cannot do it immediately. A third strategy appears: build an island.

Build an Island Before the Leap

An island is a small area of life where the Field is different: one room, one hour, one habit, one friendship, one practice, one routine.

The island does not fix the whole ocean. The island provides evidence that a different climate exists. That evidence keeps the system from surrendering. Islands are how people survive until they can move. This is also where shame must be handled carefully. Shame is not only a feeling. Shame is a constraint. Shame shrinks menu by making options socially dangerous.

A person avoids the doctor because shame says, "You will be judged." A person avoids asking for help because shame says, "You will be exposed." A person avoids changing because shame says, "You will be mocked." Shame taxes initiative. It makes the simplest moves feel impossible. This is why the social environment matters. A culture that uses humiliation as discipline is a culture that narrows Choice Set and then wonders why people behave desperately. Humiliation trains secrecy. Secrecy trains double lives. Double lives train collapse.

Choice Set work requires at least one environment where honesty does not get punished. One environment is enough to start. With Choice Set, the nervous system stops treating every decision as a threat. The body shifts from defense into curiosity. Curiosity is not a personality trait. Curiosity is a physiological state that becomes available when threat drops. Curiosity is the doorway to the next Mechanism: controlled experimentation. When curiosity is available, the person stops asking for a perfect answer and starts running tests.

That is how the menu expands further, and how the Default begins to lose its claim of inevitability. To expand Choice Set, a person does not need a perfect plan. A person needs a map of where cost lives. Cost lives in four currencies: Energy. Threat. Shame. Time.

Fewer commitments. Fewer people. Fewer apps. Fewer substances. Fewer late nights. Fewer conversations that end in heat. Fewer environments that spike the body.

Simplification is not aesthetic minimalism. Simplification is cost reduction. Sometimes it is expansion: More sleep. More protein. More daylight. More walking.

More quiet. More stable contact. More money. More skill. More language. More documentation. More distance from threat.

Not because these are "good habits," but because they widen the menu. A person with a widened menu can stop treating every decision like life-or-death. That is what capacity feels like: decisions become less theatrical. Consider a few lives, stripped of romance:

A janitor working nights knows the body is breaking, but overtime keeps food on the table. The problem is not mindset. The problem is time and money. Buffer changes everything: one saved month, one better schedule, one credential, one better contract, one second job that becomes the first. The Default does not change because the janitor becomes more enlightened. The Default changes because the price changes.

A teenager in a crowded apartment cannot "focus" the way a quiet-house child can. The problem is not discipline. The problem is environment and nervous system load. Choice Set can look like: a library, a coach, a study group, a quiet hallway, headphones, a teacher who understands, a program that provides space. Again: price changes.

A lawyer on paper has status and money, but is living inside panic because identity is tied to performance. The constraint is meaning and threat: the fear of being ordinary. Choice Set can look like boundaries, a reduced schedule, sleep, therapy, a friendship not based on competition, and a redefinition of worth. The price changes.

A recent immigrant with limited language lives inside paperwork anxiety and economic pressure. The constraint is documentation, time, and threat. Choice Set can look like language classes, legal clinics, community networks, stable employment, and a path to status. The price changes.

A PhD student in a lab is brilliant but collapsing because the Field is isolation, comparison, and uncertain reward. The constraint is social and temporal: life placed on hold for a future that is not guaranteed. Choice Set can look like structure, health, connection, and alternate paths. Again: price changes. Different lives. Same mechanics.

Increase Choice Set, and the system stops defending the old return clause as if it were life or death. Then the second lever becomes possible: experimentation. Once there is room to experiment, the problem is no longer "Why can't the person change?" The problem becomes "Which experiment produces stable evidence without blowing up the life?"

Your Choice Set is the menu you are actually ordering from. People talk about what they "could" do while ignoring what is realistically available at their current money, energy, skills, location, and social support.

The size of the Choice Set determines the kind of person you get to be. With ten options, you can be strategic. With two options, you are surviving. With one option, you are trapped. This is why constraint is not a mindset. It is geometry.

Constraint removal is often boring. It looks like learning a skill, saving money, getting a credential, building a relationship, moving neighborhoods, fixing sleep, leaving a toxic group, getting stable housing, treating an addiction. None of this is glamorous. It is how the menu expands.

People also underestimate second-order effects. Fixing sleep expands patience. Patience expands communication. Better communication expands relationships. Better relationships expand jobs and housing. One lever can widen the whole corridor.

Find the Bottleneck

The Field move is to locate the bottleneck. In systems, one bottleneck limits the whole flow. If transport is the bottleneck, you need a car, a closer job, or better transit. If childcare is the bottleneck, You need support or a different schedule. If paperwork is the bottleneck, you need help navigating institutions.

Once the bottleneck moves, new bottlenecks appear. That is not failure. That is progress. Expansion is iterative.

A life changes when the menu changes. The book is teaching you to stop arguing about the entrée and start changing the kitchen.

Choice Sets shrink under fatigue and shame. When you are exhausted, even good options feel impossible. When you are ashamed, you stop seeing options at all. Expanding the menu is not only external. It is also internal capacity: sleep, regulation, confidence earned through small wins. Sometimes the new option is simply the ability to tolerate discomfort long enough to choose well.

The Choice Set is also social. If nobody you know has done the thing, the thing feels impossible. One mentor, one friend, one example can expand options more than a thousand motivational quotes. Social proof is a term. Use it.

That is the next move. Expanding a Choice Set often looks boring: lower fixed costs, sleep, reduce dependencies. The freedom is real; it just arrives disguised as housekeeping.

20

Experiments That Work on Bad Days

MARCUS CANNOT OUT-THINK EXHAUSTION, ELENA CANNOT EXPLAIN HER WAY OUT OF RESCUE, AND RAFI CANNOT VOW HIS WAY OUT OF RELIEF. CHANGE WITHOUT DESIGN IS DEMOLITION. IMPLEMENTATION OF INTENTIONS IS A SIMPLE EXAMPLE OF WHY: WITHOUT CONCRETE PLANS, INSIGHT STAYS VERBAL.

Keep the Blast Radius Low

Many people reach a moment of insight, feel pressure, and try to escape the old life by lighting it on fire. They quit the job with no plan, end the relationship with no support, leave the city with no base, announce a new identity with no foundation, throw away the substances with no replacement stability. Sometimes the fire works. Often the fire simply moves the Default into a new room. This is why "starting over" is a dangerous phrase.

Starting over is not a reset. It is the same nervous system walking into a new environment with the same model. The Field treats change as experimentation, not as reinvention. An experiment is a small, intentional change that produces data. It is reversible when possible. It is specific. It is run long enough to be meaningful. It is evaluated by outcome, not by vibe.

A person does not need to become a scientist to use experiments.

Every life already runs experiments. Most are accidental. The difference between accidental experimentation and deliberate experimentation is whether the data is seen. Accidental experiments look like: - moving to a new neighborhood hoping it will fix the self - changing partners hoping it will fix loneliness - changing careers hoping it will fix meaning - changing substances hoping it will fix regulation - changing identity labels hoping it will fix shame Sometimes these work. Often they fail because the variable that mattered was not touched. Deliberate experiments touch the variable that matters. The key principle is blast radius.

EXPERIMENT = SMALL CHANGE + MEASURED RESULT

A blast radius is how much of life collapses if the experiment fails. Most people fear experimentation because they imagine maximum blast radius. They imagine losing everything. That means they choose recurrence, because recurrence has known damage. Known damage feels safer than unknown risk.

A person who wants to change must learn to run low-blast experiments first. A low-blast experiment changes one variable while keeping the rest stable. It treats the nervous system like an organism, not like a speech. Consider the most common variables that control behavior: Sleep.

Food. Movement. Information. Contact. Place. Money. Time structure. A person trying to change behavior without changing inputs is trying to change output while feeding the same machine.

Change Inputs Before Identity

Start with inputs because inputs are measurable. A person does not need to measure perfectly. A person needs to notice consistently. The first experiment is often boring: stabilize sleep. Not optimize. Stabilize.

Stabilize means: same bedtime window, same wake window, the same ritual that tells the body the day is ending. This is not a moral practice. It is turning down baseline threat. A nervous system that sleeps is a nervous system that can learn. The second experiment is often boring: stabilize food. Not diet. Stabilize. Stabilize means: predictable protein, predictable water, predictable timing. Hunger is not only discomfort. Hunger is a threat signal.

Threat makes the model rigid. A person who is hungry becomes the worst version of the self and then calls it identity. It is physiology. The third experiment is often boring: stabilize movement. Not aesthetic. Stabilize. Stabilize means: daily walking, stretching, carrying, breathing, some consistent load that tells the body it is alive and capable.

Movement clears stress chemistry. Without movement, stress becomes identity. The fourth experiment is often boring: stabilize information. Not purity. Stabilize. Stabilize means: reduce high-arousal media, reduce constant comparison, reduce constant catastrophe. The feed is not neutral. The feed trains the nervous system. A person cannot "think clearly" while consuming a diet designed to hijack arousal.

The fifth experiment is often boring: stabilize contact. Not popularity. Stabilize. Stabilize means: one or two people who do not escalate chaos, one or two places where the mask can come off, one or two rituals of connection that do not depend on performance. Contact is regulation. Without contact, the organism searches for relief in places that do not care.

Baseline is everything. Most people judge themselves at the peak: the fight, the craving, the collapse. The peak is built on baseline. Fixing baseline changes peaks without direct combat. Once baseline is less reactive, the next experiments can become more surgical.

This is where identity changes happen. Identity is not declared. Identity emerges from repeated behavior that becomes cheap.

Experimentation is also how the mind stops lying. A person who runs an experiment replaces opinion with evidence.

Evidence can be physical. Sleep improves, and the baseline heat drops. Caffeine decreases, and anxiety becomes readable instead of explosive. Alcohol stops, and the body reveals its true stress level. The phone leaves the bedroom, and attention returns. Walking becomes daily, and the nervous system becomes less brittle. Protein becomes consistent, and mood stops swinging so violently. An extra hour of daylight appears, and depression loosens. A boundary is held twice, and self-respect appears. A week without outrage media passes, and the world feels less hostile.

None of this is inspirational. It is input-output. Experiments can also be relational. A person stops answering every message instantly and learns who respects time. A person tells the truth once and learns who punishes honesty. A person asks for help and learns which connections are real. A person declines an invitation and learns whether belonging requires self-betrayal. A person apologizes without explanation and learns whether repair is possible. A person refuses to gossip and learns which friendships were built on shared contempt.

Relationships reveal themselves when Defaults are interrupted. This is why experimentation is threatening. It changes the social Field. The old role loses its certainty. The system responds with pressure. Pressure is information.

Subtract, Add, Substitute

Pressure tells the truth about what the system was using a person for. This is not always conscious cruelty. It is system defense. The Field does not ask for paranoia. It asks for accuracy: people and systems pay to keep familiar roles alive. Identity-neutral means: no announcement, no performance, no moral war. Just behavior. A person does not need to announce "I'm changing."

A person can simply change inputs and observe outputs. Announcement creates pressure. Pressure invites sabotage. The nervous system under social scrutiny reverts faster. Quiet change is often the fastest change because it reduces threat. There are three types of experiments that cover most of life: Subtraction. Addition. Substitution.

Subtraction experiments remove a tax. Less alcohol. Less porn. Less gambling. Less doomscroll. Less late-night chaos. Less contact with triggering people. Less multi-tasking. Less time in environments that spike threat.

Addition experiments add a buffer. More sleep. More food that stabilizes blood sugar. More movement. More daylight. More water. More skill. More money saved. More honest contact. More structure.

Substitution experiments replace a cheap regulator with a slightly better regulator. Scrolling becomes walking. Alcohol becomes a meeting, a call, a shower, a meal, a nap. Rage becomes leaving the room, lifting, writing, silence. Spending becomes planning, saving, repairing, borrowing. Sex as anesthesia becomes contact as regulation. People-pleasing becomes a neutral "No." Perfectionism becomes "good enough" delivered repeatedly.

Substitution is the hardest because it asks the body to give up immediate relief. This is why substitution requires the other two first. Subtract some taxes. Add some buffers. Then substitution becomes possible. Experiments also require a concept most people resist: lag.

Lag is the delay between input and output. Many people sabotage experiments because they expect instant results. They change one variable for two days, see no miracle, and return to the old Default. The nervous system is not an app.

It updates on a slower schedule. It needs multiple data points. It needs to trust reliability. This is why experiments require a minimum run time. A sleep experiment needs weeks. A sobriety experiment needs months. A relationship boundary experiment needs repeated cycles. A movement experiment needs a season. The time is not punishment. The time is the cost of building evidence.

Perfection destroys experimentation because perfection turns tests into verdicts. A test fails, and the mind says, "See? I can't change." That is not scientific. That is shame looking for a reason to stay.

A clean experiment treats failure as information.

If the sleep plan fails, the question becomes: what disrupted it? Noise? Anxiety? Timing? Caffeine? Screens? Social obligations? Not "What is wrong with the person?"

If the boundary fails, the question becomes: what pressure appeared? Guilt? Threat of abandonment? Financial dependence? Violence? Not "Why am I weak?"

If the sobriety attempt fails, the question becomes: what was the trigger state? Hunger? Loneliness? Shame? Fatigue? Not "Why am I broken?" This is how experiments become compassionate without becoming soft.

Dirty data comes from shame. Shame exaggerates. Shame hides. Shame performs. Shame makes a person lie to the self to protect identity. That prevents learning.

The Field treats shame as an enemy of evidence because shame distorts measurement. This is why change often accelerates when a person stops narrating and starts observing. Observation is colder than hope, but it is more useful.

A person who observes notices Defaults that the story misses: cravings spike at the same time every day, anger follows hunger, despair follows scrolling, conflict follows alcohol, numbness follows loneliness, relapse follows sleep debt, dissociation follows shame, creativity follows quiet, courage follows safety.

These are not secrets. They are just data that most people refuse to collect because data removes the fantasy of randomness.

Once data exists, experiments become sharper. A sharp experiment is simple:

Change one input.

Keep everything else as stable as possible.

Run it long enough to see a trend.

Record the outcome in plain language.

Adjust if necessary.

The record does not need to be pretty. It needs to exist. Even a few sentences a day can expose the Field in a person's life faster than years of interpretation.

High performers often change faster once they aim that skill inward. They already know iteration. They already know review Cycles. They already know that improvement is not a mood. It is repeated feedback.

Optimization without stability produces collapse. Many people chase optimization, biohacking, productivity, performance, while their baseline is still under threat. The result is brittle identity. One missed day and the whole system falls apart.

Experimentation should produce resilience, not fragility. Resilience is what happens when the system can take a hit and return to baseline without needing a self-destructive regulator. That is the real goal. Not perfection. Not constant happiness. Replacement stability.

A person knows a change is real when the old trigger happens and the body does not immediately reach for the old relief. The body pauses. The pause is everything. The pause is where a future exists. A pause is built through experiments with low blast radius. Then bigger experiments become possible: changing work, changing city, changing relationships, changing identity roles. Those are high blast moves. They should not be the first moves unless survival requires it.

For most people, the fastest path is the boring path: stabilize baseline, widen menu, run experiments, repeat. That is how a life changes without burning down every bridge that was holding it. Notice what makes these experiments difficult: they create short - term discomfort. This is why experimentation requires capacity. Capacity requires Choice Set. Choice Set creates room for discomfort without collapse. The main reason experiments fail is not lack of intelligence. It is choosing experiments that are too big for the current buffer.

People try to fix ten variables at once. They become perfect for three days. Then the system collapses and the person calls it proof of defect.

That cycle is unnecessary. A controlled experiment is humble. Humble means: one variable at a time, long enough to learn, small enough to repeat.

There is another reason experiments fail: the social system punishes them. A person starts sleeping and the friend group complains the person is boring. A person stops drinking and the family calls the person judgmental. A person sets a boundary and the partner calls the person selfish. A person stops performing and the workplace calls the person lazy.

This is not because the experiments are wrong. It is because systems defend stability. When one node changes, the network tries to restore the old configuration. That is recurrence at the social level. This is why experiments must include relationship design. A boundary is an experiment. A request is an experiment. An honest conversation is an experiment. A new role is an experiment. These experiments are higher blast radius because they can trigger conflict. But they are often required, because social systems can be the strongest constraints.

The safest way to run social experiments is to start with clarity. Clarity means: naming what is changing and why, without apology and without accusation. A person does not need to say, "You are the problem." A person can say, "This is what the body needs if the life is going to work." Bodies respond to clarity because clarity reduces uncertainty.

Uncertainty is what drives defensive behavior. This is where a simple principle appears: experiments must be run long enough for the nervous system to update. Not because people are doomed, but because models are slow. The model is protective. It waits for repetition. It waits for reliability. Real change is a boring number of repetitions. It is the same trigger met with a slightly different response, over and over, until the body stops predicting catastrophe.

Repeatable Beats Dramatic

Repeatable beats dramatic. Repeatable means: sustainable cost. A person who wants to change must become an engineer of cost.

Lower the cost of the new move. Raise the cost of the old move. Make the new move the cheapest reliable regulator. Then the system will choose it without constant war. This is where many people misunderstand discipline. Discipline is not forcing the new move forever. Discipline is running the experiment long enough for the new move to become Default. Once Default changes, willpower is no longer required at the same intensity.

The final test of an experiment is not whether it feels inspiring. The final test is whether it produces replaced stability.

That is the next mechanism: how a system stops repeating not by fighting the old Default, but by building something else that holds. There is an ethic underneath all of this: do not confuse change with chaos. Chaos can feel like freedom because chaos breaks routine. Chaos also increases threat. Threat makes the model rigid. A person chasing freedom through chaos usually ends up with the same old regulators, just louder. This is why fresh-start energy is a trap.

Fresh-start energy is often adrenaline. Adrenaline burns out. When it burns out, the old Default returns to pay the bill. Deliberate change is quieter. It protects what must be protected: health, housing, children, legal status, and the few relationships that are stabilizing. It does not gamble the whole life for a feeling.

A life becomes different when the nervous system becomes harder to hijack. That is the real definition of strength: the ability to stay coherent under pressure. Experiments build coherence. Coherence is not a personality trait. It is the outcome of repeated inputs that make the body predictable to itself. Predictability is safety. Safety is learning. Learning is freedom.

That is the chain. Once coherence exists, the final requirement becomes clear: the new stability has to replace the old one, not merely interrupt it. A person does not need to believe any of this to use it. Belief is optional. Repetition is not. Repetition is the mechanism that turns a decision into a Default. Defaults are what run a life.

That is why experimentation is not self-help. Experiments are how adults change without gambling the whole life. An experiment is a temporary change designed to produce information.

Most people either stay stuck or blow things up. They stay stuck because change feels risky. They blow things up because they finally can't tolerate the old Terms and they swing wildly. Experiments are the middle path: controlled risk.

A good experiment changes one variable at a time, runs long enough to notice a Default, and has a stop rule. "If my sleep gets worse for three nights, I stop." "If my anxiety drops, I continue." This is not rigidity. This is safety.

Experiments also protect relationships. Instead of declaring, "I am a new person now," you test a boundary. Instead of quitting your job in a rage, you update your résumé and apply for ten roles. Instead of detonating your social life, you test who can handle honest conversation.

The Field move is to treat your life like a system you can tune. Small changes compound when they are repeated. Big speeches do not.

An experiment is humility with teeth. It admits you do not know, and it still moves.

The point of an experiment is feedback. Review the results like an adult: what changed, what did not, what surprised you, what you will keep. Then run the next one. This removes drama from growth. You are not "becoming a new you." You are collecting data and making adjustments. That is what competent people do.

Do not confuse experimenting with drifting. Drifting is change without measurement. Experiments are change with learning. If you treat your life like a series of measured trials, you get smarter. If you treat it like a mood, you repeat the same year with new dates.

It is the physics of change.

21

Build Replacement Stability

Leverage Intervention

Elena wants to study each evening but scrolls instead. The Terms are obvious once they are mapped: study requires startup friction; scrolling does not. So the intervention is structural. Preload access before the day ends. Move the phone out of reach for the first hour. Segment the lesson. Put the block on the calendar. Over time, the recurrence shifts. No moral breakthrough occurred. The gradient changed.

A Default ends when it is replaced. Most people try to end Defaults through force. They fight the urge, shame the impulse, punish the relapse, and then act surprised when the system returns to the old program. Force can interrupt. Force rarely replaces.

This is why many improvements collapse into new addictions. The surface changes. The function remains. Replacement stability means the function is finally being met in a different way.

REPLACEMENT STABILITY = NEW FUNCTION + REPEAT + TIME

Coherence Is the Real Prize

The body's primary mandate is not happiness. It is coherence. Coherence means predictable regulation across time. A coherent system can forecast itself. It does not have to improvise survival every hour.

Peace is not a mood. It is the absence of constant emergency. A system trained by volatility will treat peace as suspicious at first.

A life is not a line. It is a system sitting in a return clause. Return clauses can be healthy or destructive. The system returns because the basin is deep and familiar, not because the basin is wise.

Breaking a return clause without replacing it is like digging a hole and expecting the ground to stay flat. Replacement stability means carving a new basin and deepening it until return becomes the cheapest move.

That depth is built through boring accumulation: days that do not collapse. Stability requires months, not moods.

PEACE CAN FEEL SUSPICIOUS

Some people sabotage when things are going well because calm feels unfamiliar. That is not character. It is calibration error.

Replacement stability must therefore include re-calibration, not just behavior change. The baseline has to learn that quiet, honesty, and non-catastrophic conflict are now survivable.

BUILD THE FLOOR FIRST

Replacement stability is built in layers.

First: physiology. If the body is underfed, under-slept, and overstimulated, stability is impossible.

Second: environment. If the space is chaotic, unsafe, loud, or saturated with triggers, stability is taxed before the day begins.

Third: the social layer. If the people around you punish truth, boundaries, or slowness and reward chaos, the old role will keep getting paid.

Fourth: time. If the schedule has no rhythm, the body cannot forecast. And without forecast, the nervous system stays braced.

Fifth: meaning. If the life gives the body no reason to endure boredom, stimulation will keep masquerading as aliveness.

These layers are not spiritual. They are Terms.

This is why stability is expensive in a culture that profits from volatility. Constant stimulation, outrage, comparison, and consumption are not neutral inputs.

Stability must be protected like a resource.

This is where discipline becomes an accurate word again. Discipline is protection of stability: sleep before performance, food before desperation, truth before smoothness, a calm friend before a charismatic disaster.

Maintenance separates a stable life from a lucky week. A person who has never lived stable often expects stability to arrive as a feeling. It usually arrives as a schedule.

A schedule is a container. It tells the body what happens next. That reduces uncertainty. Reduced uncertainty lowers threat. Lower threat makes learning possible.

A person who says, 'I don't do routines,' often means, 'I don't trust consistency.'

That is not freedom. It is often the avoidance of surrender. Stability requires surrender to rhythm.

This is the first win: stability is the point where a life stops taking itself hostage.

Unnecessary volatility is what turns stress into trauma. Stability creates control and support.

Repair Is the Real Test

Control does not mean dominance. It means predictability. Support does not mean being saved. It means not being alone with every shock. Repair is the real test of both.

Stable systems repair after disruption. Unstable systems escalate or detach. This is why replaced stability requires learning repair.

Replacement stability also requires dealing with identity addiction. Some people are deeply attached to being the one with the problem because the problem provides script, tribe, and explanation.

When that problem dissolves, emptiness appears. Emptiness is not the enemy. It is space.

But space can feel dangerous. This is why some people stabilize, feel dull, and go looking for fire.

Replacement stability requires learning how to feel alive without chaos. That kind of aliveness comes from depth: craft, relationships, skill, play, service, and embodiment.

Capacity is built through graded contact with life: consistent work, consistent truth, consistent conflict-handling, consistent tolerance of discomfort.

Replacement stability is the moment a person can do uncomfortable things without collapsing.

The Field describes stability as the moment possibility becomes credible.

Fantasy does not change behavior. Credibility does.

A young adult who grew up around addiction may find stability in a trade program, early mornings, predictable pay, a gym routine, and a small circle that does not use. The person did not become a saint. The person built a basin: rhythm, body, money, people. The old return clause loses depth. A mid-career professional who has been living on caffeine, anxiety, and praise may find stability in reducing workload, sleeping, ending a relationship that feeds performance, and rebuilding friendships that are not competitive. The person loses some status heat and gains coherence.

The person becomes less impressive and more free. A caregiver who has been drowning in obligation may find stability in formal support - respite care, childcare, community resources - plus boundaries that stop exploitation. The person becomes stable not because love decreases but because the menu widens.

A person who has survived violence may find stability in place: a safer neighborhood, a locked door, therapy, a support group, training in self-defense or legal resources, and routines that signal safety to the body. The person becomes stable by reducing threat and adding support.

Different lives. Same mechanism: a new basin deepened through repeated regulation. Once stability exists, another truth becomes unavoidable: freedom is not permission. It is capacity.

Chaos is stimulating. Many people confuse aliveness with chaos because the only time they felt sharp was when they were in danger.

Replacement stability teaches the body that quiet is not death. Quiet is where integration happens.

Without a floor, the nervous system cannot reliably choose anything else. Choice requires slack. Slack is stability.

This is also why many apparently successful people are not stable. Success can be a high-functioning Default built on fear, control, and performance.

Viability is the central word. A stable system is a viable system. A viable system can continue without destroying itself.

Replacement stability also requires grief. The old Default did something. It gave relief, identity, belonging, power, stimulation, or survival. If that function is not grieved, the system will keep trying to reinstall it.

Loneliness matters here. Leaving an old Default often means losing a role, a ritual, a schedule, or a whole social climate. The nervous system reads those losses as danger.

Community Makes Stability Hold

Replacement stability often looks like community. Not a crowd. A structure: meetings, teams, classes, rituals, work with dignity, and friendships that do not depend on self-destruction.

The most effective change often includes boring commitments. Boring commitments are stabilizers because they create rhythm. Rhythm trains the body. The body then stops improvising. Improvisation is exhausting. Exhaustion fuels relapse.

Meaning is not philosophy. It is a reason the body agrees to pay the cost of change. Without meaning, change feels like deprivation. With meaning, it starts to feel like investment.

History means something trained a loop. Prophecy means the loop still owns the future. Replacement stability is how history stops masquerading as destiny.

Identity is what happens when a problem repeats long enough. Replacement stability breaks repetition. This is why the Field insists on the sequence:

First: widen Choice Set.

Then: run low-blast experiments.

Then: build replaced stability.

Then: let identity catch up.

When identity is forced ahead of stability, the system collapses under shame. When stability comes first, identity changes quietly and holds.

Pressure will hit. Illness happens. Breakups happen. Money collapses. Death happens. Systems change. The question is not whether life will shake the system. The question is whether the system knows how to stabilize again without destroying itself.

A stable person does not avoid disruption. A stable person repairs faster. Repair speed is the real advantage.

Once stability exists, the next question becomes unavoidable: what is freedom inside a constrained world?

Permission Is Not Power

Freedom is not permission. Freedom is capacity: the ability to hold a choice without collapse.

Replacement is a law of replacement. Remove a behavior without replacing its function and the system will reinstall it, or install something worse.

People quit one addiction and pick up another, leave one toxic relationship and enter a similar one, or stop one coping strategy and develop a new compulsion. The underlying need did not disappear.

Replacement stability means the new behavior has to hold under stress. It has to work on a bad day, not only on a good one.

The Field move is to build replacements that are cheap and available: water before alcohol, walking before doomscrolling, calling one friend before spiraling, sleep before grand decisions.

Over time, stable replacements become identity. Not because you "manifested," but because you trained your nervous system to reach for different levers.

Design replacements for your worst day, not your best one. On your best day, you can do almost anything. On your worst day, you Default.

Replacement stability also requires patience. The old relief is credible because it has history. The new behavior has to earn that credibility through repetition. You do not need a perfect replacement. You need a reliable one. Reliability beats intensity. Replace a bad habit with nothing and the old system snaps back. Replace it with a stable substitute and the nervous system finally gets another place to land.

22

Freedom Is Capacity, Not Permission

Elena can be told to leave, Marcus can be told to slow down, and Rafi can be told to stop. Permission is not the same as capacity. Freedom is not permission. Permission says a move is allowed. Capacity determines whether the move is usable under real load.

Power, in the Field, means usable options under pressure. That is why freedom is capacity. Capacity is the set of resources that makes a choice repeatable. Repeatable is the real test. Anyone can do almost anything once.

Freedom is doing it again next week when the nervous system is tired. A person can have permission to quit a job and still be unable because rent is due. A person can have permission to leave a relationship and still be unable because violence is a threat. A person can have permission to eat well and still be unable because time is gone and food is expensive.

A person can have permission to rest and still be unable because shame is trained and safety depends on being useful. A person can have permission to be sober and still be unable because the body has no other regulator. A person can have permission to study and still be unable because the home is chaotic. This is why freedom talk becomes insulting when it ignores capacity. It turns structural constraints into personal failure. The Field refuses that lie. Capacity has components.

Philosophy has argued about free will for centuries. The argument often misses the lived mechanism.

A person feels free when choices are usable. A person feels trapped when choices are merely theoretical. That is why capacity, not rhetoric, is the operating measure.

When load exceeds resources, the system runs survival programs. Survival programs are narrow. They prioritize immediate regulation. They do not prioritize values. The truth is harsh: overload reveals character is partly a function of capacity. This is not to erase responsibility. It is to define responsibility accurately: build capacity so that values can be executed even under stress. This is why capacity is the hidden layer behind "self-control." Self-control is not a personality trait floating in space.

It is a biological function dependent on energy, sleep, glucose regulation, stress chemistry, and social context. When the body is depleted, self-control becomes expensive. When self-control is expensive, the system chooses cheaper regulators. This is predictable, not shameful. A person who slept four hours, skipped meals, and is running on caffeine does not have the same Choice Set as a person who slept eight and ate breakfast. The first person can still behave well. But the cost is higher.

Higher cost means less repeatability. Repeatability is the point. Stable routines are not "boring lifestyle content." They are capacity production.

Capacity is produced, not discovered. A person is not "born disciplined" in any simple sense. A person is born into a Field that either supports capacity or taxes it from childhood. A child who sleeps, eats, and feels safe develops executive function with less friction. A child who lives in noise, threat, and unpredictability develops executive function under load. The function may still develop, but it develops with scars and compensations.

Those compensations are often called personality. This is why capacity work can feel like becoming a different person. In reality, it is removing the load that was distorting the person.

There is an existing framework in economics and ethics that points toward this: the capability approach. It argues that freedom should be measured by real capabilities - what people are actually able to do and be - not by abstract rights alone. The Field converges on the same conclusion from a different angle: rights without capacity are decoration. Capacity is also where privilege becomes measurable.

Pre-paid capacity looks like: - a family that can catch a fall - a neighborhood with safety - a school with resources - a body that is not constantly inflamed - citizenship and clean documents - access to transportation - language fluency - healthcare access - time not consumed by survival labor - social networks that open doors Multipliers widen menus. This is why some people can take "risks" and call it bravery. The risk is buffered. The fall is cushioned. The same action in a different life would be suicidal.

A person who tells someone else to "take the leap" without checking buffer is not inspirational. That person is careless.

Capacity also explains why some people appear to "waste" Opportunity.

Opportunity is not usable if the body cannot hold it. A person offered a promotion may panic because visibility triggers threat. A person offered love may sabotage because closeness triggers loss. A person offered stability may create chaos because calm triggers suspicion. The opportunity exists on paper. Capacity to hold the opportunity does not. This is why capacity includes emotional regulation, not just resources. Regulation is the ability to stay coherent while feeling.

Many people were trained to treat feeling as danger. Feeling triggers survival programs. Survival programs narrow menu. Narrow menu reduces freedom. This is why freedom begins in the body. A person can know the right move and still be unable to execute because the nervous system is in threat mode. The body is protecting survival, not executing values. In that moment, the person is not evil.

The person is under capacity. Capacity restoration is what allows choice to return. This is why people who learn to restore capacity become free faster. They stop treating depletion as identity.

States change. But only if the inputs change. This is why freedom talk that ignores physiology becomes useless.

The mind cannot outtalk a body that is depleted. Capacity is also the reason some people become rigid even with money and education. Money reduces some constraints and increases others. Money can increase Choice Set and also increase temptation. Temptation is not moral weakness. Temptation is the nervous system noticing available regulators. A person with money has access to more regulators: substances, travel, sex, status purchases, distraction. If internal capacity is low, abundance can become another Field of addiction. Freedom requires the capacity to use resources without being owned by them. Self-governance is impossible without regulation.

Regulation is capacity. Capacity also explains why some people choose "small lives" and are not failures. The Field defines maturity as accurate tradeoff-making. Tradeoffs are unavoidable. The question is whether they are conscious. A person with low capacity often makes unconscious tradeoffs: trading long-term health for immediate relief, trading long-term trust for immediate control, trading long-term future for immediate regulation. This is not stupidity. It is survival economics.

A person who builds capacity gains the ability to choose tradeoffs consciously. Conscious tradeoffs are freedom.

A person can become 10% more free. Then 20%. Then 30%. That does not sound heroic. It is the realistic path.

A person who becomes 30% more free changes the trajectory of a decade. That is why capacity work is worth doing even inside constraints that cannot be removed immediately. Capacity turns the same world into a different menu. That is the point. And once the menu exists, the choices made inside that menu become training data. Choices are not only outcomes. Choices are signals that shape the future.

These capacities create degrees of freedom. This does not deny personal responsibility. It clarifies what responsibility is.

Responsibility is not pretending the menu is equal. Responsibility is building capacity where possible and refusing to waste it when it exists.

A person with low capacity should not be bullied into miracle behavior. That bullying produces shame. Shame produces threat. Threat reduces capacity further. The result is recurrence. Wasting capacity looks like living as if the future does not exist. It looks like constant self-sabotage while having every tool required to build. It looks like treating boredom as an emergency and consuming to fill it. It looks like using privilege as insulation from self-awareness.

Capacity can be squandered. Many do. This is why freedom is not a moral badge. It is a system state. The clearest way to see capacity is to watch what happens under stress. Under stress, does the person have Stress exposes capacity. Under pressure, the useful questions are blunt: Do you have enough sleep, buffer, support, regulation, and meaning to keep the better move available? If not, the answer is design, not self-contempt.

Freedom Has to Be Usable

Freedom is not an abstract right. It is a lived state. A person can be legally free and physiologically trapped. A person can be politically oppressed and still build internal freedom through regulation and meaning, but the external constraints still matter. A person can be externally privileged and still live inside a nervous system prison. The Field holds both truths at once. Freedom is multi-layered. It exists on scales. There is individual freedom: the ability to regulate, choose, and act.

There is relational freedom: the ability to speak, set boundaries, repair, and be safe. There is economic freedom: the ability to survive without humiliation. There is civic freedom: the ability to move through institutions without being hunted. There is cultural freedom: the ability to exist without being erased or punished for identity. These layers interact. Weakness in one layer taxes the others. This is why "personal responsibility" arguments and "systemic oppression" arguments often talk past each other. Both are describing real constraints at different scales.

The Field is not interested in winning that argument. Capacity can be built, increased, repaired, protected, and redistributed. That is where hope lives, without fluff. Not all constraints. Many. A person cannot change genetics, but can change behavior and environment around those genetics. A person cannot change childhood, but can change how the body predicts danger now.

A person cannot change every institution, but can change which institutions are entered and how. A person cannot change history, but can change what is passed forward. Freedom is what becomes possible when the system stops spending all resources on defense.

Defense is costly. Defense shrinks menu. Menu shrinks future. Freedom expands future.

Capacity also creates a quieter form of dignity: the ability to stop bargaining with the self all day.

Low-capacity lives are full of bargaining: "I'll sleep later." "I'll eat later." "I'll call later." "I'll handle it later." "I'll stop tomorrow."

Later becomes the dumping ground for needs. Needs do not disappear. They accumulate. Accumulation becomes pressure. Pressure triggers survival programs. The person then uses the cheapest relief and calls it failure.

It was not failure. It was debt collecting. Capacity interrupts the debt cycle. Consistency creates predictability. Predictability creates safety. Safety creates learning. Learning creates freedom.

This chain is why capacity work is not selfish. It is preventative. A person with no capacity becomes a hazard to the self and to others, not because of evil but because survival programs are contagious. Panic spreads. Rage spreads. Collapse spreads. A person who stabilizes becomes less contagious. This is how private capacity becomes public good.

MICRO-CAPACITIES STILL COUNT

Even inside hard constraint, micro-capacities matter. A person in a hostile environment can still practice a small form of freedom: not lying to the self. Not inflating shame. Not escalating conflict. Choosing one stabilizing habit. Choosing one honest relationship. Choosing one hour that is not owned by the feed. These are not cute. They are seeds. Seeds become buffer over time. Freedom begins as small resistance to being programmable.

Programmability is what the Field is trying to reduce. Not because control is evil, but because a programmable nervous system becomes a tool for any system willing to pay for it. Capacity is the refusal to be easily bought.

Freedom is the ability to choose the hard thing now because the system can hold the consequences.

Permission does not deliver this. Capacity does. This is why the Field makes the work brutally concrete.

No slogans. No fantasies. Capacity is built from sleep, food, movement, money, relationships, place, and meaning. Those are the levers.

Once capacity exists, choice stops being mostly reaction and starts behaving like signal. Repetition begins to sign the future. That is the bridge to the next chapter.

The Field move is to ask: what capacity am I missing? Is it skills? Is it childcare? Is it transportation? Is it mental health treatment? Is it community? Is it legal status? Then you stop moralizing and start building.

Public Goods Create Real Freedom

Capacity also scales. A community with strong public goods produces more free people: libraries, parks, transit, healthcare, education. Those are freedom infrastructure. People call them "politics." They are conditions.

As systems grow more complex, permission will not be enough. People will need capacity to navigate data, institutions, and stress without selling the self for relief.

Freedom is the ability to act without destroying yourself. That is the definition that survives reality.

Capacity is visible in the simplest example: a ramp. The law can say "equal access," but without a ramp, the wheelchair user is still locked out. That is freedom in one image. Build ramps in your own life too: habits, savings, skills, community, treatment, and design that make the right action physically possible.

Capacity is not just individual. A society that denies healthcare, education, or safety is a society that manufactures unfree people. You cannot "mindset" your way out of broken infrastructure. You can survive it, but freedom requires building conditions that allow people to act well.

Capacity is the metric: can you actually do the thing without breaking? When you build capacity, permission stops feeling theoretical and starts feeling usable. Build capacity and the world opens. Then choice becomes real.

Permission is cheap; capacity is expensive. You can be "allowed" to rest and still be unable to rest without guilt, withdrawal, or fear.

23

Choice as Signature

EVERY DAY ELENA SIGNS WITH RESPONSIBILITY, MARCUS WITH PERFORMANCE, AND RAFI WITH RELIEF OR REPAIR. EVERY CHOICE IS TRAINING DATA.

CHOICE TRAINS THE FUTURE

Every choice is training data. People treat choices as isolated moral moments. That framing is too small. A choice is a signal sent into the future. The future answers by becoming easier or harder to live inside. This is not mystical.

It is accumulation. A human nervous system learns from what is repeated. Repetition creates expectation. Expectation creates Default behavior. Default behavior creates identity. Identity creates the life. This is why small choices matter more than dramatic ones.

Dramatic choices are rare. Small choices are daily. The daily is what trains the system. A person who sleeps one night is tired. A person who sleeps consistently becomes a different organism. A person who tells the truth once is brave. A person who tells the truth consistently becomes reliable.

A person who moves once is sore. A person who moves consistently becomes regulated. A person who saves once is cautious. A person who saves consistently becomes buffered. Consistency is the hidden lever because it changes expectation. Expectation is the brain's prediction model. The brain is always guessing what comes next. It uses past data to predict future cost. When the past data shows chaos, the brain predicts chaos and braces. When the past data shows stability, the brain predicts stability and relaxes.

TRAINING = CHOICE × REPETITION

Relaxed systems can choose. Braced systems defend. This is why consistency is not aesthetics. It is neuroeconomics.

The simplest way to understand this is through reinforcement learning, the same family of logic used in many modern algorithms.

An agent takes an action. The environment returns an outcome. If the outcome reduces cost, the action becomes more likely. If the outcome increases cost, the action becomes less likely. Over time, the agent learns a policy: a set of actions that tends to reduce cost. Humans are agents. Life is the environment. The policy is what most people call personality.

The mind prefers to think of choice as a courtroom: guilty or innocent, good or bad, strong or weak. The body experiences choice as training: more of this, less of that. Training language is more useful Because it is forward-looking. A courtroom looks backward. Training looks forward. This is why the same action can be interpreted differently depending on the frame. A person says, "I failed." Training frame says, "The old policy ran. The conditions favored it."

Training frame does not absolve responsibility. It makes responsibility practical. Practical responsibility means changing what is repeated, not punishing what already happened. Signals have strength. A signal is strong when it is repeated under the same trigger. A signal is weak when it is performed only in easy conditions.

People overestimate change after a good day. A good day is an easy condition. The real test is a hard day. The system notices which signals survive pressure. Those are the ones it stores as policy. This is why change is often invisible for a while. The person is collecting strong signals. The person is repeating the new move under pressure until the body begins to trust it.

Trust is a physiological phenomenon. It is the moment the nervous system predicts safety.

People think trust is romantic. Trust is prediction. This is why betrayal hurts. Betrayal changes prediction abruptly. The nervous system experiences that as threat. Choice as signal also explains why "willpower" is unreliable.

Willpower is a short-term resource. It behaves like muscle: it can be trained, but it is also depleted by load. Under high load, willpower becomes expensive. When willpower becomes expensive, the system chooses habits. Habits are stored policies that do not require conscious effort. This is why building habits is not self-help. It is cost reduction.

A habit is a choice that became cheap. The goal is not to become a robot. The goal is to make the right choices cheap so that conscious effort can be saved for situations that truly require it: emergencies, moral decisions, complex tradeoffs, caregiving, creativity, strategy. A person with no habits spends consciousness on basics, then has no energy left for the life that needs thought. This is why stability creates intelligence. Stability frees cognitive bandwidth.

Cognitive bandwidth is the ability to hold multiple variables at once. Bandwidth shrinks Under stress. This is well-known in behavioral economics and cognitive science: scarcity - of money, time, safety - consumes attention. The mind becomes tunnel vision. Tunnel vision is not stupidity. It is the brain trying to survive. A person in scarcity makes choices that look short-sighted.

Again: that is not moral failure. It is a predictable effect of load. When load decreases, the person appears to become smarter. The person did not get a new brain. The person got bandwidth. Bandwidth is a form of freedom. Choice as signal is also why small financial decisions matter beyond money. A person who saves even small amounts is not only preparing financially. The person is training a new identity: "I can create buffer." That identity changes how risk is perceived.

Risk becomes less fatal. Less fatal risk expands Choice Set. Expanded Choice Set allows better choices. Better choices compound. This is why people underestimate the psychological value of buffer. Buffer is not only protection. Buffer is a signal that the future exists.

The same is true for health. A person who walks daily is not only burning calories. The person is training the body to expect movement. The body becomes less anxious because movement is one of the oldest signals of agency. Movement tells the nervous system: "The organism can act." That reduces helplessness. Reduced helplessness reduces the craving for cheap regulators.

Small physical routines often reduce depression and anxiety. The body feels less trapped because it has proof of movement. Choice as signal also explains relationship outcomes. Every time a person chooses to repair instead of punish, the relationship becomes safer. Every time a person chooses to punish instead of repair, the relationship becomes brittle. Safety is not a feeling. Safety is the expectation that conflict will not become catastrophe.

People talk about "communication." The real variable is repair. Repair is a repeated signal: "The bond can survive disruption." Without that signal, closeness becomes dangerous. The nervous system stays guarded. Guarded systems cannot be intimate. They can only negotiate.

Some couples talk for years and never become close. They communicate without repair. The bond never receives evidence that it can survive honesty. Choice as signal also creates reputation. Reputation is not only what others think. Reputation is how others predict you will behave. Prediction determines how they treat you.

How they treat you changes your environment. Environment changes your options. Options change your future behavior. This is a feedback loop. A person who shows up repeatedly becomes trusted. Trusted people get access: opportunities, patience, support. A person who disappears repeatedly becomes distrusted. Distrusted people get gates: restrictions, suspicion, exclusion.

This is harsh but true. The Field prices predictability. Predictable people are safer to invest in.

The most powerful signal is reliability. Reliability is not being perfect. Reliability is being consistent enough that others can plan.

A person cannot control every outcome. A person can control whether the next move is the same move.

Choice as signal also clarifies why "one big decision" rarely changes a life. One big decision is a spike. Spikes are not baselines. Baselines come from the slope: the daily rate of doing the thing.

A person who wants to change should stop worshiping spikes and start respecting slope.

Slope Beats Spikes

Slope is what compounds. This is why small changes are not trivial. Small changes are slope adjustments. Over time they create different destinations. A person who adjusts slope by one degree ends up in a different city a year later. That is geometry, not inspiration. Choice as signal becomes even more serious when viewed across generations. A stable baseline is a signal that becomes inheritance.

That is why the question of the future is not abstract. The future is built in kitchens, bedrooms, hallways, workplaces, and neighborhoods through repeated choices that train what the next generation expects.

And that brings the work to the next level. The policy is trained. This means a person is not only choosing in the moment. A person is teaching the system what to choose next time. That teaching happens whether it is conscious or not. Every time a person scrolls to avoid feeling, the system learns: scrolling is a regulator. Every time a person lies to avoid conflict, the system learns: lying is safety. Every time a person explodes to regain control, the system learns: violence is power. Every time a person disappears to avoid shame, the system learns: absence is protection.

Every time a person drinks to soften loneliness, the system learns: alcohol is connection.

Repetition Makes the Future Feel Inevitable

The system does not judge. It stores data. Then the future arrives and behaves like the data. This is why choice is a signal. The most dangerous signals are the ones that train inevitability.

Inevitability is not fate. Inevitability is a model that expects no other option. A person repeats a Default enough times and the system stops offering alternatives. It stops offering pause. It stops offering imagination. It moves from choice into reflex. The person then says, "That's just who I am." That sentence is usually the moment the person surrendered to training.

Training can be reversed. But training does not reverse by arguing with it. It reverses by sending new signals.

New signals are small at first. Repeatable signals become policies. Policies become lives. This is how the future becomes structured.

A person can change without anyone noticing at first. The person is changing the training data. The outputs shift quietly. Later, the identity story updates and everyone pretends the change was sudden. It was not sudden. It was accumulation. Accumulation is also why tiny betrayals matter. A person betrays sleep night after night and teaches the body: depletion is normal. A person betrays hunger day after day and teaches the body: urgency is normal.

A person betrays boundaries conversation after conversation and teaches the body: collapse is normal. A person betrays truth lie after lie and teaches the body: fear is normal. A person betrays the future dollar after dollar and teaches the body: scarcity is normal. Then the person wonders why life feels narrow.

The body is living in the model it was taught. Choice as signal also explains compounding. Baseline is everything.

Baseline determines what triggers look like, what stress looks like, what love looks like, what boredom looks like, what silence looks like.

A person who changes baseline often loses compatibility with old environments. The old environment was calibrated to the old baseline. When baseline shifts, the old environment feels loud, unsafe, or empty. This is not arrogance. This is calibration.

This is also why relapse often occurs in familiar places. The place is a cue. Cues activate policies. The body remembers what to do there.

Choice as signal means that cues can be redesigned. This is how the Field can be re-trained. Choice as signal also forces a hard truth: neutrality does not exist.

Not choosing is a choice. Avoiding is a choice. Waiting is a choice. Every day teaches the system what is normal. This is why time is expensive. Time is the medium through which training occurs. Every day that passes is training data, whether the person likes it or not. This is not meant to create guilt. Guilt is useless training data. Guilt teaches threat. Threat teaches recurrence.

The purpose is Leverage. Once choice is clear as signal, the person stops using decisions as self-judgment and starts using decisions as design. Design is this: choose signals that build capacity and widen the menu. Signals can be tiny.

A person chooses to drink water first and teaches the body: care exists. A person chooses to step outside for five minutes and teaches the body: air exists. A person chooses to text one friend honestly and teaches the body: contact exists. A person chooses to shut the phone at night and teaches the body: rest is allowed. A person chooses to save ten dollars and teaches the body: buffer is possible. A person chooses not to escalate a fight and teaches the body: power without violence exists. A person chooses to eat before crisis and teaches the body: urgency is not required. Tiny signals become trend. Trend becomes baseline. Baseline becomes life.

There is one more correction that prevents this idea from becoming toxic: not every action is a signal of identity.

Noise exists. A person can have a bad day, snap, and still be a fundamentally safe person. A person can miss a workout and still be a disciplined person. A person can relapse and still be in recovery. A person can disappoint someone and still be reliable. A system is not defined by one data point. A system is defined by trend.

The Field emphasizes repetition. Repetition separates signal from noise. If shame tries to weaponize this, it will say, "Every mistake defines you." That is false. Mistakes are data. Identity is the aggregate.

The useful question after any mistake is not "Who am I?" The useful question is "What did this mistake train, and what signal will be sent next?" This keeps responsibility forward-facing. It also keeps compassion honest. Compassion does not deny cost. Compassion refuses to turn cost into destiny.

Signals can be repaired. Repair is itself a signal: "Even when I fall, I return." That return is the difference between a life that spirals and a life that stabilizes. Spirals are the result of compounding in the wrong direction: one mistake triggers shame, shame triggers threat, threat triggers more mistakes, and the slope steepens. Breaking the spiral is not about never slipping. It is about refusing to convert slips into identity. Trend beats theater.

This is how choice becomes a tool instead of a weapon. This is why the Field treats the day as the unit of change.

A decade is built out of days. A life is built out of decades. A lineage is built out of lives.

That last line matters because choice does not only train the self. Choice trains children, partners, coworkers, and communities. Choice becomes culture. Culture becomes inheritance.

What you sign repeatedly does not stay private. Repeated choice becomes someone else's environment. That is where signature turns into legacy.

SIGN DELIBERATELY

A signature is how you make something official. Choice is your signature on the terms of your life.

Every day you sign something, even if it is silent: the job you keep, the relationship you tolerate, the health habit you ignore, the narrative you repeat, the boundary you refuse to set. Silence is a signature too.

This is not meant to shame you. It is meant to return agency. Agency is not the fantasy of total control. Agency is choosing what you will pay for and what you will not.

The Field move is to sign deliberately. If you are going to suffer, suffer for something that builds. If you are going to sacrifice, sacrifice for something that compounds. If you are going to endure, endure on purpose.

People underestimate the dignity of deliberate choice because they are trained to wait for permission or rescue. The book is not rescuing you. It is teaching you to read the page you are signing.

A signature changes history. Your choices become someone else's environment. That is how the Field evolves.

Sign well. A signature is repeated. One signature on a page is a moment. A thousand signatures is a life. Small signatures matter because they set trajectory: the extra hour of sleep, the honest text, the boundary, the walk, the quiet no. They do not feel dramatic. They change the Field by accumulation.

If you want to know what you truly believe, look at what you repeatedly do when no one is watching. That is your signature. Change the repetition and your signature changes. Over time, the person changes. This is not philosophy. It is training.

You sign with repetition. Make repetition worthy. Make the next signature small and repeatable. That is how you become credible to yourself. Sign daily. A single day rarely changes a life. A thousand small signals do. Signatures repeat. If you want a new one, make it easy to repeat: smaller commitment, clearer cue, immediate feedback.

24

Being a Good Ancestor

ELENA KNOWS THAT WHAT A PERSON NORMALIZES TODAY BECOMES SOMEBODY ELSE'S STARTING POINT. EVERY LIFE IS A HANDOFF.

People live as if experience ends at the skin. It does not. Behavior becomes environment for other people. Environment becomes training. Training becomes somebody else's baseline.

That is why good intentions are not enough. Good intentions do not prevent inherited damage. A person can mean well and still make volatility feel normal. A person can love deeply and still train the room to brace. A person can call something temporary while a child's body records it as climate.

A good ancestor is someone who reduces transmitted volatility.

LEGACY = TODAY'S NORMAL × TOMORROW'S BASELINE

Most people inherit defaults long before they inherit money. They inherit a nervous system's expectations about what life will cost. Some inherit repair. Some inherit silence. Some inherit rules. Some inherit fear. Some inherit adults who apologize. Some inherit adults who explain nothing and demand gratitude for confusion.

What moves through a life is rarely dramatic at first. It is whether promises are kept. Whether money is discussed honestly. Whether rest is allowed. Whether someone can say no without the room turning hostile. Whether a mistake becomes a lesson or a humiliation. Whether recovery is normal or always delayed. Whether one person's panic becomes everybody else's assignment.

A child should not have a job inside adult chaos. Not peacekeeper. Not translator. Not witness. Not emotional employee. When adults hand that labor downward, they call it maturity. The body experiences it as load.

What becomes normal becomes baseline. Baseline becomes the next person's idea of reality. That is how volatility becomes lineage.

Ancestry is larger than parenting. A teacher becomes an ancestor through what is normalized in a classroom. A supervisor becomes an ancestor through what is rewarded and what is punished. A manager becomes an ancestor through what a team learns to fear. A partner becomes an ancestor through the rules of closeness. A friend becomes an ancestor through what is tolerated. A landlord, pastor, coach, nurse, older sibling, uncle, and neighbor all become ancestors when their repeated behavior becomes somebody else's weather.

Functional legacy is what remains when speeches are forgotten. Children, coworkers, students, friends, and communities copy the baseline, not the explanation.

What you tolerate becomes tradition. Nice without boundary often transmits danger. A child who watches adults smile through harm learns that harm is acceptable if it is polite. A worker who watches a team treat exhaustion as professionalism learns that self-erasure is the price of belonging. A partner who learns that truth triggers punishment starts pricing honesty as dangerous.

No is an inheritance. A child who learns no learns agency. A person who learns that truth can survive contact learns dignity. A room where repair happens on purpose becomes a room that teaches reality without terror.

When Elena stops treating rescue as proof of love, her younger sibling inherits a different rule: care can include limits, and love does not require self-erasure. That change is small at first. It is a shorter phone call. A refused bailout. A boundary spoken sooner. A ride not given. A lie not covered. A different baseline begins not as a speech but as a repeated refusal to train the next person into confusion.

Ancestry also runs inside one lifetime. Your future self-inherits the body, the money, the habits, the friendships, the reputation, and the unfinished business you are building now. Short-term relief can therefore become a form of theft from the future self. It spends tomorrow's capacity for tonight's numbness. That does not make relief evil. It makes cost accounting non-negotiable.

A good ancestor does not constantly rob the future self. The practical aim is to leave behind more stability than panic.

Buffer is legacy in practical form: documents in order, money that does not vanish at the first shock, repair before resentment becomes climate, homes where no one has to earn safety by disappearing, schedules with margin, systems that do not collapse when one person gets sick, and relationships that can survive honest information.

Public goods are ancestry at scale. Clear forms, fair process, breathable air, functional transit, safe public space, and reliable institutions widen the next person's Choice Set. When people romanticize personal virtue while stripping public goods, they misunderstand legacy. Legacy is not only character. Legacy is structure.

A society becomes ancestral through what it makes normal. It can normalize bureaucratic humiliation, impossible rents, permanent exhaustion, and untreated trauma. Or it can normalize sleep, repair, transparency, access, and margin. Both are inheritances. Both train bodies before bodies have language for what is happening.

Marcus sees this at work. Teams do not inherit mission statements. They inherit response time, penalty patterns, emotional weather, meeting logic, and the cost of telling the truth. If leadership says burnout matters but rewards panic, panic becomes policy. If leadership says family matters but treats boundaries as lack of commitment, self-betrayal becomes culture. Institutions reproduce through repetition the same way families do.

Rafi sees it in recovery. Nobody inherits slogans. They inherit whether honesty is survivable, whether relapse becomes abandonment, whether help can be requested without humiliation, whether structure exists before collapse, and whether somebody taught them that the body deserves a future. Recovery is not just abstinence. It is the transmission of a different baseline.

This is why the phrase good ancestor only sounds sentimental until it is translated into mechanics. It means reducing avoidable volatility. It means passing forward more buffer and less chaos. It means making repair normal. It means making truth cheaper. It means leaving the next nervous system with a slightly wider menu than the one you inherited.

A good ancestor transmits a wider future by reducing avoidable volatility and leaving the next person more usable options.

Many people grow up in environments where the future does not feel real. Plans get mocked. Hope gets treated as naivete. Adults live as if nothing can improve, which means the child learns that planning is pointless. That child becomes an adult who cannot hold a long arc and then gets called lazy. Often the deeper truth is trained hopelessness.

Transmitting future looks boring from the outside. It looks like keeping promises. Showing up consistently. Telling the truth about money. Making the home predictable. Protecting sleep, food, and recovery.

Apologizing when wrong. Refusing to make one person carry the whole room. Saying no to chaos before chaos becomes climate. Saving small amounts repeatedly. Fixing paperwork before it becomes a crisis. Building routines that still work on bad days.

It also looks like refusing false heroism. Some people are so addicted to being needed that they train dependency everywhere they go. They mistake indispensability for love. They call exhaustion devotion. They create systems that only function when they are overextended and then complain that nobody helps. That is not noble. It is unstable. A good ancestor builds systems that do not require collapse to prove care.

This chapter is not asking whether you are morally pure. It is asking a structural question: what does your repetition train in the people around you?

Do you train predictability or scanning? Repair or silence? Truth or performance? Margin or chronic emergency? Agency or helplessness? Rest or exhaustion-as-identity? Limits or access without end?

Your life is teaching even when you are not speaking.

That is why legacy is not mainly about memory. It is about mechanics. A speech disappears. A pattern remains. A child may forget a lecture and still remember in the body that the door slams before the anger does. An employee may forget the values memo and still remember that bad news gets punished. A partner may forget the apology and still remember whether the next conflict feels safer than the last one.

Mechanics outlive explanations.

The adult task is therefore not to become impressive. It is to become reliable in the right ways. Reliability in this sense is not perfection. It is not emotional flatness. It is not sterile control. It is the repeated reduction of unnecessary chaos. It is the creation of structures other people can live inside without shrinking.

A person can inherit damage and still interrupt transmission. That is one of the most important truths in the book. You do not need a pure past to become a better ancestor. You need visibility, responsibility, and repetition. You need to tell the truth about what trained you. You need to stop calling inevitability what is actually repetition under old Terms. And you need to build new Terms small enough to hold under load.

Elena does not become a good ancestor by becoming endlessly available. She becomes one by making care more honest. Marcus does not become one by giving another speech about values. He becomes one by lowering the price of candor and raising the price of chaos. Rafi does not become one by winning a dramatic battle once. He becomes one by making recovery more ordinary than self-destruction.

What people inherit from you will not mainly be your intentions. It will be your repeated standards.

That means the question is not whether you will leave a mark. Repetition guarantees that you will. The question is what kind.

The Field Seen Whole

This is where the Field comes fully into focus as one object. Terms are the invisible prices. State is what the body can currently pay. Time changes cost. Place changes cost. Power changes who sets the prices and who absorbs them. Repetition turns the affordable move into identity. Identity gets mistaken for essence. Then that patterned identity becomes another person's training data.

Everything in this book has been one face of that same mechanism. The body was never separate from the room. The room was never separate from law, money, migration, work, family, or meaning. The personal and the structural were never different species of explanation. They were different elevations of the same map.

A unified theory is not a claim of omniscience. It is a refusal to keep pretending these domains are unrelated. A human life is the output of inputs interacting over time. Biology, early environment, relationships, institutions, attention, money, schedule, and culture meet in one place: a nervous system trying to survive without becoming its own prison.

The Field does not abolish responsibility. It makes responsibility accurate. Explanation without responsibility becomes excuse. Responsibility without explanation becomes punishment. The Field insists on a harder middle path: name the conditions honestly, then design what comes next.

That is why ancestry is the right final frame. It turns growth into transmission. You are not only improving a private life. You are deciding what your body, your habits, your calendar, your honesty, your consumption, your boundaries, your work, and your love will teach forward.

You are also an ancestor to your future self. Tomorrow inherits the body you train today, the buffer you build or drain today, the relationships you repair or corrode today, the paperwork you handle or avoid today, the truths you speak or keep pricing as dangerous. Short-term relief can be a form of cruelty to that future self. A good ancestor does not keep robbing tomorrow to numb today.

Leave the Field better than you found it is not a slogan. It is the simplest serious ethic in this model. Make truth less dangerous. Make repair more normal. Make rest more legitimate. Make planning more believable. Make children less employable as emotional staff. Make shame less available as a tool of control. Make the better move cheaper for the people who come after you.

You do not need to become a hero to do that. You need to become honest enough to stop passing your unexamined pattern forward as destiny.

That is the whole Field seen at human scale: what you inherit, what you repeat, what you redesign, and what your redesign makes possible for people you may never meet.

25

Different Terms, Different Lives

BY THE TIME MOST PEOPLE ASK WHY THEIR LIFE KEEPS CIRCLING THE SAME PAIN, THE PATTERN IS ALREADY OLD. THE BODY HAS PRACTICED IT. THE RELATIONSHIPS AROUND IT HAVE ADAPTED TO IT. THE INSTITUTIONS AROUND IT MAY EVEN PROFIT FROM IT. WHAT FEELS PERSONAL IS USUALLY PARTLY STRUCTURAL.

That is the argument of this book: repeated behavior under stable Terms becomes structured life.

People do not choose from an infinite menu. They choose from a priced one. Terms shape State. State narrows the Choice Set. The system then reaches for the cheapest survivable move. Relief reinforces it. Repetition stabilizes it. That is what makes lives rhyme.

Once you can see that sequence, a great deal of confusion stops posing as fate.

The point was never to deny responsibility. It was to locate responsibility where it can work. Shame is a poor engineer. It intensifies pain more reliably than it redesigns the system that keeps making the same move cheap.

Different Terms, different lives.

That sentence is neither excuse nor slogan. It is a practical law of human behavior. Change the Terms and different actions become cheaper. Change the available support and different risks become tolerable. Change sleep, time, money, friction, enforcement, shame, recovery, or truth, and you change what can realistically repeat.

This is true in private life. It is also true in family systems, workplaces, schools, neighborhoods, courts, markets, and states. A person can be bright and still be trapped inside expensive honesty. A person can be good and still be priced into harm. A person can be sincere and still be surrounded by Terms that make collapse predictable.

That is why moral language often fails. It describes the scene from a distance but not the machinery inside it.

Call a person lazy and you still do not know whether sleep is broken, money is unstable, the commute is punishing, the body is inflamed, the task is ambiguous, the room is humiliating, or the cost of failure has become so loaded that avoidance now feels cheaper than action.

Structural language is slower at first. It is more useful later.

Marcus treated exhaustion as proof. It made him legible inside ambitious rooms. The job kept making self-erasure profitable in the short term. Praise arrived faster than recovery. Visibility arrived faster than margin. The Invoices arrived later.

The solution was not a speech about self-worth. It was structural renegotiation: clearer scope, slower yes, protected time, fewer false urgencies, more honest cost accounting. The man did not become a new species. The menu changed.

Elena treated rescue as the family tax for being competent. Everyone else's crisis kept landing on the same doorstep. She did not need deeper insight into resentment. She needed a different bill.

Rafi confused relief with rescue. Under loneliness, shame, and agitation, the old move kept offering immediate discount. Recovery began when the better move stopped being absurdly expensive.

More structure before nightfall. More honest contact. Less access to cash in the wrong window. A room that did not punish truth. Friction on the destructive move. Support on the stabilizing one. Different Terms, different nights. Different nights, different life.

This is why the book has insisted that freedom is not mainly the absence of rules. Freedom is capacity plus design. It is a body that can choose and a Field that does not immediately punish the better move out of existence.

The fantasy version of adulthood says you should be able to override any environment through force of character. That fantasy flatters institutions because it converts structural failure into personal inadequacy. The Field interrupts that lie. It puts agency back on real ground.

Real ground is where patterns are priced, not where systems pretend choice is frictionless.

The point of reading the Field is not to become cynical. It is to become less confused. Cynicism says everything is rigged and nothing can change. The Field says something harder: much more is designed than you were taught to notice, and because design exists, redesign is possible.

Some readers will want something more flattering. They will want the book to tell them they are secretly limitless. But lives do not improve because a sentence sounds noble. Lives improve when the better move becomes cheaper often enough to repeat.

That is why the most important changes in adulthood are often boring to outsiders: the automatic transfer, the earlier boundary, the meal prepped before hunger becomes chaos, the legal form submitted on time, the bottle not purchased, the script prepared before panic.

A meeting shortened. A room left sooner. A script prepared in advance. A notebook kept near the bed. A weekly money review. A ride arranged before panic. A friend told the truth before the story mutates. Boring changes are what survive the weather.

People still worship spikes: the dramatic confession, the reinvention, the perfect Monday, the one heroic act that supposedly cancels years of repetition. Spikes are memorable. Slope is what compounds.

A good day proves almost nothing. A hard day reveals the real policy. That is why the right question is not whether a move works in ideal conditions. It is whether it survives contact with fatigue, shame, inconvenience, loneliness, time pressure, and the body you actually live in.

If the better move only works on a good day, it is not designed yet.

People constantly mistake aspiration for architecture. They think wanting is the same as planning and planning is the same as readiness. It is not. Readiness means the first step is visible, the cost is survivable, and the better move still exists when the hard hour arrives.

This is true for people. It is equally true for systems. Design beats declaration.

The deepest implication of the Field is therefore political as much as personal. Private struggle is real. Structural design is real. These are not competing truths. They are layered ones.

That means compassion has to become more exact. Compassion is not pretending every outcome is equally avoidable. Compassion is learning to ask better questions about cost, threat, reinforcement, and the hidden bill.

A serious politics of this model would judge schools, workplaces, platforms, neighborhoods, and states by one test: what behavior do they make cheap under load, and who is forced to carry the delayed invoice?

That question does not erase accountability. It sharpens it.

Some readers will first use this model on themselves. Good. Some will use it on family, work, law, housing, money, school, healthcare, or addiction and realize that what looked like personal failure was often a system charging hidden fees. Good. Nothing durable happens before legibility.

The book has also argued for a harder kind of hope. Not fantasy. Not denial. Hard hope: the kind that starts once the mechanism is visible enough that you can stop wasting time fighting ghosts.

Hope becomes adult when it stops requiring magic and starts requiring visible mechanisms and workable plans.

DIFFERENT TERMS, DIFFERENT LIVES

That applies backward as well as forward. If earlier Terms helped produce the life you have, then present Terms are already teaching the life you are becoming.

The closing question of the book is not, 'Who am I really?' That question often invites mythology. The more useful one is: what does my current Field keep making likely?

If the answer is more debt, more panic, more secrecy, more self-erasure, more volatility, more drift, or more fake urgency, then the work is not to invent a new personality. The work is to alter what keeps feeding that answer.

Build friction where useful. Protect sleep. Tell the truth earlier. Save a little. Prepare the script. Make the next honest move easier than the next false one.

Elena's future changes when care stops requiring self-erasure. Marcus's future changes when achievement stops pricing life out of the room. Rafi's future changes when relief no longer has to arrive through self-destruction.

The argument of the book can therefore be stated in one line.

You do not repeat what you love. You repeat what the Field keeps making affordable.

And the practical answer follows in one more line.

If you want a different life, make different lives affordable.

That is the work. Not performance. Not purity. Pricing. Design. Repetition. A wider Choice Set. A body that trusts a better move because the better move no longer feels like punishment.

The final dignity of the model is that it does not ask you to lie. It does not ask you to claim freedom where you do not have it. It asks you to become more exact about where freedom can be built.

The life in front of you is not infinitely open. It is also not fixed. It is priced. Read the prices. Change what you can. Protect what matters. Make the next move cheaper to repeat. Then repeat it until the body stops calling it foreign.

That is how change begins: repeated, workable moves the body can actually learn.

Epilogue

What Changes When You Read the Field

What changes when you know is not what happens to you. It is what you stop misnaming.

Before the Field is visible, experience gets interpreted in the smallest possible way. Failure feels like character. Relapse feels like weakness. Collapse feels like proof. Success feels like luck. The mind builds a courtroom inside the head and spends years prosecuting the self.

The Field replaces the courtroom with a map.

A map does not remove grief or erase injustice. It ends a particular kind of confusion. It ends the fantasy that repetition is random, that self-hatred is a strategy, and that insight alone is architecture.

Once the map is visible, the work becomes more honest. You stop asking why you are like this in the abstract and start asking what keeps making this move cheap. You stop treating recurrence as betrayal and start treating it as information.

That shift matters because so much adult suffering is intensified by misdiagnosis. People keep applying moral pressure to structural problems and then call the predictable outcome personal failure.

The Field does not remove moral life. It clarifies it.

Moral seriousness begins with accurate description. If a person is trapped, say trapped. If a system is predatory, say predatory. If a room trains fear, say fear. If a move lowers immediate pain while increasing long-term damage, say both.

That is why the book has insisted on anti-shame without becoming anti-responsibility. Shame clouds the mechanism. Responsibility studies it.

You do not need to solve every part of your life at once. You need to see the current pattern clearly enough to stop paying for confusion. Name the Default. Price the relief. Track the Invoice. Find one leverage point. Build one protocol that works on a bad day.

That is enough to begin.

Many readers will want certainty beyond that. They will want to know whether the model explains everything. It does not. No useful model explains everything. Traits matter. Biology matters. History matters.

Luck matters. Culture matters. Love matters. Tragedy matters. Singular decisions matter. The Field is strongest where recurrence under constraint is strongest. It is a practical model, not a total cosmology.

Its usefulness is still considerable. It explains why insight is common and durable change is rare. It explains why the same conflict returns wearing different clothes. It explains why one small structural edit can change more than a month of motivational speech.

It also offers a different standard of dignity.

Dignity is not pretending you were free in every moment you were trapped. Dignity is telling the truth about the trap without turning the trap into identity.

That is why the book keeps returning to one practical line: design beats willpower.

Willpower matters. But it is expensive, unstable, and easily defeated by chronic load. Design lasts longer. Design conserves energy. Design is how one good intention becomes a repeatable condition.

The final use of the Field is therefore not self-analysis for its own sake. It is redesign.

Make one gate clearer. Make one harmful move harder to reach. Make one honest move cheaper. Put one bill on autopay. Set one boundary one hour earlier. Protect one hour of sleep. Write one script before the stressful call. Add one support before the crash instead of after it.

Small design is still design. Repeated design becomes a different life.

The point is not perfection. The point is trajectory. One day rarely changes a life. A thousand repetitions do.

That means read the Field carefully: in your body, your home, your work, your habits, your relationships, your sleep, your institutions, your city, and your calendar. Read where the pressure is. Read where the relief is. Read where the hidden bills are.

Then make one better move cheaper.

That is enough to justify the model. That is enough to begin again. That is enough to make the next life less expensive than the last one.

The engineer replaces the hostile manager.

Read the Field well enough and you stop bargaining with yourself in the dark. You stop asking for a different personality and start building different conditions.

That is not glamorous. It is better than glamorous. Durable change, repeated long enough, becomes a different life.

The Model

YOU ARE NOT LAZY. YOU ARE PRICED.

Human behavior is best read as priced adaptation under load. Before any decision is felt as a decision, conditions are already in force: body, state, time, money, relationships, law, environment, culture, attention, and enforcement. Some moves are cheap. Some are expensive. Some are visible only in theory. What repeats is usually what the Field keeps affordable.

CORE CHAIN

TERMS → STATE → CHOICE SET →

DEFAULT → REINFORCEMENT → RECURRENCE

UNCHOSEN TERMS + REPEATED COSTS = THE LIFE YOU ARE LIVING.

DEFINITIONS

- **Terms:** the conditions in force - body, place, money, law, schedule, relationships, culture, and enforcement.
- **State:** what the body can currently carry - sleep, stress, fatigue, hunger, pain, grief, stimulation, and regulation.
- **Choice Set:** the menu actually usable under those conditions, not the menu that exists in theory.
- **Default:** the lowest-cost reliable move under pressure.
- Reinforcement: what makes the move stick, often through immediate relief.
- **Recurrence:** what appears when the same priced move is learned and repeated.

EQUATIONS

CAPACITY = RESOURCES - CURRENT LOAD

VISIBLE CHOICE = OPTIONS PRICED BY HIDDEN TERMS

RECURRENCE = FAMILIAR RELIEF + LOW CHOICE SET

REPLACEMENT STABILITY = NEW FUNCTION + REPETITION + TIME

LAWS

1. Behavior follows cost.
2. Relief reinforces faster than ideals.
3. State determines the usable Choice Set.
4. Environment sets price before choice exists.
5. Recurrence is priced stability.
6. Freedom is capacity, not permission.
7. Remove a behavior without replacing its function and it returns.
8. What repeats becomes someone else's baseline.

COROLLARIES

- Design beats lecture.
- A better move that fails on a bad day is not designed yet.
- A smaller, cleaner Choice Set beats a larger chaotic one.
- Low-blast experiments outperform dramatic reinvention.
- Buffer widens what you can afford.

- Planning is load moved forward in time.
- Choice is a signature before it becomes a story.
- If you want a different life, make different lives affordable.

METHOD

- Start with recurrence.
- Price the behavior honestly.
- Name the Terms in force.
- Find the hidden cost.
- Reduce one constraint.
- Add one buffer.
- Raise friction on the old regulator.
- Lower friction on the better move.
- Replace function, not form.
- Test the sequence on a bad day.
- Repeat until the better move becomes the cheap, reliable move.

The model does not abolish responsibility. It makes responsibility accurate. Explanation without responsibility becomes excuse. Responsibility without explanation becomes punishment. The Field insists on a harder middle path: name the conditions honestly, then design what comes next.

Limitations of the Model

NO EXPLANATORY FRAMEWORK CAPTURES THE FULL RANGE OF HUMAN BEHAVIOR. THE INVISIBLE FIELD MODEL IS NO EXCEPTION.

SCOPE AND APPLICATION

The model is strongest when analyzing recurrence under constraint. It is less effective when applied to singular, novel, or unusually high-deliberation decisions where reinforcement history and environmental pricing play a smaller role.

INFLUENCE VS. INEVITABILITY

This framework emphasizes environmental conditions, State, reinforcement gradients, and structural design. It describes patterned influence, not mechanical inevitability. It does not deny:

- Trait Variation / Individual differences.
- Cultural Difference / Socialized norms.
- Moral Responsibility / Agency and ethics.
- The Role of Chance / Unpredictability.

PRACTICALITY OVER COMPLETENESS

The model simplifies complex biological and social processes to keep the machinery legible. It is designed for practical intervention, not laboratory-level completeness.

CORE INTENT

The purpose of this model is illumination, not reduction. It is built to help the reader see recurring structures more clearly. By identifying the architecture of the Field, one can intervene more intelligently.

Endnotes

1. Herbert A. Simon, "A Behavioral Model of Rational Choice," The Quarterly Journal of Economics 69, no. 1 (1955): 99 - 118. doi: 10.2307/1884852.; Naomi I. Eisenberger, Matthew D. Lieberman, and Kipling D. Williams, "Does Rejection Hurt? An fMRI Study of Social Exclusion," Science 302, no. 5643 (2003): 290 - 292. doi: 10.1126/science.1089134.
2. Bruce S. McEwen, "Protective and damaging effects of stress mediators," New England Journal of Medicine 338, no. 3 (1998): 171 - 179.; Hans P. A. Van Dongen et al., "The cumulative cost of additional wakefulness: dose-response effects on neurobehavioral functions and sleep physiology from chronic sleep restriction and total sleep deprivation," Sleep 26, no. 2 (2003): 117 - 126.
3. William Samuelson and Richard Zeckhauser, "Status Quo Bias in Decision Making," Journal of Risk and Uncertainty 1, no. 1 (1988): 7 - 59. doi: 10.1007/BF00055564.; W. Brian Arthur, "Competing Technologies, Increasing Returns, and Lock-In by Historical Events," The Economic Journal 99, no. 394 (1989): 116 - 131. doi: 10.2307/2234208.
4. Lee Ross, "The Intuitive Psychologist and His Shortcomings: Distortions in the Attribution Process," in Advances in Experimental Social Psychology, vol. 10, ed. Leonard Berkowitz (New York: Academic Press, 1977), 173 - 220.; Anuj K. Shah, Sendhil Mullainathan, and Eldar Shafir, "Some Consequences of Having Too Little," Science 338, no. 6107 (2012): 682 - 685. doi: 10.1126/science.1222426.
5. Urie Bronfenbrenner, The Ecology of Human Development: Experiments by Nature and Design (Cambridge, MA: Harvard University Press, 1979).; Douglass C. North, Institutions, Institutional Change and Economic Performance (Cambridge: Cambridge University Press, 1990).
6. Robert Plomin and Denise Daniels, "Why Are Children in the Same Family so Different From One Another?" Behavioral and Brain Sciences 10, no. 1 (1987): 1 - 16. doi: 10.1017/S0140525X00055941.; Urie Bronfenbrenner, The Ecology of Human Development: Experiments by Nature and Design (Cambridge, MA: Harvard University Press, 1979).
7. W. Thomas Boyce and Bruce J. Ellis, "Biological Sensitivity to Context: I. An Evolutionary-Developmental Theory of the Origins and Functions of Stress Reactivity," Development and Psychopathology 17, no. 2 (2005): 271 - 301. doi: 10.1017/S0954579405050145.
8. W. Thomas Boyce and Bruce J. Ellis, "Biological Sensitivity to Context: I. An Evolutionary-Developmental Theory of the Origins and Functions of Stress Reactivity," Development and Psychopathology 17, no. 2 (2005): 271 - 301. doi: 10.1017/S0954579405050145.; Bruce S. McEwen and Eliot Stellar, "Stress and the Individual: Mechanisms Leading to Disease," Archives of Internal Medicine 153, no. 18 (1993): 2093 - 2101.
9. Vincent J. Felitti et al., "Relationship of Childhood Abuse and Household Dysfunction to Many of the Leading Causes of Death in Adults: The Adverse Childhood Experiences (ACE) Study," American Journal of Preventive Medicine 14, no. 4 (1998): 245 - 258. doi: 10.1016/S0749-3797(98)00017-8.; Bruce S. McEwen and Eliot Stellar, "Stress and the Individual: Mechanisms Leading to Disease," Archives of Internal Medicine 153, no. 18 (1993): 2093 - 2101.
10. Bruce S. McEwen and Eliot Stellar, "Stress and the Individual: Mechanisms Leading to Disease," Archives of Internal Medicine 153, no. 18 (1993): 2093 - 2101.; Vincent J. Felitti et al., "Relationship of Childhood Abuse and Household Dysfunction to Many of the Leading Causes of Death in Adults: The Adverse Childhood Experiences (ACE) Study," American Journal of Preventive Medicine 14, no. 4 (1998): 245 - 258. doi: 10.1016/S0749-3797(98)00017-8.
11. Robert A. Rescorla and Allan R. Wagner, "A Theory of Pavlovian Conditioning: Variations in the Effectiveness of Reinforcement and Nonreinforcement," in Classical Conditioning II: Current Research and Theory, ed. A. H. Black and W. F. Prokasy (New York: Appleton-Century-Crofts, 1972),

64 - 99.; Dylan G. Gee, "Caregiving influences on emotional learning and regulation: applying a sensitive period model," Current Opinion in Behavioral Sciences 36 (2020): 177 - 184. doi: 10.1016/j.cobeha.2020.11.003.

12. Albert Bandura, "Self-Efficacy: Toward a Unifying Theory of Behavioral Change," Psychological Review 84, no. 2 (1977): 191 - 215. doi: 10.1037/0033-295X.84.2.191.; Robert A. Rescorla and Allan R. Wagner, "A Theory of Pavlovian Conditioning: Variations in the Effectiveness of Reinforcement and Nonreinforcement," in Classical Conditioning II: Current Research and Theory, ed. A. H. Black and William F. Prokasy (New York: Appleton-Century-Crofts, 1972), 64 - 99.
13. John Bowlby, Attachment and Loss, Vol. 1: Attachment (New York: Basic Books, 1969).; Cindy Hazan and Phillip R. Shaver, "Romantic Love Conceptualized as an Attachment Process," Journal of Personality and Social Psychology 52, no. 3 (1987): 511 - 524. doi: 10.1037/0022-3514.52.3.511.
14. W. James Gauderman et al., "The Effect of Air Pollution on Lung Development from 10 to 18 Years of Age," New England Journal of Medicine 351, no. 11 (2004): 1057 - 1067. doi: 10.1056/NEJMoa040610.
15. Andy Clark, "Whatever Next? Predictive Brains, Situated Agents, and the Future of Cognitive Science," Behavioral and Brain Sciences 36, no. 3 (2013): 181 - 204. doi: 10.1017/S0140525X12000477.; Robert A. Rescorla and Allan R. Wagner, "A Theory of Pavlovian Conditioning: Variations in the Effectiveness of Reinforcement and Nonreinforcement," in Classical Conditioning II: Current Research and Theory, ed. A. H. Black and W. F. Prokasy (New York: Appleton-Century-Crofts, 1972), 64 - 99.
16. Andy Clark, "Whatever Next? Predictive Brains, Situated Agents, and the Future of Cognitive Science," Behavioral and Brain Sciences 36, no. 3 (2013): 181 - 204. doi: 10.1017/S0140525X12000477.; Richard E. Nisbett and Timothy D. Wilson, "Telling More Than We Can Know: Verbal Reports on Mental Processes," Psychological Review 84, no. 3 (1977): 231 - 259. doi: 10.1037/0033-295X.84.3.231.
17. Bruce S. McEwen, "Protective and damaging effects of stress mediators," New England Journal of Medicine 338, no. 3 (1998): 171 - 179.; Stevan E. Hobfoll, "Conservation of Resources: A New Attempt at Conceptualizing Stress," American Psychologist 44, no. 3 (1989): 513 - 524. doi: 10.1037/0003-066X.44.3.513.
18. Hans P. A. Van Dongen et al., "The cumulative cost of additional wakefulness: dose-response effects on neurobehavioral functions and sleep physiology from chronic sleep restriction and total sleep deprivation," Sleep 26, no. 2 (2003): 117 - 126.; Bruce S. McEwen and Eliot Stellar, "Stress and the Individual: Mechanisms Leading to Disease," Archives of Internal Medicine 153, no. 18 (1993): 2093 - 2101.
19. Peter M. Gollwitzer, "Implementation Intentions: Strong Effects of Simple Plans," American Psychologist 54, no. 7 (1999): 493 - 503. doi: 10.1037/0003-066X.54.7.493.; Richard H. Thaler and Shlomo Benartzi, "Save More Tomorrow™: Using Behavioral Economics to Increase Employee Saving," Journal of Political Economy 112, no. S1 (2004): S164 - S187. doi: 10.1086/380085.
20. Stevan E. Hobfoll, "Conservation of Resources: A New Attempt at Conceptualizing Stress," American Psychologist 44, no. 3 (1989): 513 - 524. doi: 10.1037/0003-066X.44.3.513.; Bruce S. McEwen and Eliot Stellar, "Stress and the Individual: Mechanisms Leading to Disease," Archives of Internal Medicine 153, no. 18 (1993): 2093 - 2101.
21. Terry E. Robinson and Kent C. Berridge, "The neural basis of drug craving: an incentive-sensitization theory of addiction," Brain Research Reviews 18, no. 3 (1993): 247 - 291.; Terry E. Robinson and Kent C. Berridge, "The Incentive Sensitization Theory of Addiction: Some Current Issues," Philosophical Transactions of the Royal Society B: Biological Sciences 363, no. 1507 (2008): 3137 - 3146.
22. June Price Tangney, "Situational Determinants of Shame and Guilt in Young Adulthood," Personality and Social Psychology Bulletin 18, no. 2 (1992): 199 - 206. doi: 10.1177/0146167292182011.; Janell L. Mensinger, Tracy L. Tylka, and Mary E. Calamari, "Mechanisms Underlying Weight Status and Healthcare Avoidance in Women: A Study of Weight Stigma, Body-Related Shame and Guilt, and Healthcare Stress," Body Image 25 (2018): 139 - 147. doi: 10.1016/j.bodyim.2018.03.001.
23. Paul Pierson, "Increasing Returns, Path Dependence, and the Study of Politics," American Political Science Review 94, no. 2 (2000): 251 - 267.; W. Brian Arthur, "Competing Technologies, Increasing Returns, and Lock-In by Historical Events," The Economic Journal 99, no. 394 (1989): 116 - 131.
24. Margaret Stroebe and Henk Schut, "The dual process model of coping with bereavement: rationale and description," Death Studies 23, no. 3 (1999): 197 - 224.; Laura L. Carstensen, Derek M. Isaacowitz, and

Susan T. Charles, "Taking Time Seriously: A Theory of Socioemotional Selectivity," American Psychologist 54, no. 3 (1999): 165 - 181.

25. W. Thomas Boyce and Bruce J. Ellis, "Biological Sensitivity to Context: I. An Evolutionary-Developmental Theory of the Origins and Functions of Stress Reactivity," Development and Psychopathology 17, no. 2 (2005): 271 - 301. doi: 10.1017/S0954579405050145.; Lawrence D. Frank, Peter O. Engelke, and Thomas L. Schmid, "Many Pathways from Land Use to Health: Associations between Neighborhood Walkability and Active Transportation, Body Mass Index, and Air Quality," Journal of the American Planning Association 72, no. 1 (2006): 75 - 87.

26. Robert J. Sampson, Great American City: Chicago and the Enduring Neighborhood Effect (Chicago: University of Chicago Press, 2012).; Raj Chetty et al., "Where Is the Land of Opportunity? The Geography of Intergenerational Mobility in the United States," The Quarterly Journal of Economics 129, no. 4 (2014): 1553 - 1623.

27. Stephen A. Stansfeld et al., "Aircraft and road traffic noise and children's cognition and health: a cross-national study," The Lancet 365, no. 9475 (2005): 1942 - 1949. doi: 10.1016/S0140-6736(05)67174-7.; Philippa Howden-Chapman et al., "Effect of insulating existing houses on health inequality: cluster randomised study in the community," BMJ 334, no. 7591 (2007): 460. doi: 10.1136/bmj.39070.573032.80.; Frank A. J. L. Scheer, Michael F. Hilton, Christos S. Mantzoros, and Steven A. Shea, "Adverse metabolic and cardiovascular consequences of circadian misalignment," Proceedings of the National Academy of Sciences 106, no. 11 (2009): 4453 - 4458. doi: 10.1073/pnas.0808180106.

28. United Nations, Department of Economic and Social Affairs, Population Division, World Urbanization Prospects 2025: Summary of Results (New York: United Nations, 2025).

29. U.S. Census Bureau, State Population Totals and Components of Change: 2020-2025 (Washington, DC: U.S. Census Bureau, January 2026); Annual Estimates of the Resident Population for the United States, Regions, States, District of Columbia and Puerto Rico: April 1, 2020 to July 1, 2025 (NST-EST2025-POP).

30. John W. Berry, Uichol Kim, Thomas Minde, and Doris Mok, "Comparative Studies of Acculturative Stress," International Migration Review 21, no. 3 (1987): 491 - 511.; Christine J. Yeh and Mayuko Inose, "International Students' Reported English Fluency, Social Support Satisfaction, and Social Connectedness as Predictors of Acculturative Stress," Counselling Psychology Quarterly 16, no. 1 (2003): 15 - 28. doi: 10.1080/0951507031000114058.; Jean Lee, Gary F. Koeske, and Esther Sales, "Social Support Buffering of Acculturative Stress: A Study of Mental Health Symptoms among Korean International Students," International Journal of Intercultural Relations 28, no. 5 (2004): 399 - 414. doi: 10.1016/j.ijintrel.2004.08.005.

31. Douglass C. North, Institutions, Institutional Change and Economic Performance (Cambridge: Cambridge University Press, 1990).; James C. Scott, Seeing Like a State: How Certain Schemes to Improve the Human Condition Have Failed (New Haven: Yale University Press, 1998).

32. Marc Wittmann, Jenny Dinich, Martha Merrow, and Till Roenneberg, "Social Jetlag: Misalignment of Biological and Social Time," Chronobiology International 23, nos. 1 - 2 (2006): 497 - 509. doi: 10.1080/07420520500545979.; John W. Berry, "Immigration, Acculturation, and Adaptation," Applied Psychology 46, no. 1 (1997): 5 - 34. doi: 10.1111/j.1464-0597.1997.tb01087.x.

33. Anandi Mani, Sendhil Mullainathan, Eldar Shafir, and Jiaying Zhao, "Poverty Impedes Cognitive Function," Science 341, no. 6149 (2013): 976 - 980. doi: 10.1126/science.1238041.; Anuj K. Shah, Sendhil Mullainathan, and Eldar Shafir, "Some Consequences of Having Too Little," Science 338, no. 6107 (2012): 682 - 685. doi: 10.1126/science.1222426.

34. Anandi Mani, Sendhil Mullainathan, Eldar Shafir, and Jiaying Zhao, "Poverty Impedes Cognitive Function," Science 341, no. 6149 (2013): 976 - 980. doi: 10.1126/science.1238041.; Stevan E. Hobfoll, "Conservation of Resources: A New Attempt at Conceptualizing Stress," American Psychologist 44, no. 3 (1989): 513 - 524. doi: 10.1037/0003-066X.44.3.513.

35. Anuj K. Shah, Sendhil Mullainathan, and Eldar Shafir, "Some Consequences of Having Too Little," Science 338, no. 6107 (2012): 682 - 685.; Anandi Mani, Sendhil Mullainathan, Eldar Shafir, and Jiaying Zhao, "Poverty Impedes Cognitive Function," Science 341, no. 6149 (2013): 976 - 980. doi: 10.1126/science.1238041.

36. Eytan Bakshy, Solomon Messing, and Lada A. Adamic, "Exposure to Ideologically Diverse News and Opinion on Facebook," Science 348, no. 6239 (2015): 1130 - 1132. doi: 10.1126/science.aaa1160.; Adam D. I. Kramer, Jamie E. Guillory, and Jeffrey T. Hancock, "Experimental evidence of massive-scale emotional contagion through social networks," Proceedings of the National Academy of Sciences 111, no. 24 (2014): 8788 - 8790. doi: 10.1073/pnas.1320040111.
37. Paul E. Meehl, Clinical Versus Statistical Prediction: A Theoretical Analysis and a Review of the Evidence (Minneapolis: University of Minnesota Press, 1954).; Robyn M. Dawes, David Faust, and Paul E. Meehl, "Clinical Versus Actuarial Judgment," Science 243, no. 4899 (1989): 1668 - 1674. doi: 10.1126/science.2648573.
38. Eytan Bakshy, Solomon Messing, and Lada A. Adamic, "Exposure to Ideologically Diverse News and Opinion on Facebook," Science 348, no. 6239 (2015): 1130 - 1132. doi: 10.1126/science.aaa1160.; Adam D. I. Kramer, Jamie E. Guillory, and Jeffrey T. Hancock, "Experimental Evidence of Massive-Scale Emotional Contagion through Social Networks," Proceedings of the National Academy of Sciences 111, no. 24 (2014): 8788 - 8790. doi: 10.1073/pnas.1320040111.
39. Herbert A. Simon, "A Behavioral Model of Rational Choice," The Quarterly Journal of Economics 69, no. 1 (1955): 99 - 118.; Amos Tversky and Daniel Kahneman, "Judgment under Uncertainty: Heuristics and Biases," Science 185, no. 4157 (1974): 1124 - 1131.
40. Mark Freeston et al., "Why do people worry?" Personality and Individual Differences 17, no. 6 (1994): 791 - 802.; Michel J. Dugas et al., "Generalized anxiety disorder: A preliminary test of a conceptual model," Behaviour Research and Therapy 36, no. 2 (1998): 215 - 226.
41. Douglass C. North, Institutions, Institutional Change and Economic Performance (Cambridge: Cambridge University Press, 1990).; Robert A. Karasek Jr., "Job Demands, Job Decision Latitude, and Mental Strain: Implications for Job Redesign," Administrative Science Quarterly 24, no. 2 (1979): 285 - 308.
42. James C. Scott, Seeing Like a State: How Certain Schemes to Improve the Human Condition Have Failed (New Haven: Yale University Press, 1998).; W. Brian Arthur, "Competing Technologies, Increasing Returns, and Lock-In by Historical Events," The Economic Journal 99, no. 394 (1989): 116 - 131.
43. Joseph E. Stiglitz and Andrew Weiss, "Credit Rationing in Markets with Imperfect Information," American Economic Review 71, no. 3 (1981): 393 - 410.; Douglass C. North, Institutions, Institutional Change and Economic Performance (Cambridge: Cambridge University Press, 1990).
44. Donald Moynihan, Pamela Herd, and Hope Harvey, "Administrative Burden: Learning, Psychological, and Compliance Costs in Citizen-State Interactions," Journal of Public Administration Research and Theory 25, no. 1 (2015): 43 - 69. doi: 10.1093/jopart/muu009.; Tom R. Tyler, "Procedural Justice, Legitimacy, and the Effective Rule of Law," Crime and Justice 30 (2003): 283 - 357.
45. Robert A. Karasek Jr., "Job Demands, Job Decision Latitude, and Mental Strain: Implications for Job Redesign," Administrative Science Quarterly 24, no. 2 (1979): 285 - 308.
46. Arlie Russell Hochschild, The Managed Heart: Commercialization of Human Feeling (Berkeley: University of California Press, 1983).
47. Hans P. A. Van Dongen et al., "The cumulative cost of additional wakefulness: dose-response effects on neurobehavioral functions and sleep physiology from chronic sleep restriction and total sleep deprivation," Sleep 26, no. 2 (2003): 117 - 126.; Laura K. Barger et al., "Extended work shifts and the risk of motor vehicle crashes among interns," PLoS Medicine 3, no. 12 (2006): e487.
48. Max Weber, "Politics as a Vocation" (1919), in From Max Weber: Essays in Sociology, ed. H. H. Gerth and C. Wright Mills (New York: Oxford University Press, 1946).; Richard M. Ryan and Edward L. Deci, "Self-Determination Theory and the Facilitation of Intrinsic Motivation, Social Development, and Well-Being," American Psychologist 55, no. 1 (2000): 68 - 78. doi: 10.1037/0003-066X.55.1.68.
49. Max Weber, "Politics as a Vocation" (1919), in From Max Weber: Essays in Sociology, ed. H. H. Gerth and C. Wright Mills (New York: Oxford University Press, 1946).; H. L. A. Hart, The Concept of Law, 3rd ed. (Oxford: Oxford University Press, 2012).
50. Tom R. Tyler, "Procedural Justice, Legitimacy, and the Effective Rule of Law," Crime and Justice 30 (2003): 283 - 357.
51. Donald Moynihan, Pamela Herd, and Hope Harvey, "Administrative Burden: Learning, Psychological, and Compliance Costs in Citizen-State Interactions," Journal of Public Administration Research and Theory 25, no. 1 (2015): 43 - 69. doi: 10.1093/jopart/muu009.

52. Tom R. Tyler, Why People Obey the Law (New Haven: Yale University Press, 1990).; Amanda Sheely and Shawn M. Kneipp, "The Effects of Collateral Consequences of Criminal Involvement on Employment, Use of Temporary Assistance for Needy Families, and Health," Women & Health 55, no. 5 (2015): 548 - 565. doi: 10.1080/03630242.2015.1022814.
53. Murray Bowen, Family Therapy in Clinical Practice (New York: Jason Aronson, 1978).; Salvador Minuchin, Families and Family Therapy (Cambridge, MA: Harvard University Press, 1974).
54. Murray Bowen, Family Therapy in Clinical Practice (New York: Jason Aronson, 1978).; Albert Bandura, "Self-Efficacy: Toward a Unifying Theory of Behavioral Change," Psychological Review 84, no. 2 (1977): 191 - 215. doi: 10.1037/0033-295X.84.2.191.
55. John M. Gottman and Robert W. Levenson, "Marital processes predictive of later dissolution: Behavior, physiology, and health," Journal of Personality and Social Psychology 63, no. 2 (1992): 221 - 233. doi: 10.1037/0022-3514.63.2.221.; James A. Coan and David A. Sbarra, "Social Baseline Theory: The Social Regulation of Risk and Effort," Current Opinion in Psychology 1 (2015): 87 - 91.
56. James A. Coan, Hillary S. Schaefer, and Richard J. Davidson, "Lending a hand: Social regulation of the neural response to threat," Psychological Science 17, no. 12 (2006): 1032 - 1039.; John M. Gottman and Robert W. Levenson, "Marital processes predictive of later dissolution: Behavior, physiology, and health," Journal of Personality and Social Psychology 63, no. 2 (1992): 221 - 233. doi: 10.1037/0022-3514.63.2.221.
57. John Bowlby, Attachment and Loss, Vol. 1: Attachment (New York: Basic Books, 1969).; Mary D. S. Ainsworth et al., Patterns of Attachment: A Psychological Study of the Strange Situation (Hillsdale, NJ: Lawrence Erlbaum, 1978).
58. Cindy Hazan and Phillip R. Shaver, "Romantic Love Conceptualized as an Attachment Process," Journal of Personality and Social Psychology 52, no. 3 (1987): 511 - 524. doi: 10.1037/0022-3514.52.3.511.; John M. Gottman and Robert W. Levenson, "Marital processes predictive of later dissolution: Behavior, physiology, and health," Journal of Personality and Social Psychology 63, no. 2 (1992): 221 - 233. doi: 10.1037/0022-3514.63.2.221.
59. James A. Coan, Hillary S. Schaefer, and Richard J. Davidson, "Lending a Hand: Social Regulation of the Neural Response to Threat," Psychological Science 17, no. 12 (2006): 1032 - 1039. doi: 10.1111/j.1467-9280.2006.01832.x.
60. John Bowlby, Attachment and Loss, Vol. 1: Attachment (New York: Basic Books, 1969).; Cindy Hazan and Phillip R. Shaver, "Romantic Love Conceptualized as an Attachment Process," Journal of Personality and Social Psychology 52, no. 3 (1987): 511 - 524. doi: 10.1037/0022-3514.52.3.511.
61. Terry E. Robinson and Kent C. Berridge, "The neural basis of drug craving: an incentive-sensitization theory of addiction," Brain Research Reviews 18, no. 3 (1993): 247 - 291.; Terry E. Robinson and Kent C. Berridge, "The Incentive Sensitization Theory of Addiction: Some Current Issues," Philosophical Transactions of the Royal Society B: Biological Sciences 363, no. 1507 (2008): 3137 - 3146.
62. Jennifer Katz and Vanessa Tirone, "Going Along With It: Sexually Coercive Partner Behavior Predicts Dating Women's Compliance With Unwanted Sex," Violence Against Women 16, no. 7 (2010): 730 - 742. doi: 10.1177/1077801210374867.
63. John Bancroft and Erick Janssen, "The Dual Control Model of Male Sexual Response: A Theoretical Approach to Centrally Mediated Erectile Dysfunction," Neuroscience & Biobehavioral Reviews 24, no. 5 (2000): 571 - 579. doi: 10.1016/S0149-7634(00)00024-5.; Cindy Hazan and Phillip R. Shaver, "Romantic Love Conceptualized as an Attachment Process," Journal of Personality and Social Psychology 52, no. 3 (1987): 511 - 524. doi: 10.1037/0022-3514.52.3.511.
64. Ernest Becker, The Denial of Death (New York: Free Press, 1973).; Abram Rosenblatt, Jeff Greenberg, Sheldon Solomon, Tom Pyszczynski, and Deborah Lyon, "Evidence for Terror Management Theory: I. The Effects of Mortality Salience on Reactions to Those Who Violate or Uphold Cultural Values," Journal of Personality and Social Psychology 57, no. 4 (1989): 681 - 690. doi: 10.1037/0022-3514.57.4.681.
65. Ernest Becker, The Denial of Death (New York: Free Press, 1973).; Jeff Greenberg, Tom Pyszczynski, and Sheldon Solomon, "The Causes and Consequences of a Need for Self-Esteem: A Terror Management Theory," in Public Self and Private Self, ed. Roy F. Baumeister (New York: Springer, 1986), 189 - 212.
66. Laura L. Carstensen, Derek M. Isaacowitz, and Susan T. Charles, "Taking Time Seriously: A Theory of Socioemotional Selectivity," American Psychologist 54, no. 3 (1999): 165 - 181.; Jeff Greenberg, Tom

Pyszczynski, and Sheldon Solomon, "The Causes and Consequences of a Need for Self-Esteem: A Terror Management Theory," in Public Self and Private Self, ed. Roy F. Baumeister (New York: Springer, 1986), 189 - 212.

67. Laura L. Carstensen, Derek M. Isaacowitz, and Susan T. Charles, "Taking Time Seriously: A Theory of Socioemotional Selectivity," American Psychologist 54, no. 3 (1999): 165 - 181.; Abram Rosenblatt, Jeff Greenberg, Sheldon Solomon, Tom Pyszczynski, and Deborah Lyon, "Evidence for Terror Management Theory: I. The Effects of Mortality Salience on Reactions to Those Who Violate or Uphold Cultural Values," Journal of Personality and Social Psychology 57, no. 4 (1989): 681 - 690. doi: 10.1037/0022-3514.57.4.681.
68. Laura L. Carstensen, Derek M. Isaacowitz, and Susan T. Charles, "Taking Time Seriously: A Theory of Socioemotional Selectivity," American Psychologist 54, no. 3 (1999): 165 - 181.
69. Richard E. Nisbett and Timothy D. Wilson, "Telling More Than We Can Know: Verbal Reports on Mental Processes," Psychological Review 84, no. 3 (1977): 231 - 259. doi: 10.1037/0033-295X.84.3.231.
70. Robert A. Rescorla and Allan R. Wagner, "A Theory of Pavlovian Conditioning: Variations in the Effectiveness of Reinforcement and Nonreinforcement," in Classical Conditioning II: Current Research and Theory, ed. A. H. Black and W. F. Prokasy (New York: Appleton-Century-Crofts, 1972), 64 - 99.; Dylan G. Gee, "Caregiving influences on emotional learning and regulation: applying a sensitive period model," Current Opinion in Behavioral Sciences 36 (2020): 177 - 184. doi: 10.1016/j.cobeha.2020.11.003.
71. Robert A. Rescorla and Allan R. Wagner, "A Theory of Pavlovian Conditioning: Variations in the Effectiveness of Reinforcement and Nonreinforcement," in Classical Conditioning II: Current Research and Theory, ed. A. H. Black and W. F. Prokasy (New York: Appleton-Century-Crofts, 1972), 64 - 99.; Albert Bandura, "Self-Efficacy: Toward a Unifying Theory of Behavioral Change," Psychological Review 84, no. 2 (1977): 191 - 215. doi: 10.1037/0033-295X.84.2.191.
72. Peter M. Gollwitzer, "Implementation Intentions: Strong Effects of Simple Plans," American Psychologist 54, no. 7 (1999): 493 - 503. doi: 10.1037/0003-066X.54.7.493.; Robert A. Rescorla and Allan R. Wagner, "A Theory of Pavlovian Conditioning: Variations in the Effectiveness of Reinforcement and Nonreinforcement," in Classical Conditioning II: Current Research and Theory, ed. A. H. Black and W. F. Prokasy (New York: Appleton-Century-Crofts, 1972), 64 - 99.
73. Amartya Sen, Development as Freedom (Oxford: Oxford University Press, 1999).; Martha C. Nussbaum, Women and Human Development: The Capabilities Approach (Cambridge: Cambridge University Press, 2000).
74. Terry E. Robinson and Kent C. Berridge, "The Neural Basis of Drug Craving: An Incentive-Sensitization Theory of Addiction," Brain Research Reviews 18, no. 3 (1993): 247 - 291.; Anuj K. Shah, Sendhil Mullainathan, and Eldar Shafir, "Some Consequences of Having Too Little," Science 338, no. 6107 (2012): 682 - 685. doi: 10.1126/science.1222426.
75. Stevan E. Hobfoll, "Conservation of Resources: A New Attempt at Conceptualizing Stress," American Psychologist 44, no. 3 (1989): 513 - 524. doi: 10.1037/0003-066X.44.3.513.; Hans P. A. Van Dongen et al., "The cumulative cost of additional wakefulness: dose-response effects on neurobehavioral functions and sleep physiology from chronic sleep restriction and total sleep deprivation," Sleep 26, no. 2 (2003): 117 - 126.
76. Hans P. A. Van Dongen et al., "The cumulative cost of additional wakefulness: dose-response effects on neurobehavioral functions and sleep physiology from chronic sleep restriction and total sleep deprivation," Sleep 26, no. 2 (2003): 117 - 126.; Stevan E. Hobfoll, "Conservation of Resources: A New Attempt at Conceptualizing Stress," American Psychologist 44, no. 3 (1989): 513 - 524. doi: 10.1037/0003-066X.44.3.513.
77. Peter M. Gollwitzer, "Implementation Intentions: Strong Effects of Simple Plans," American Psychologist 54, no. 7 (1999): 493 - 503. doi: 10.1037/0003-066X.54.7.493.; Albert Bandura, "Self-Efficacy: Toward a Unifying Theory of Behavioral Change," Psychological Review 84, no. 2 (1977): 191 - 215. doi: 10.1037/0033-295X.84.2.191.
78. Phillippa Lally, Cornelia H. M. van Jaarsveld, Henry W. W. Potts, and Jane Wardle, "How Are Habits Formed? Modelling Habit Formation in the Real World," European Journal of Social Psychology 40, no. 6 (2010): 998 - 1009. doi: 10.1002/ejsp.674.; Hans P. A. Van Dongen et al., "The cumulative cost of

additional wakefulness: dose-response effects on neurobehavioral functions and sleep physiology from chronic sleep restriction and total sleep deprivation," Sleep 26, no. 2 (2003): 117 - 126.

79. Donella H. Meadows, Thinking in Systems: A Primer (White River Junction, VT: Chelsea Green Publishing, 2008).; Richard E. Nisbett and Timothy D. Wilson, "Telling More Than We Can Know: Verbal Reports on Mental Processes," Psychological Review 84, no. 3 (1977): 231 - 259. doi: 10.1037/0033-295X.84.3.231.
80. Peter M. Gollwitzer, "Implementation Intentions: Strong Effects of Simple Plans," American Psychologist 54, no. 7 (1999): 493 - 503. doi: 10.1037/0003-066X.54.7.493.; Phillippa Lally, Cornelia H. M. van Jaarsveld, Henry W. W. Potts, and Jane Wardle, "How Are Habits Formed? Modelling Habit Formation in the Real World," European Journal of Social Psychology 40, no. 6 (2010): 998 - 1009. doi: 10.1002/ejsp.674.
81. Carlos Blanco et al., "Testing the drug substitution switching-addictions hypothesis: A prospective study in a nationally representative sample," JAMA Psychiatry 71, no. 11 (2014): 1246 - 1253. doi: 10.1001/jamapsychiatry.2014.1206.; Terry E. Robinson and Kent C. Berridge, "The Incentive Sensitization Theory of Addiction: Some Current Issues," Philosophical Transactions of the Royal Society B: Biological Sciences 363, no. 1507 (2008): 3137 - 3146.
82. Albert Bandura, "Self-Efficacy: Toward a Unifying Theory of Behavioral Change," Psychological Review 84, no. 2 (1977): 191 - 215. doi: 10.1037/0033-295X.84.2.191.; Stevan E. Hobfoll, "Conservation of Resources: A New Attempt at Conceptualizing Stress," American Psychologist 44, no. 3 (1989): 513 - 524. doi: 10.1037/0003-066X.44.3.513.
83. Amartya Sen, Development as Freedom (Oxford: Oxford University Press, 1999).; Martha C. Nussbaum, Women and Human Development: The Capabilities Approach (Cambridge: Cambridge University Press, 2000).
84. Amartya Sen, Development as Freedom (Oxford: Oxford University Press, 1999).; Martha C. Nussbaum, Women and Human Development: The Capabilities Approach (Cambridge: Cambridge University Press, 2000).
85. Stevan E. Hobfoll, "Conservation of Resources: A New Attempt at Conceptualizing Stress," American Psychologist 44, no. 3 (1989): 513 - 524. doi: 10.1037/0003-066X.44.3.513.; Bruce S. McEwen and Eliot Stellar, "Stress and the Individual: Mechanisms Leading to Disease," Archives of Internal Medicine 153, no. 18 (1993): 2093 - 2101.
86. Martha C. Nussbaum, Women and Human Development: The Capabilities Approach (Cambridge: Cambridge University Press, 2000).; Stevan E. Hobfoll, "Conservation of Resources: A New Attempt at Conceptualizing Stress," American Psychologist 44, no. 3 (1989): 513 - 524. doi: 10.1037/0003-066X.44.3.513.
87. Martha C. Nussbaum, Women and Human Development: The Capabilities Approach (Cambridge: Cambridge University Press, 2000).; Raj Chetty et al., "Where Is the Land of Opportunity? The Geography of Intergenerational Mobility in the United States," The Quarterly Journal of Economics 129, no. 4 (2014): 1553 - 1623.
88. Bruce S. McEwen and Eliot Stellar, "Stress and the Individual: Mechanisms Leading to Disease," Archives of Internal Medicine 153, no. 18 (1993): 2093 - 2101.; James A. Coan and David A. Sbarra, "Social Baseline Theory: The Social Regulation of Risk and Effort," Current Opinion in Psychology 1 (2015): 87 - 91.
89. Douglass C. North, Institutions, Institutional Change and Economic Performance (Cambridge: Cambridge University Press, 1990).; Albert Bandura, "Self-Efficacy: Toward a Unifying Theory of Behavioral Change," Psychological Review 84, no. 2 (1977): 191 - 215. doi: 10.1037/0033-295X.84.2.191.
90. Albert Bandura, "Self-Efficacy: Toward a Unifying Theory of Behavioral Change," Psychological Review 84, no. 2 (1977): 191 - 215. doi: 10.1037/0033-295X.84.2.191.; Urie Bronfenbrenner, The Ecology of Human Development: Experiments by Nature and Design (Cambridge, MA: Harvard University Press, 1979).
91. J. R. Norris, Markov Chains (Cambridge: Cambridge University Press, 1998).; Albert Bandura, "Self-Efficacy: Toward a Unifying Theory of Behavioral Change," Psychological Review 84, no. 2 (1977): 191 - 215. doi: 10.1037/0033-295X.84.2.191.
92. Robert A. Rescorla and Allan R. Wagner, "A Theory of Pavlovian Conditioning: Variations in the Effectiveness of Reinforcement and Nonreinforcement," in Classical Conditioning II: Current

Research and Theory, ed. A. H. Black and W. F. Prokasy (New York: Appleton-Century-Crofts, 1972), 64 - 99.; Albert Bandura, "Self-Efficacy: Toward a Unifying Theory of Behavioral Change," Psychological Review 84, no. 2 (1977): 191 - 215. doi: 10.1037/0033-295X.84.2.191.

93. Phillippa Lally, Cornelia H. M. van Jaarsveld, Henry W. W. Potts, and Jane Wardle, "How Are Habits Formed? Modelling Habit Formation in the Real World," European Journal of Social Psychology 40, no. 6 (2010): 998 - 1009. doi: 10.1002/ejsp.674.; Richard H. Thaler and Shlomo Benartzi, "Save More Tomorrow™: Using Behavioral Economics to Increase Employee Saving," Journal of Political Economy 112, no. S1 (2004): S164 - S187. doi: 10.1086/380085.

94. Robert A. Rescorla and Allan R. Wagner, "A Theory of Pavlovian Conditioning: Variations in the Effectiveness of Reinforcement and Nonreinforcement," in Classical Conditioning II: Current Research and Theory, ed. A. H. Black and W. F. Prokasy (New York: Appleton-Century-Crofts, 1972), 64 - 99.; Albert Bandura, "Self-Efficacy: Toward a Unifying Theory of Behavioral Change," Psychological Review 84, no. 2 (1977): 191 - 215. doi: 10.1037/0033-295X.84.2.191.

95. Phillippa Lally, Cornelia H. M. van Jaarsveld, Henry W. W. Potts, and Jane Wardle, "How Are Habits Formed? Modelling Habit Formation in the Real World," European Journal of Social Psychology 40, no. 6 (2010): 998 - 1009. doi: 10.1002/ejsp.674.; Albert Bandura, "Self-Efficacy: Toward a Unifying Theory of Behavioral Change," Psychological Review 84, no. 2 (1977): 191 - 215. doi: 10.1037/0033-295X.84.2.191.

96. Urie Bronfenbrenner, The Ecology of Human Development: Experiments by Nature and Design (Cambridge, MA: Harvard University Press, 1979).; Albert Bandura, "Self-Efficacy: Toward a Unifying Theory of Behavioral Change," Psychological Review 84, no. 2 (1977): 191 - 215. doi: 10.1037/0033-295X.84.2.191.

97. Vincent J. Felitti et al., "Relationship of Childhood Abuse and Household Dysfunction to Many of the Leading Causes of Death in Adults: The Adverse Childhood Experiences (ACE) Study," American Journal of Preventive Medicine 14, no. 4 (1998): 245 - 258. doi: 10.1016/S0749-3797(98)00017-8.; Bruce S. McEwen and Eliot Stellar, "Stress and the Individual: Mechanisms Leading to Disease," Archives of Internal Medicine 153, no. 18 (1993): 2093 - 2101.

98. Albert Bandura, "Self-Efficacy: Toward a Unifying Theory of Behavioral Change," Psychological Review 84, no. 2 (1977): 191 - 215. doi: 10.1037/0033-295X.84.2.191.; John Bowlby, Attachment and Loss, Vol. 1: Attachment (New York: Basic Books, 1969).

99. Albert Bandura, "Self-Efficacy: Toward a Unifying Theory of Behavioral Change," Psychological Review 84, no. 2 (1977): 191 - 215. doi: 10.1037/0033-295X.84.2.191.; Urie Bronfenbrenner, The Ecology of Human Development: Experiments by Nature and Design (Cambridge, MA: Harvard University Press, 1979).

100. Albert Bandura, "Self-Efficacy: Toward a Unifying Theory of Behavioral Change," Psychological Review 84, no. 2 (1977): 191 - 215. doi: 10.1037/0033-295X.84.2.191.; Stevan E. Hobfoll, "Conservation of Resources: A New Attempt at Conceptualizing Stress," American Psychologist 44, no. 3 (1989): 513 - 524. doi: 10.1037/0003-066X.44.3.513.

101. Richard H. Thaler and Shlomo Benartzi, "Save More Tomorrow™: Using Behavioral Economics to Increase Employee Saving," Journal of Political Economy 112, no. S1 (2004): S164 - S187. doi: 10.1086/380085.; Stevan E. Hobfoll, "Conservation of Resources: A New Attempt at Conceptualizing Stress," American Psychologist 44, no. 3 (1989): 513 - 524. doi: 10.1037/0003-066X.44.3.513.

102. Donald Moynihan, Pamela Herd, and Hope Harvey, "Administrative Burden: Learning, Psychological, and Compliance Costs in Citizen-State Interactions," Journal of Public Administration Research and Theory 25, no. 1 (2015): 43 - 69. doi: 10.1093/jopart/muu009.; Lawrence D. Frank, Thomas L. Schmid, James F. Sallis, James Chapman, and Brian E. Saelens, "Linking Objectively Measured Physical Activity with Objectively Measured Urban Form: Findings from SMARTRAQ," American Journal of Preventive Medicine 28, no. 2 Suppl 2 (2005): 117 - 125. doi: 10.1016/j.amepre.2004.11.001.; Tom R. Tyler, Why People Obey the Law (New Haven: Yale University Press, 1990).

103. Douglass C. North, Institutions, Institutional Change and Economic Performance (Cambridge: Cambridge University Press, 1990).; Robert A. Karasek Jr., "Job Demands, Job Decision Latitude, and Mental Strain: Implications for Job Redesign," Administrative Science Quarterly 24, no. 2 (1979): 285 - 308.

104. Amartya Sen, Development as Freedom (Oxford: Oxford University Press, 1999).; Albert Bandura, "Self-Efficacy: Toward a Unifying Theory of Behavioral Change," Psychological Review 84, no. 2 (1977): 191 - 215. doi: 10.1037/0033-295X.84.2.191.
105. Phillippa Lally, Cornelia H. M. van Jaarsveld, Henry W. W. Potts, and Jane Wardle, "How Are Habits Formed? Modelling Habit Formation in the Real World," European Journal of Social Psychology 40, no. 6 (2010): 998 - 1009. doi: 10.1002/ejsp.674.; Richard H. Thaler and Shlomo Benartzi, "Save More Tomorrow™: Using Behavioral Economics to Increase Employee Saving," Journal of Political Economy 112, no. S1 (2004): S164 - S187. doi: 10.1086/380085.
106. Albert Bandura, "Self-Efficacy: Toward a Unifying Theory of Behavioral Change," Psychological Review 84, no. 2 (1977): 191 - 215. doi: 10.1037/0033-295X.84.2.191.; Phillippa Lally, Cornelia H. M. van Jaarsveld, Henry W. W. Potts, and Jane Wardle, "How Are Habits Formed? Modelling Habit Formation in the Real World," European Journal of Social Psychology 40, no. 6 (2010): 998 - 1009. doi: 10.1002/ejsp.674.
107. Albert Bandura, "Self-Efficacy: Toward a Unifying Theory of Behavioral Change," Psychological Review 84, no. 2 (1977): 191 - 215. doi: 10.1037/0033-295X.84.2.191.; John Bowlby, Attachment and Loss, Vol. 1: Attachment (New York: Basic Books, 1969).
108. Albert Bandura, "Self-Efficacy: Toward a Unifying Theory of Behavioral Change," Psychological Review 84, no. 2 (1977): 191 - 215. doi: 10.1037/0033-295X.84.2.191.; Stevan E. Hobfoll, "Conservation of Resources: A New Attempt at Conceptualizing Stress," American Psychologist 44, no. 3 (1989): 513 - 524. doi: 10.1037/0003-066X.44.3.513.
109. James A. Coan, Hillary S. Schaefer, and Richard J. Davidson, "Lending a Hand: Social Regulation of the Neural Response to Threat," Psychological Science 17, no. 12 (2006): 1032 - 1039. doi: 10.1111/j.1467-9280.2006.01832.x.; Phillippa Lally, Cornelia H. M. van Jaarsveld, Henry W. W. Potts, and Jane Wardle, "How Are Habits Formed? Modelling Habit Formation in the Real World," European Journal of Social Psychology 40, no. 6 (2010): 998 - 1009. doi: 10.1002/ejsp.674.
110. Donella H. Meadows, Thinking in Systems: A Primer (White River Junction, VT: Chelsea Green Publishing, 2008).; Albert Bandura, "Self-Efficacy: Toward a Unifying Theory of Behavioral Change," Psychological Review 84, no. 2 (1977): 191 - 215. doi: 10.1037/0033-295X.84.2.191.
111. Urie Bronfenbrenner, The Ecology of Human Development: Experiments by Nature and Design (Cambridge, MA: Harvard University Press, 1979).; Douglass C. North, Institutions, Institutional Change and Economic Performance (Cambridge: Cambridge University Press, 1990).; Jack P. Shonkoff et al., "The Lifelong Effects of Early Childhood Adversity and Toxic Stress," Pediatrics 129, no. 1 (2012): e232 - e246. doi: 10.1542/peds.2011-2663.
112. Amartya Sen, Development as Freedom (Oxford: Oxford University Press, 1999).; Douglass C. North, Institutions, Institutional Change and Economic Performance (Cambridge: Cambridge University Press, 1990).
113. Phillippa Lally, Cornelia H. M. van Jaarsveld, Henry W. W. Potts, and Jane Wardle, "How Are Habits Formed? Modelling Habit Formation in the Real World," European Journal of Social Psychology 40, no. 6 (2010): 998 - 1009. doi: 10.1002/ejsp.674.; Stevan E. Hobfoll, "Conservation of Resources: A New Attempt at Conceptualizing Stress," American Psychologist 44, no. 3 (1989): 513 - 524. doi: 10.1037/0003-066X.44.3.513.
114. Urie Bronfenbrenner, The Ecology of Human Development: Experiments by Nature and Design (Cambridge, MA: Harvard University Press, 1979).; Douglass C. North, Institutions, Institutional Change and Economic Performance (Cambridge: Cambridge University Press, 1990).; Stevan E. Hobfoll, "Conservation of Resources: A New Attempt at Conceptualizing Stress," American Psychologist 44, no. 3 (1989): 513 - 524. doi: 10.1037/0003-066X.44.3.513.
115. Urie Bronfenbrenner, The Ecology of Human Development: Experiments by Nature and Design (Cambridge, MA: Harvard University Press, 1979).; Douglass C. North, Institutions, Institutional Change and Economic Performance (Cambridge: Cambridge University Press, 1990).
116. Amartya Sen, Development as Freedom (Oxford: Oxford University Press, 1999).; Stevan E. Hobfoll, "Conservation of Resources: A New Attempt at Conceptualizing Stress," American Psychologist 44, no. 3 (1989): 513 - 524. doi: 10.1037/0003-066X.44.3.513.
117. Lee Ross, "The Intuitive Psychologist and His Shortcomings: Distortions in the Attribution Process," in Advances in Experimental Social Psychology, vol. 10, ed. Leonard Berkowitz (New York: Academic

Press, 1977), 173 - 220.; Anuj K. Shah, Sendhil Mullainathan, and Eldar Shafir, "Some Consequences of Having Too Little," Science 338, no. 6107 (2012): 682 - 685. doi: 10.1126/science.1222426.

118. Amartya Sen, Development as Freedom (Oxford: Oxford University Press, 1999).; Robert J. Sampson, Great American City: Chicago and the Enduring Neighborhood Effect (Chicago: University of Chicago Press, 2012).

119. Bruce S. McEwen and Eliot Stellar, "Stress and the Individual: Mechanisms Leading to Disease," Archives of Internal Medicine 153, no. 18 (1993): 2093 - 2101.; Stevan E. Hobfoll, "Conservation of Resources: A New Attempt at Conceptualizing Stress," American Psychologist 44, no. 3 (1989): 513 - 524. doi: 10.1037/0003-066X.44.3.513.

120. Peter M. Gollwitzer, "Implementation Intentions: Strong Effects of Simple Plans," American Psychologist 54, no. 7 (1999): 493 - 503. doi: 10.1037/0003-066X.54.7.493.; Albert Bandura, "Self-Efficacy: Toward a Unifying Theory of Behavioral Change," Psychological Review 84, no. 2 (1977): 191 - 215. doi: 10.1037/0033-295X.84.2.191.

121. Raj Chetty et al., "Where Is the Land of Opportunity? The Geography of Intergenerational Mobility in the United States," The Quarterly Journal of Economics 129, no. 4 (2014): 1553 - 1623.; Robert J. Sampson, Great American City: Chicago and the Enduring Neighborhood Effect (Chicago: University of Chicago Press, 2012).

122. Urie Bronfenbrenner, The Ecology of Human Development: Experiments by Nature and Design (Cambridge, MA: Harvard University Press, 1979).; Douglass C. North, Institutions, Institutional Change and Economic Performance (Cambridge: Cambridge University Press, 1990).; Stevan E. Hobfoll, "Conservation of Resources: A New Attempt at Conceptualizing Stress," American Psychologist 44, no. 3 (1989): 513 - 524. doi: 10.1037/0003-066X.44.3.513.

123. Anandi Mani, Sendhil Mullainathan, Eldar Shafir, and Jiaying Zhao, "Poverty Impedes Cognitive Function," Science 341, no. 6149 (2013): 976 - 980. doi: 10.1126/science.1238041.; Herbert A. Simon, "A Behavioral Model of Rational Choice," The Quarterly Journal of Economics 69, no. 1 (1955): 99 - 118.

124. Amartya Sen, Development as Freedom (Oxford: Oxford University Press, 1999).; Martha C. Nussbaum, Women and Human Development: The Capabilities Approach (Cambridge: Cambridge University Press, 2000).

125. Peter M. Gollwitzer, "Implementation Intentions: Strong Effects of Simple Plans," American Psychologist 54, no. 7 (1999): 493 - 503. doi: 10.1037/0003-066X.54.7.493.; Phillippa Lally, Cornelia H. M. van Jaarsveld, Henry W. W. Potts, and Jane Wardle, "How Are Habits Formed? Modelling Habit Formation in the Real World," European Journal of Social Psychology 40, no. 6 (2010): 998 - 1009. doi: 10.1002/ejsp.674.; Albert Bandura, "Self-Efficacy: Toward a Unifying Theory of Behavioral Change," Psychological Review 84, no. 2 (1977): 191 - 215. doi: 10.1037/0033-295X.84.2.191.

126. Amartya Sen, Development as Freedom (Oxford: Oxford University Press, 1999).; Douglass C. North, Institutions, Institutional Change and Economic Performance (Cambridge: Cambridge University Press, 1990).

127. Albert Bandura, "Self-Efficacy: Toward a Unifying Theory of Behavioral Change," Psychological Review 84, no. 2 (1977): 191 - 215. doi: 10.1037/0033-295X.84.2.191.; Peter M. Gollwitzer, "Implementation Intentions: Strong Effects of Simple Plans," American Psychologist 54, no. 7 (1999): 493 - 503. doi: 10.1037/0003-066X.54.7.493.

Glossary

CORE TERMS

- **Choice Set:** The set of actions you can actually take under your current conditions. Not what is theoretically possible. What is usable under pressure.
- **Default:** The lowest-cost behavior you return to when pressure rises. It stabilizes you. It repeats because it works under the conditions you are in.
- **Field:** The system of conditions shaping your behavior at all times. It includes your body, your environment, and the structures around you. It is not seen directly. It is seen through what repeats.
- **Pricing:** What actions cost. Not just in money, but in time, energy, risk, shame, belonging, safety, and identity. Pricing is set by your conditions. It is not neutral.
- **Recurrence:** What repeats. The outcomes that show up again and again because the underlying conditions have not changed.
- **Reinforcement:** What makes something stick. Relief, not pleasure, is the strongest form. What reduces pressure gets repeated.
- **State:** Your current condition. What you can carry right now. Sleep, stress, fatigue, emotion, and load all shape it.
- **Terms:** The conditions you are inside of. Where you live. Who you are around. What resources you have. What systems you are subject to.

VARIABLES

- **Allostatic Load:** The accumulated cost of carrying stress over time.
- **Baseline:** Your default level of stability when nothing acute is happening.
- **Buffer:** What protects you from collapse. Savings. Rest. Support. Time. Stability.
- **Capacity:** What you can actually do and sustain. Not once. Repeatedly.

- **Constraint:** Anything that limits your options or raises the cost of action.
- **Cost:** The full burden of an action across all currencies. Always relative to your conditions.
- **Environmental Load:** What your surroundings are doing to you. Noise. Instability. Density. Threat.
- **Load:** Everything you are carrying. Obligations, stress, pressure, and demand.

SYSTEM DYNAMICS

- **Choice Compression:** When your options shrink under pressure.
- **Default Loop:** The pattern of trigger, state shift, behavior, and reinforcement that repeats.
- **Misattribution:** When you blame yourself for what is being produced by your conditions.
- **Noise:** What looks like a pattern but is not.
- **Overfitting:** Seeing meaning where there is none.
- **Recurrence Pattern:** A repeated outcome that signals stable conditions underneath.
- **Relief Loop:** A pattern where what helps now makes things worse later, but still gets repeated.
- **Return Clause:** The pull back to what is familiar when pressure rises.
- **Signal:** A pattern that actually predicts what will happen.
- **Underfitting:** Missing the pattern even when it is clear.

TOOLS & INTERVENTIONS

- **Buffer Building:** Increasing what protects you so you do not collapse under pressure.
- **Capacity Expansion:** Increasing what you can actually sustain.
- **Co-regulation:** How other people stabilize or destabilize you.
- **Constraint Reduction:** Removing or lowering what makes action costly.
- **Experiment:** Changing one thing to see what happens.
- **Friction:** Making something harder so it happens less.
- **Leverage:** A small change that shifts everything.
- **Low-Blast Experiment:** A change that teaches you something without risking everything.
- **Regulation:** Returning to stability after disruption.
- **Replacement Stability:** A better pattern that does the same job at a lower long-term cost.
- **Stabilization:** Creating conditions that hold.

Acknowledgments

THIS BOOK WAS SHARPENED BY PEOPLE WHO ANSWERED CONFUSION WITH PRECISION AND CARE.

To the readers, friends, editors, and first listeners who kept asking the useful question, not "why," but "how," thank you. Your patience is inside the pages.

To those who lived through expensive conditions and still insisted on building wider ones for other people: this argument belongs to you too.

About the Author

A. H. Reynoso writes about behavior the way an analyst reads a balance sheet: follow the incentives, the constraints, and the hidden costs, and the outcome stops looking mysterious.

Raised in Upper Manhattan and educated at The Bronx High School of Science and Colgate University, Reynoso translates complex systems into plain-language models people can actually use under pressure.

His work focuses on structural leverage - how to change what people can afford to do, not just what they intend to do. He is the founder of Obvious Things Publishing and the creator of The Invisible Field, a framework for understanding recurring patterns across work, money, relationships, and personal systems.

www.ingramcontent.com/pod-product-compliance
Lightning Source LLC
LaVergne TN
LVHW020509100826
845148LV00003B/728